How to Find Money Online

An Internet-Based Capital Guide for Entrepreneurs

Alan Joch

McGRAW-HILL

New York   San Francisco   Washington, D.C.   Auckland   Bogotá
Caracas   Lisbon   London   Madrid   Mexico City   Milan
Montreal   New Delhi   San Juan   Singapore
Sydney   Tokyo   Toronto

McGraw-Hill

A Division of The McGraw·Hill Companies

1 2 3 4 5 6 7 8 9 0   DOC/DOC   0 9 8 7 6 5 4 3 2 1 0

ISBN 0-07-136060-3

It was set in Minion by Pro-Image Corporation.

Printed and bound by R. R. Donnelley & Sons Company.

McGraw-Hill books are available at special quantity discounts to use as premiums and sales promotions, or for use in corporate training programs. For more information, please write to the Director of Special Sales, Professional Publishing, McGraw-Hill, Two Penn Plaza, New York, NY 10121-2298. Or contact your local bookstore.

This publication is designed to provide accurate and authoritative information in regard to the subject matter covered. It is sold with the understanding that neither the author nor the publisher is engaged in rendering legal, accounting, futures/securities trading, or other professional service. If legal advice or other expert assistance is required, the services of a competent professional person should be sought.

> —*From a Declaration of Principles jointly adopted by a Committee of the American Bar Association and a Committee of Publishers.*

This book is printed on recycled, acid-free paper containing a minimum of 50% recycled, de-inked fiber.

For Anne, Matt, and Alex

Contents

Preface

Why read a book about using the Internet to find business financing when the Internet is there, ready to be explored? After all, dozens of search engines will let you use keywords to quickly locate a particular venture capital firm, angel investor network, incubator, commercial bank, or other capital source.

The problem is that search engines are at once too efficient and too narrow for collecting the information entrepreneurial ventures need. You may be able to easily find mountains of information on the Internet about financing private seed-stage, start-up, expansion-stage, and pre-IPO companies, but locating the right investor for your particular business is almost impossible with traditional search engines.

This book is designed as a search aid to be used hand-in-mouse with the Internet. For example, numerous directories of venture capital funds exist online, but in most cases investors appear alphabetically. The best way to find the right venture fund is to sort through candidates according to which markets they specialize in funding, what minimum and maximum investments they typically make, and what geographical areas they target their investments. "How to Find Money Online" sorts and summarizes essential criteria like these to help you identify the right funding sources in six main categories of equity and debt financing, including more than 400 equity investment sources. The write-ups also tell you how each funding source prefers to receive proposals and information about your company. You then just point your computer's Web browser to the appropriate links to start the process of soliciting funding, rather than wading through mounds of search engine pages.

In the end, a guidebook to funding sources on the Internet can save time and help you do what you do best—build a successful company and communicate your enthusiasm for it to potential investors.

A WEB OF MONEY

Money can't buy you happiness, but too little money can buy you failure and years of frustration if you're an entrepreneur in today's "winner take all" economy. Experienced entrepreneurs know that even the deepest pockets can't make up for a management team without vision, experience, and talent. And even the savviest entrepreneurs can't turn a new service or product into gold if target customers don't need it.

Nevertheless, hunting for capital is a task entrepreneurs never seem to be free of, whether they're trying to research a new market or add production equipment to keep pace with unexpected demand. Money isn't a guarantee for success, but without enough of it at critical development stages, entrepreneurs are almost guaranteed to see their visions become fantasies.

Fortunately, there's help.

The Internet is changing how companies market, conduct, and grow their business. It's also making it easier for entrepreneurs to connect with investors who want a piece of growing private companies. Best of all, the Internet is democratic when it comes to helping entrepreneurs thrive. You don't have to run a high-tech company—or even be a computer expert—to let the Web connect you with capital. Accountants, gourmet food shops, clothiers, aromatherapy boutiques, dry cleaners, and hardware stores all have a chance to find money online to open strong and grow market share.

The tools you need are simple: A PC with a modem and a Web browser, standard items on most computers today. Then, just plug the system into a commercial Internet connection from national service providers like AOL and Microsoft Network, or a small, local ISP (Internet Service Provider), and the door to a wide range of capital sources will open for you.

This book will guide you to find the right capital sources, depending on your market, the maturity of your company, your location, and your sales territory. Beyond that you'll only need the basic entrepreneurial tools—a killer idea, a comprehensive business plan, and entrepreneurial drive—to begin surfing for dollars.

GETTING STARTED

The Internet's world-wide resources can save hours of time tracking down investors interested in your company's development stage and market, but when it comes to nailing down funding, you'll still need to rely on some old fashioned techniques and tools. No amount of salesmanship on your part will be successful if you haven't scouted out the investors most likely to deal with you. Once you've developed a viable short list of funding sources, you'll need a comprehensive and well-executed business plan to reach the first major goal: A face to face meeting with an entrepreneur-friendly investor. Here's an overview on how to pick the right capital sources and present them with a business plan worth betting your dreams on.

CHOOSE INVESTORS CAREFULLY

If you believe everything you read in business magazines about the so-called New Internet Economy, you might think that your fate and that of thousands of other entrepreneurs lies in the hands of a cadre of Silicon Valley venture capitalists housed on Sand Hill Road in Menlo Park, CA. This legendary stretch of offices on the edge of Stanford University holds the highest concentration of venture capital funds anywhere in the world. It's true that within this stretch of office buildings are the headquarters of investors that backed the Silicon Valley elite when they were just garage operations.

But venture capital is a good source of money, primarily if you have a growing business that can achieve $50 million or more in revenues over the next five years, or if you need between $3 million to $10 million to jumpstart a company. Entrepreneurs also must be prepared to give up control—perhaps 20 percent to 50 percent of their company in equity shares, along with a seat on the board of directors—to the investment fund. Approximately 2.5 percent of new companies go this route, according to OffRoad Capital, an online matchmaker for entrepreneurs and investors. Today, more than 350 venture funds have detailed

Web sites that tell you what types of businesses they're interested in and what they expect in return for their investment dollars. The trouble is, combing through all these sites single-handedly can take weeks of effort to find a handful of venture funds that would be willing to consider your proposal.

We've already done that work and organized hundreds of sites by industry focus so you can easily find candidates (see page 153). The capsule summaries (beginning on page 36) also include contact information and tell you the preferred way to reach each fund.

But don't grab a Latte and point your browser to Valley investors just yet. The venture capital industry is brimming with money—some funds have more capital than good start ups to invest in—but it's only one source in a large pool of potential funding sources available to entrepreneurs. That's good news, especially if you're not working the Web, selling computer hardware and software, next generation medical systems, or other leading edge markets that grab a disproportionate share of venture capital attention.

You can also be touched by an angel. This prosaic name is for rich and investment savvy individuals who buy a piece of the action in almost 5 percent of young companies, OffRoad says Angels often don't look for a management role, just a return on their investment. Our directory of angel investors (see page 169) can put you in touch with the right investors, whether your business is high tech or a nuts-and-bolts basic manufacturer.

Business incubators, both non-profit and for-profit entities, are becoming an increasingly important source for entrepreneurial financing and critical resources—office space, for instance (see page 199).

Commercial banks account for nearly 20 percent of business cash. Today, in a fraction of the time it takes to sit down with a loan manager at a brick-and-mortar bank, you can use the Web to comparison shop for the best rates and the highest credit lines (see page 244).

Other sources include, of course, personal savings, which accounts for 27 percent of small-business funding, by far the lion's share, OffRoad says. Relatives and friends ante up another

13 percent. The Internet probably won't help you with the latter two categories, beyond distributing your well-crafted pleas as e-mail or perhaps initiating a heartfelt videoconference session with a rich uncle. But the Web can help you find investors in all the other categories, and in some cases, help you speed up the process with electronic application forms and easy comparison shopping.

Business Plans: The Key to Sealing the Deal

The Internet can help you find potential investors and put you in touch with them quickly. But it doesn't change the fundamental tools you need to win over a skeptical funding source. The key element in your business plan to attract an investor is a viable description of the size of the potential market, which, of course, helps the backer estimate the possible return on investment, according to Timothy Dineen, a business consultant and principle of Trinity Capital, Norcross, GA, (lepcap@mindspring.com).

Market potential will also help you narrow down the type of investor you should be courting. For example, angel investors typically focus on smaller markets—companies with the chance to reach annual sales of $15 million to $25 million in two to five years. Venture funds set their sights higher: they traditionally invest between $3 million to $10 million initially in companies that appear capable of hitting $50 million to $100 million in five years or less, Dineen says. If profits are still far in the future, you might try a seed fund—often a venture fund that specializes in infant companies. These sources can spot you as little as $100,000 up to $1.5 million for test marketing or building a prototype techno-toy. More and more seed-fund sources and universities also offer incubators: office space, business advice, and basic services like telephone lines to help fledgling ventures dry their wings.

If you're young enough to thrive in an incubator, you may not have a fully developed business plan yet. All others will find this document essential for introducing your company to potential investors. What's more, the task—or in some cases, the pain—of putting your vision, goals, financial projections, and market analysis down on paper is valuable for thinking through in detail all aspects of your business.

The Web can help you craft your business plan, too. Some sites, like www.bizplan.com, are run by publishers of business plan software, and offer advice and templates for creating your own document. Business consultants and universities also provide plenty of advice. The free, Business Plan Template, from Old Dominion University's Entrepreneurship Center (Norfolk, VA; www.odu.edu), includes the essential elements that experts say should be included in a comprehensive business plan.

THE BUSINESS PLAN TEMPLATE

Old Dominion University Entrepreneurship Center.

A. Title Page

The title page should identify the name of the company, the name of the principals (i.e., the team members) and their affiliations, and the date the business plan is submitted.

B. Executive Summary—2–3 Pages

The Executive Summary should be prepared **after** the body of the plan has been completed. Gather information for each of the following elements throughout the planning process. Many professionals assign certain parts of the plan to respective department leaders. However, one person should coordinate all of the information and then prepare the Executive Summary. That single coordinator provides style continuity and acts as the "glue" that keeps the plan together.

1. **Purpose of the Plan**
   Why are you writing this document, and who is the intended audience?
2. **Products or Services Offered**
   Describe your company's products in terms of what the customer buys—not necessarily what you produce. For example: "My business provides access subscriptions to the Internet"—not, "My business connects computers to the Internet".

3. **Market Analysis—Characteristics, Scope**

   What has caused the market for your products or services to exist in each of the countries in which it operates? How big is the market in $ sales, population, units consumed, etc.?

4. **Market and Sales Strategy**

   What specific practices will you employ in competing within each of the companies in your business' market? Will you offer more services for a premium price or fewer services for a lower price? How will your potential customers learn about your product? When will the sale actually occur—who will conduct the sale?

5. **Key Personnel**

   Most investors look at the management team for its expertise in a given business or market. Who are the key personnel in your company and what unique or special skills do they bring to the team? (Note: In your business plan *YOU* are the management team).

6. **Financial Data**

   Include highlights of your financial data. Current assets, and future projections especially. (Note: This section need not be comprehensive. A cursory financial analysis is sufficient).

7. **Return on Investment**

   Any serious investor will want to know what to expect in return for any financial contribution to the company. Highlight the expectation in the summary.

C. Table of Contents

D. Background

If the company is very new, background descriptions can include information about the industry, the key personnel, or the unique strength of the newly formed venture.

1. Company description—past and present
2. Distinctive skills, uniqueness, protection

E. Market Analysis

A complete review and analysis of the market conditions, behavior, and trends in each country is an essential part of a good marketing plan. Many new companies have indications about market conditions, but very little evidence to support the intuition. Evidence to support each of the following sections is the key to a thorough market analysis.

1. **Industry Description, Scope and Trends**
   Include a review of the business system and market analysis within each section.
2. **Major Customer Profile**
   List the most important potential and current customers in each country that the company operates in. Include the percentage of market share represented by each, and as much operational and "personality" information as is available.
3. **Target Market—Market Penetration**
   Explain why certain customers or groups have been targeted and show the current level of customers of sales within the target group.
4. **Predominant Sales Techniques**
   Describe the methods your company will use in its sales strategies in each country. Will you be telemarketing, making direct sales presentations, or using a distributor or sales agent, etc?
5. **Problems, Obstacles and Opportunities**
   Don't gloss over obstacles in the business plan. Present them in their proper perspective and show your strategies and plans for overcoming them.
6. **Market Research—General and Specific**
   Include recent findings and important data as well as the interpretation of this information.
7. **Competition—Strengths and Weaknesses**
   Present your competition from the perspective of the customer. What strength does the marketplace view the competition as having? Then, what will your company do to compete effectively? Again, provide this analysis for each of the countries that your team members are from.

F. Product and/or Services—Specific

Include a description of what jobs or problems your product or service eliminates for the customer. Pictures and illustrations are helpful.

1. **Benefits—Customer Needs Satisfied**
   Show evidence of the need as well as the satisfaction.
2. **Present Stage—Idea, Prototype, Small Sales, etc.**
   If your product is not market ready, show steps necessary to take it from its current status to ready.
3. **Life Cycle**
   How long will your product or service be suitable for the market?
4. **Intellectual Property—Patents, Trade Secrets, etc.**
   Any properties owned or in application should be included. Describe the unique marketability of the property for the business.

G. Market Strategy

A good market strategy is dynamic and your plan should include contingencies for change. Include the following in your strategy.

1. Specific growth strategy for at least 5 years
2. Distribution
3. Advertising—institutional and product specific
4. Specific sales strategies—personnel, compensation, sales calls, closing ratios, average sales/communications

H. Operations

Operational plans should describe how the product or service will be produced. If unique abilities are a key part of the product, their production should be described in detail here.

1. Key personnel—allocation of their resources, major strengths
2. Production and/or service delivery—capacity techniques, cost factors, logistics, quality control, economies of scale
3. Supplies needed
4. Legal structure

5. Stockholders, board of directors
6. Organization chart
7. Future human resource requirements

I. Financial
The financial description of the plan should present a fiscal picture of the operational plans. Include complete assumptions for every category explaining the growth assumptions.

1. Funding requirements—amount, type, term, etc.
2. Use of funds
3. Payout to investors—timing, return on investment
4. Past and present financials—3 years
   • Cashflow
   • Profit and loss statement
   • Balance sheet
5. Future Projects—3 years
   • Cashflow
   • P&L
   • Balance sheet
6. Explanation of assumptions in projections

J. Appendices
Make most references in the body of the plan. Use the appendices for the following extra information, making reference to them in the body of the plan.

1. Key managers resumes
2. Pictures
3. Professional reference (letters of recommendation)
4. Published information
5. Contracts and agreements

You can also hire business plan specialists to write your plan, based on your ideas and experience. Dineen, who says he's written 50 plans over the last 10 years, charges between $5000 to $25000 for a from-scratch plan, depending on how much data and analysis of the target industry an entrepreneur provides and how much Dineen must accumulate to give the plan teeth. Alternately, Dineen will critique an already written plan for about $500.

Beyond the basics, experts all have different ideas about what should be emphasized.

Dineen suggests that you consider how investors typically read a business plan so you know which sections to spend the most time on. He says the executive summary is the most-read and thus the most influential part of a plan. Second, investors tend to go directly to the financial projections at the back of the plan. "Only if those two things pass muster do they go on to read the body," Dineen says. To succeed, the financial data has to be realistic and believable, but large enough to interest the investor with a profitable return on the investment. Also, don't balk at showing realistic "burn rates," the period in perhaps the first year or two when the venture loses money. "Don't show profitability too soon," Dineen advises. "That can shoot a business plan down because it demonstrates that the management is not realistic."

For a reality check to make sure your numbers are realistic, research your target industry and competitors by taking advantage of public-company data. Also, research the size of the total market and the number of companies that sell to it, to estimate your potential market share and how much money you'll need to spend to achieve it. If you don't have the experience and analytical abilities to make these judgments, hire a professional business consultant to do the work. It's a costly up front expense, but it will help guarantee investors take your proposals seriously, Dineen says.

Bela Musits, director of the Incubator Program at Rensselaer Polytechnic Institute, Troy, NY, considers three elements key to a successful plan. The first is a well articulated discussion of the product's or service's benefits. "Explain why the customer is going to buy it—that's where you make the sale to a potential investor," according to Musits. Next, explain the market opportunity in a way that identifies which segments of a market have the most potential. "The worst thing you can do is say 'if I capture x percent of the market, I'll be successful.' You've got to say which segment of the market. People often are not focused enough," Musits says. Third, sell the entrepreneurial team. Has it launched a start up before? What relevant business experience does it have? Many investors consider managerial talent as important when committing capital as the business idea itself. If you're lacking in entrepreneurial experience, admit it rather than trying to hide it, and then hire people to fill any gaps, Musits says. "It's like a baseball team: If don't have a left fielder, you go out and find one."

Finally, remember that a business plan has a short shelf life. As your business grows, when you reach a product development milestone, or when a new technology shakes up your target market, update the plan to keep it relevant. Experts also warn that you shouldn't wait to start shopping the plan around when the delivery trucks are unloading new computer equipment or an injection molding machine onto the shop floor. From start to finish, it may take a few weeks to nine months or more to close an investment partnership, so start knocking on doors approximately a year before you'll need to pay your suppliers.

VENTURE CAPITAL: FUEL FOR GROWING COMPANIES

For many young companies, venture capital funding can mean the difference between a successful start up and great idea that never gets off the ground. Money isn't the only reason. The cachet of a top name venture capital fund is a vote of confidence in an unproven business plan that can open doors to other investors, distribution pipelines, and customers. If you choose a venture partner successfully, he or she will have a ready Rolodex of business connections that will replace weeks of cold-calling on your part.

Since no single entrepreneur is an expert in all phases of launching a business—from product or service development, to financing, to sales and marketing—you'll probably need to assemble a team of executives who will complement your strengths and fill in any gaps in your expertise. The business tentacles of a thriving venture capital fund can help put you in contact with executives of other companies and other entrepreneurs looking for new challenges.

Our directory of venture capital firms lists more than 350 companies throughout the country that target private, pre-IPO (initial public offering), and in some cases public companies. How do you narrow the list to find the one that's best for you?

There are no exact formulas for determining the right venture capital fund, partly because the personal chemistry between an entrepreneur and the managing partners—a highly subjective criterion—is one of the keys to finding the right fit. Nevertheless, there are a number of important factors to consider that must also be in place before you get down to gut feelings.

First, make sure the potential venture capital firm has a track record in your target market. Remember the primary trade-off you're making in accepting venture capital cash: You're relinquishing a piece of your company and probably a seat on your board of directors. Giving this kind of control to an investor can be a good thing if the person understands your market and its competitive challenges, as well as having connections to the network of other investors, attorneys, and potential employees that could help your company as it grows. Most venture capital Web sites list the names of current investments, called portfolio companies. Use this information to help you track down portfolio-company managers to hear what other entrepreneurs say about the fund you're considering.

Second, locate funds that understand your development stage. Most venture funds will consider attractive business opportunities in a range of growth phases, from start ups looking for their first funding rounds, to established businesses approaching a public offering. Probe fund managers to find which stages they have concentrated on in the last year or two. Market conditions change rapidly, and you'll want a partner who understands your particular challenges.

Third, consider geography. While Menlo Park, CA, is ground zero for the venture capital industry, a number of regional funds—or satellite offices of California funds—invest outside of Silicon Valley. Close proximity to your fund manager means he or she will have a better understanding of your market and your company, making it easier for you to sell yourself in the beginning and to derive as much business insight as possible once you tie the knot.

Next, see if a potential fund can supply the amount of money you need. Young, seed stage companies may need $250,000 to finish a prototype, but many funds won't invest less than $1 million in a venture. Alternately, the $10 million you need for expensive production equipment may be beyond what some funds bankroll in their initial investment. Check the directory summaries to find the right fit.

Once you've narrowed down the field to a working list of funds to pursue, you're ready to make your initial contacts. If possible find another entrepreneur, attorney, business consultant, or client who has a connection with the fund and can introduce you. Any entrée will improve your chances over having your executive summary or business plan arrive along with the pile of other ideas fund managers receive every day. While not as effective as a personal introduction, the Web can improve your chances of becoming noticed. Many sites list the e-mail addresses of managing partners or provide electronic forms that let you sketch an overview of your company. Establish e-mail contact with a manager or associate partner, and you'll have someone on the lookout for your proposal when it arrives.

VENTURE CAPITAL RESOURCES

Turn to the Web when it's time to investigate possible sources of venture capital and to initiate contacts with the nation's leading venture-capital fund managers. You'll find details about funding criteria, the backgrounds of fund managers, and the best ways to quickly get your proposal to the proper person. The downside of shopping for capital on the Web? Today, there are so many funds with an online presence, your search engine queries will bury you with scores of "hits," although only a fraction of them may be relevant for your market or stage of development.

To streamline the search process, comb through the "Focus" headings in the following alphabetized list of venture capital funds to find the funds most active in your particular market niche. A second directory, "Venture Fund Market-Focus Index," follows the alphabetized list to make it easier to match funds and markets. The fund summaries in the main directory will tell you about any special criteria each fund considers when evaluating potential clients. In the "How to Apply" sections of these summaries, you'll find contact information as well as tips on what to include in your proposal when you're making an initial contact to a particular fund.

FROM INSIDE: WHAT SELLS A VENTURE CAPITALIST

M. R. Rangaswami and Constantin Delivanis accomplished a domain-name coup four years ago when they registered their Web site as www.sandhill.com. Until then, no one had thought about using the reference to the prestigious Sand Hill Road, the most fashionable address in the venture capital industry. It's fitting and ironic that Rangaswami and Delivanis's venture company, the Sand Hill Group, ended up with this URL: their's is a virtual office with no actual physical location. Rangawami and his partner fund young companies with their own money and conduct business in person, over the Internet, and via cell phones.

For Rangaswami, virtual offices are just a normal part of business in the Internet Age. Today, he's a sought after investor, not only for the money he can pump into a growing business, but also for his business acumen. In an average year, Ranga-swami reads 500 business plans. Here's his advice for getting your proposals to the top of a venture capitalist's stack.

"There's more junk hitting me than ever before. Two years ago, I used to receive 100 business plans a year, now I'm getting 500 a year. With e-mail, the same plan can be sent around to hundreds of different venture capital funds. The challenge from an entrepreneur's viewpoint is how to separate his or her business plan from vast number of plans out there.

"Entrepreneurs need to grab us, they need to show us why the plan is unique, innovative, and not a me-too idea. I look for a one- to two-page executive summary to do this. Next, I like a concept that's simple, but one where people haven't done it before. I saw a plan a some months ago that described a simple concept for direct mail. You send a Microsoft Word document and your mailing list to their Web site, and they print, sort, and mail the letters. The beauty of the plan was its simplicity. It used a new medium, the Internet, to do something different. That's a pretty successful company now.

"The business plan should be straight forward, matter of fact. Too many plans are overly promotional, all hype. Let the numbers and facts speak for themselves, not a lot of superlatives.

"Nobody has enough time. I spend about five minutes reading an executive summary, and about 10 minutes on the financial details in a plan. The executive summary is much harder to write than a 50-page business plan. Include three or four things in the executive summary. A summary paragraph on the market. Define who the customer is and the size of the market. Have a compelling value proposition—the product should either increase revenue for customers or decrease costs. Demonstrate that. Include your time-to-market strategy—if you get funded, how long will it take to get to market? The faster the better—I don't like a plan that says the product will be out two years from now. We look for something that will be available in the next six months, even if it's being phased in. We want to see actions and the ability to meet milestones.

"At that point, if I like the idea, I'll send an e-mail and say, let's chat on the phone, maybe for 10 to 15 minutes while I'm driving in my car. Within that time, the entrepreneur has got to set up a deal with me. Can he push me to a meeting? He has to be a little pushy and say, when can we get together? Once you get in front of someone, you're harder to ignore. Out of the 500 plans I read a year, perhaps 50 will get face time. Of those, maybe one gets funded.

"We like to see people who show a commitment to the venture: The person who says, 'I had a high paying job that I quit to do this,' versus an individual who says, 'I'm working now, but I'll quit if I get funded.' We like people who've taken the plunge and are living on a credit card and savings. That tells you he or she believes in the idea.

"A track record in running a business usually helps, but if someone has already done a successful start up, there is no dearth of funding available. Ninety-nine percent of the population hasn't done that. In those cases, we look for patterns of success.

"The first meeting establishes whether there's some chemistry between us. I give the entrepreneur a to-do list. Pitch the idea to this individual to see if they'll buy your product or service. It's a way to validate the business plan. It's also a test to see if the entrepreneur has follow up capabilities. Twenty-five percent of them disappear after the first meeting and we never hear from them again.

"Let's say it's someone who has done the to-dos. He or she has impressed us. So we have another meeting and get more details. That's a couple-hour meeting where we sit down and brainstorm how the business might work. This is when they see the value add we can bring. We bring business acumen from having done this before, from the network we have. We also look at the exit strategy to make sure our goals are aligned. We're unorthodox investors in that we don't look for five-year plans—in this market, you're lucky if you have an accurate one-year plan.

"But the biggest thing that happens at this meeting is chemistry—we either have it or we don't. If we don't feel anything, we tell them up front, 'Go find another fund.'

"Finally, entrepreneurs shouldn't feel dejected or disappointed when they get turned down. If you really believe in your stuff, keep at it. Someone is going to believe in you."

FROM THE TRENCHES: "SERIAL ENTREPRENEURS" SHARE THEIR SECRETS

When it comes to raising money for a growing company, nothing succeeds like success. This may sound obvious, and even frustrating if you're trying to build your first business, but your track record, or the records of people who have signed on to your vision, can outweigh any other business factor, including the quality of your business plan or your venture's market potential. The reason: Investors such as venture capitalists, angels, incubator directors, and bank loan officers search for comfort factors that will help convince them in the middle of the night that their hundreds-of-thousands or millions of dollar investments won't ultimately dissipate like the ratings for last year's sitcom hit. A battle-tested business manager provides this comfort.

The need for business veterans, combined with the high-speed entrepreneurial market of the last five years, has forged a new kind of business specialist—the "serial entrepreneur." These men and women haven't been through the start-up process just once, instead they have thrived on the leading edge of company development by guiding the creation of two, three, or more companies. Among the most famous serial entrepreneurs is Jim Clark, who founded the computer graphics firm Silicon Graphics, then parlayed the proofs of that successful business into Netscape Communications, a Web browser developer and the first clear winner in the emerging Internet market thanks to a wildly successful initial public offering (IPO) in 1996. Later, Netscape famously tangled with software giant Microsoft as one of the main protagonists in Microsoft's anti-trust case. Now Clark and a close group of investors and software developers are trying to merge the Web with the multi-billion dollar healthcare industry with Healtheon/WebMD, an unproven yet well funded venture thanks to Clark's reputation as a start-up manager with a golden touch.

Other, less famous, entrepreneurs throughout the world quietly accomplish similar feats of serial entrepreneurship. The sequence starts with the cocktail napkin idea that's developed enough to excite a small group of early collaborators, who pool their money and business expertise to hone the idea into a viable commercial service or product. The start-up circle expands to include friends, relatives, and business associates who contribute additional talent and money to take the fledgling business to the next level: A business strategy polished enough to interest an angel investor. With an infusion of outside money, the business team hones the business plan and creates a prototype that proves the business concept, earns a patent, if appropriate, or proves that this group has a proprietary asset that will deter future competitors from easily squashing the company if and when it starts to pull in profits.

At this point, serial entrepreneurs are ready to walk the walk into a venture capital conference room, after pulling strings from investors or anyone else plugged into the regional investment community who can make an influential introduction. If successful, subsequent funding rounds over the next months or years come as the young business periodically doubles its growth and prepares for a "liquidity event," also known as paying the piper. This could be a purchase by a larger company or, often more lucratively, an IPO, which lets investors realize a payoff for their early involvement.

For a true serial entrepreneur, working for the new parent company or managing the now public company's growth through the thicket of shareholder demands is as fulfilling as holding a million shares in the latest dotcom flame out. The real action is when he or she is hunched over the cocktail napkin, sketching out a newest idea to change the world.

STILL LEARNING THE THIRD TIME AROUND

Serial entrepreneur Bill O'Farrell knows the start-up drill. He's now in the early rounds of launching his third company and is relearning a lesson he discovered 10 years ago: Finding funding for a new venture isn't a scientific, paint-by-numbers exercise.

His first venture, the Company of Science and Art (COSA), emerged in 1990, after O'Farrell and a small group of partners worked the financial system using all of their people savvy and personal connections. At each phase of its evolution, COSA attracted more and more formal financing, finally convincing "smart money" to buy into their main product, software to edit digital video, in 1993.

Initial seed money came from personal savings of each of the founders, plus cash from family. "This was a total bootstrap," O'Farrell recalls. "If we had $100,000, that was about it." As meager as COSA's financial resources were, the company faced an even bigger problem: All of the founding team was in its 20s and none had ever run a business before. O'Farrell, the oldest member, was a 28-year-old attorney out of law school for just a year. The other founders had even less experience in the business world: All were fresh out of college with less than a year's worth of seasoning in the real world.

To help convince even supportive relatives to trust their money with business neophytes, the company mangers used their connections to engage some professors from the prestigious Ivy League school, Brown University, who agreed to sit on COSA's board of advisors.

Still, the collective inexperience of the day-to-day management team showed in both COSA's initial business plan and its ultimate goals. The engineering contingent among the founders envisioned a new kind of publishing company that used emerging computer multimedia technology to publish magazines that arrived to subscribers on CD-ROM discs instead of old-fashioned paper and ink. With hubris common to both college graduates and technology pioneers, one of the founding engineers declared that COSA would be a failure if all it achieved was success on a par with the multinational, multi-billion-dollar entertainment conglomerate, Sony. "We had a business plan that, if successful, would have produced a combination of AT&T, America Online, and Sony," O'Farrell recalls. "Frankly, if I were an investor, I never would have backed us."

Although O'Farrell had been knocking on the doors of venture capitalists from the beginning, he never got anyone to close a deal. "I had at least ten meetings with venture capitalists," O'Farrell says. "They never said no, but I never got my follow-up phone calls returned. Getting to an answer impossible."

Gradually, "the more sober of us" realized the business strategy needed to be more focused than the rule-the-world approach that the young managers initially created, O'Farrell recalls. As time went on, the company better defined its technology strengths and the area where it offered the high-tech market some unique capabilities. "We had a good grasp of the digital video market in general," O'Farrell says.

This realization forced COSA to constantly narrow its vision of itself, so that the initial fantasy of becoming an instant media giant soon became more modest and attainable: COSA would offer multimedia consulting services to business clients that wanted to produce company training films and promotional materials. COSA would also use its technical talents to write software applications that would make the task of editing digital movies easier. "We soon had a couple of products that were generating revenue and some consulting gigs," O'Farrell says.

He remains philosophical about COSA's early mistakes and says he and his associates would not have eventually achieved success if they hadn't endured this learning experience and remained flexible enough to work through their problems. "We were incredibly early in a market that didn't exist yet," he says, referring to the plan for distributing magazines on discs. "But in the process of creating the CD-ROM, we became aware of the restraints that multimedia developers faced. This allowed us to come out with an incredibly useful product."

That product became AfterEffects, digital video editing software that arrived on the market in December of 1992. "We sort of knew the product was going to do well because in October and November we were testing it and folks raved about it," says O'Farrell. Six months after the premiere of AfterEffects, the graphics arts company Aldus Corp. purchased the technology for $4 million; it continues to be marketed by Adobe Systems Inc., San Jose, California, which acquired Aldus in 1994.

Considering the multi-national strategy that some COSA founders argued for early on, the decision to sell out to a larger company showed how much the entrepreneurs matured in two and a half years. "We just couldn't convince ourselves that we knew how to make this a big business," says O'Farrell. "Besides, we'd been running on macaroni and cheese for too many years."

In addition to putting a sizable chunk of money in his bank account, the COSA experience also taught O'Farrell the finer points of managing a start up. And although his encounters with venture capitalists weren't successful, his financing efforts added a number of important names and numbers to his Rolodex. So that by the time COSA's buyer became part of Adobe in the fall of 1994, O'Farrell was ready to leave the corporate world behind and wrestle in the entrepreneurial dirt once again.

Among the introductions O'Farrell received in his high-tech networking efforts were researchers with the famously innovative multimedia lab at the Massachusetts Institute of Technology. MIT continues to hold regular venture forums where entrepreneurs looking for money make short presentations to an audience of inventors, business people, and investors (see the MIT Enterprise Forum at www.mitforum-cambridge.org/). In 1994, O'Farrell accepted an invitation to tell the audience about his COSA experiences, and after his presentation met an MIT researcher doing work in speech recognition, the ability for computers to process human speech. "It was a perfect time for me to leave the corporate world," O'Farrell says.

Knowing the value of having a group of Brown University professors anoint COSA's early efforts, O'Farrell used his partner's MIT associations to enlist MIT computer scientists as members of the board for the budding efforts to commercialize speech recognition technology.

O'Farrell and other COSA veterans, as well as some friends and family, pooled about $250,000 in seed money to get the new venture running for the next year. By August of 1995, SpeechWorks, the new company's name, was already signing deals from potential clients who wanted to become early adopters of its telephone-based information system, which is now being used by airline customers to confirm flights, among other applications. With a small revenue stream already in place, SpeechWorks prepared for it's first formal financing round and started shopping around its business concept to venture capital firms.

O'Farrell and his associates finally found themselves sitting across the conference table from venture capitalists interested in making a deal. Atlas Venture (www.atlasventure.com) and Charles River Ventures (www.crv.com/), two Boston-area venture capital funds, eventually committed $2.5 million to SpeechWorks. The tone of the meetings was no comparison to what O'Farrell experienced when he was trying to fund COSA. "Given that I had done one start up—a painful one—my management skills were less suspect. I'd proven myself as a manager."

A number of other factors, many of them lessons learned the hard way from the COSA experience, also helped seal venture capital deals for SpeechWorks. First, the new company was more focused, O'Farrell says. Willing to concede the planet to established multinationals, SpeechWorks began life with a clear business plan that showed how the company would apply speech recognition to business telephone systems, where the significant financial milestones for the company existed, and what the company's burn rate would be at any point in time. "We had a focus. We said exactly what we were going to do, and we pretty much did it," says O'Farrell. "[Our progress] was measurable. There never was a point when we couldn't show why things weren't better than yesterday."

Another validation for SpeechWorks was a 30-year technology licensing agreement with MIT, attained with the help of O'Farrell's business partner. The willingness of two well-known venture capitalists gave SpeechWorks a ready-for-prime-time aura: People who fancy themselves intelligent about start ups gave the company their seal of approval, which greased the wheels for later financing rounds and technology alliances, O'Farrell says.

In all, SpeechWorks fueled its pre-IPO growth with a total of $75 million in venture capital, including the early commitments for preferred stock by Charles River and Atlas. In four later funding rounds, SpeechWorks added BankAmerica Ventures (at press time, the fund didn't maintain a Web site), the European-based enterprise software publisher SAP, microprocessor giant Intel, and Questmark Partners (www.questmark.com) to its list of investors. SpeechWorks also entered a partnership with AT&T, which received stock in exchange for telephony technology that dovetailed with what SpeechWorks was developing. A final private investment round to provide "our launching pad for the IPO" included funds from GE Equity (www.geequity.com) and iGate Ventures (http://www.igatecapital.com/igateventures.html), O'Farrell says.

SpeechWorks ultimately relied heavily on venture capital, but throughout its funding stage considered—and in some cases discarded—other options, too. The company found the paperwork involved with applying for Small Business Administration loans too "traumatic" to pursue. Government technology grants, which did provide some capital for SpeechWorks, were valuable but were saddled with time consuming paper work, O'Farrell recalls.

As venture funds anted up to participate in SpeechWorks' future, the start up found more and more investor representatives sitting on the board of directors, offering opinions and business advice about how to move to the next growth level. For O'Farrell the experience was new—because no formal investors helped fund COSA its board remained a reflection of the founders and the Brown University professors. Having regular board meetings with outside investors sitting in "felt different," according to O'Farrell, but "underscored the business element" of the enterprise. "Having a formal board, with the discipline of board meetings, emphasized that this was a business venture. This was about making something commercial out of a sophisticated technology."

As the company makes its preparations for its IPO, which it expects to occur in late 2000, its managers say they feel like they have a valid business strategy in place. Funding wasn't the only hurdle SpeechWorks had to overcome. It also had to convince potential customers that they needed speech recognition technology and that the SpeechWorks applications would work as advertised. "In the beginning it wasn't like people didn't want our stuff, but we had to prove to customers that the technology worked well enough. Every time we got people to a point where we thought we would close a deal, they wanted something else. We're finally beginning to see market demand for the product taking off."

By the summer of 2000, the company employed more than 250 people and added to its cachet with contracts from marquee customers like United Airlines, which will use SpeechWorks speech recognition systems for a customer flight-information systems. Other customers include the securities brokers E-Trade, and Donaldson, Lufkin & Jenrette, which will incorporate SpeechWorks into their financial systems.

With two start ups under his belt, O'Farrell might appear the model of entrepreneurial expertise, able to guide companies from inception to IPO with ease. But as a reminder that financing a new venture is never easy, he encountered some setbacks with his third enterprise that show even serial entrepreneurs aren't beyond learning additional lessons in humility.

OpenAir uses a hot Internet business strategy, known as the application service provider (ASP) model, to deliver software applications over the Web instead of requiring customers to install and periodically upgrade the applications on their own computers. The target market, small businesses across virtually all industry segments, can potentially save on technology costs using ASP-based software applications because the companies don't have to hire in-house experts to install, run, and fix the software when problems pop up. OpenAir's suite of applications, which became available in the summer of 1999, currently includes programs for automating financial and administrative tasks for small companies.

OpenAir founders completed their first seed financing round in the spring of 1999 with a total of $500,000 from close associates and from O'Farrell's personal savings. That fall, the company received additional funds totaling about $2.5 million from angel investors and two seed funds, Rex Capital (www.rexcapital.com) and I-Hatch (www.ihatch.com). O'Farrell thinks back to that period near the turn of the century as a time as wild and treacherous as the Alaskan Gold Rush was in the previous century. "Things were zooy," he says. "People were throwing money at us. We raised the money pretty easily. But that was just a moment in time."

Nevertheless, as 2000 approached OpenAir needed a significant infusion of cash, to the tune of $10 million, which would require the participation of one or more venture capital funds. But when the founders put feelers out to obvious first-choice funds—the ones that had a track record with O'Farrell and SpeechWorks—they received a lukewarm response. "We just didn't have enough progress to get venture guys psyched for $10 million," O'Farrell says. "I learned with OpenAir that no matter how much you've done, even if [previous venture capital investors] still very much like you, they won't invest if something doesn't feel right yet."

O'Farrell believes that because he was in a transition from working full time with SpeechWorks and moving over to OpenAir, he wasn't clear in his own mind how much of a commitment he could make to OpenAir as its chief executive officer. His venture-capital associates clearly read O'Farrell's ambivalence and refused to take it on faith that something as critical as the CEO role would eventually be worked out effectively. "I had said that I'd be CEO until OpenAir was formed, then I'd see what would happen after that. I was naïve. I was complacent. I didn't appreciate the institutional part of venture capital funding. I walked in there believing we had a set of issues we had to work out, and believed we'd figure them out. I overlooked the fact that these guys have a process they work through: You have to answer every one of their questions, and I didn't spend enough time focusing on the questions the venture capitalists were asking. You have to jump. I didn't jump enough."

Being familiar with a group of venture capitalists from his previous start up also led to misunderstandings that may not have arisen if the relationships were more formal and at arms length. According to O'Farrell, his earlier venture investors invited him to let them in early on his next project, which was OpenAir. O'Farrell confidently took their advice and ended up regretting it. Giving investors an early peek at a fledgling company opened him up to criticisms that were obvious to O'Farrell, but appeared to be management oversights when considered around an investor's conference table. "They said, 'Well, your plan is a little unfocused,'" O'Farrell recalls. "I said, 'But you told me to come early!'" This initial bump got the talks off to a poor start, O'Farrell explains. "What I should have done is not said anything. We took the idea in really early on, before our angel financing round. I didn't even know what all the questions were at that point. I spent the summer and part of the early fall addressing the issues those guys brought up. We all spent a fair amount of time talking, but we never got comfortable."

So he started banging on the doors of other venture capitalists, but O'Farrell discovered what he calls a perception problem. "People were asking us 'Why aren't those [previous investors] backing this?'" OpenAir decided that the only way to win over venture capitalists was with concrete growth from the company. It's goal was to sign 10,000 users by the end of the year and roll out a total of three applications in the same time period. "We did that and then went back to the venture guys. We went through the fundamentals of the business and started raising money in January." By March, the financing round was completed and OpenAir had $12.5 million in venture money, although with new funds, including Fidelity Ventures.

REAL-LIFE ADVICE

After guiding three companies, O'Farrell has a working list of five lessons he's learned, sometime from strategies that worked, sometimes from ones that failed. They include:

- Shopping a start up around to investors too early can make entrepreneurs look unprepared and stymie the investment relationship.
- The motivation of the founders, especially the CEO, has to be clear.
- Don't approach angel or venture-capital investors with a "lifestyle" business. One of the biggest turnoffs for investors, whether early-round angels or "smart money" venture capitalists, is a pitch by an entrepreneur who wants to build a so-called lifestyle business. These companies are characterized by

a small group of founders who want to retain close control of the company's management and draw a regular, comfortable income from the enterprise's profits. Although a perfectly viable business model for an entrepreneur, lifestyle businesses should be financed from savings of close associates rather than private equity investments. "Almost by definition, you can't expect other people to back you" because there's no strategy for a profit-rich IPO or acquisition, says O'Farrell. "The notion of building a big company that makes investors money, on the other hand, suggests you're taking other people's money in a way that makes some sense."

- Don't be overly concerned about company dilution and valuation at an early stage. If an entrepreneur overvalues a start up, potential investors will shy away. "It sets everyone's expectations artificially high," says O'Farrell. "Discussions with early investors should go along the lines of 'We don't really know what the company is worth, but we're putting our life into it, and you're putting lots of money into it. Let's be reasonable.' If I'm giving up a third of my company in the first investment round, that doesn't feel like too much."

- Opt for angel money versus venture capital in early investment rounds. "One of hardest things anyone can do is move an idea off the drawing board and make it into something tangible," O'Farrell says. Venture capitalists may have trouble seeing the value of a fledgling idea because they're evaluating in terms of something that can sustain high long-term growth. An early-stage company may not be developed enough to provide such growth assurances. However, according to O'Farrell, an angel investor may be more willing to make a smaller bet based on his or her regard for the founders and their dedication to the project, rather than to a cold evaluation of the venture's immature business fundamentals. "I prefer to raise a half million dollars from a number of angels and get a six month [strategic] plan in place," O'Farrell explains. "Then, I can begin to build a track record. When it's time to go to the venture capitalists, we can say, 'This is what we did, this is what we learned. Here are our beta customers. Here's our proof of concept.'" That record, rather than a cocktail napkin sketch of a business idea, is more apt to attract first round venture funds.

BORN IN THE DORM

Generation Y entrepreneurs that build a dotcom business using a PC in their college dorm are favorite subjects of "new economy" magazines that want to show how wide open the opportunities are in today's Internet economy. However, college-aged entrepreneurs have been around longer than the current crop of cover boys and girls. Witness Michael Dell, the computer impresario who used $1000 to create the now $27 billion Dell Computer Corp., Round Rock, Texas, a computer manufacturer, while he was a student at the University of Texas in 1984.

Sam Kellett, founder and chief executive officer of eAttorney, Atlanta, got a similar early start, so that by the time he started his first company, it felt like he'd already been through the process once before. In 1996, as part of an MBA project at the University of Georgia, Kellett was required to become a virtual entrepreneur by recruiting four classmates and developing a business plan for a commercially viable company. The students were given 25 minutes to pitch the plan to a group of actual venture capitalists from the Atlanta area, who would give a thumbs up or down evaluation of the proposal (but no actual money). "It's the closest academic experience you can get to what it's like meet with venture capitalists in the real world," Kellett says.

From that experience, eAttorney was born. The Web business uses the rent-an-application ASP model to deliver a legal recruiting program over the Internet. "We were an ASP before ASPs were cool," Kellett says. At first, the company focused just on matching law students with potential-employer attorney partnerships and companies. In time, eAttorney evolved full-blown business applications geared for the legal community. They include administrative and financial applications for the legal profession, all available on a rent-as-needed basis, as well as programs to automate billing, time keeping, contact management, and presenting bills to clients. The company targets small legal firms with 50 or fewer employees, which Kellett says represents 97 percent of the legal community. Today, the company says 400 law offices, 55 law schools, and 70,000 law students and practicing attorneys now use the recruiting software.

Despite the collegiate jump start Kellett received in his MBA class, he admits he had a lot to learn about being an entrepreneur in the real world. Just 24 when he hit the streets with his ASP idea, Kellett has developed a strategy of surrounding himself with seasoned business veterans, who validate the business strategy in the eyes of formal investors. "I got Robert P. Guyton, Inktomi co-founder, on our board. He's been there and done it. He's helped us with multiple partners. Your deal has to be that much better to attract the right folks."

Kellett also exploited the venture capital contacts he made in college. "I went around the local business community and met with people I was introduced to through the venture capitalists we presented to in college," he recalls. He and his business partner stoked the business with initial seed capital, and it wasn't until three years later, in 1999, that eAttorney tried for its first round of venture funding. The delay was part of Kellett's strategy. "I needed to meet some key people around town who are the gatekeepers of the club," the close-knit investment community in Atlanta, which is mirrored in metropolitan centers across the country and ultimately tie into the vaulted venture funds headquartered on Sand Hill Road in Menlo Park, California.

"Getting into the investment community is important for start ups, especially in the cocktail-napkin stage. You need to find people who can make an introduction because there are so many deals. One firm in town gets pitched 200 deals a day. Surrounding yourself with people considered to be 'smart money' validates your the deal," Kellett says. "Ideally, you want someone to make an introduction for you. The venture capital market is relationship oriented. They reward each other."

Nothing—even the lack of a beneficial introduction to a key investor—should stop an entrepreneur who believes in his or her company from knocking on important doors. In addition to making presentations at local angel investors forums, Kellett also singled out a business leader in Atlanta, Martin Tilson of Kilpatrick Stockton LLP, a corporate law firm. "I knew Mart Tilson was one of the guys I needed to know," he says. But none of Kellett's networking efforts resulted in finding a contact who could set up a meeting with Tilson. Undeterred, Kellett decided to cold-call Tilson. Luckily, he says, Tilson gave him 20 seconds on the phone to make his pitch; Kellett used the time to interest Tilson enough in eAttorney to agree to set up a face-to-face meeting. The combination of forum presentations and getting face time with important financial leaders paid off. "Now we're part of the dotcom community," Kellett says. One of the benefits of this resident status is the possibility for ongoing relationships that may not blossom immediately, but may take off later. "If [a venture fund] says no this go around, it may say yes in the future. They'll help you sooner or later," Kellett believes.

Nevertheless, the process of exposing your fledgling business idea to hardened investors can be akin to a job interview from hell, only worse. "These meetings aren't good for your self es-teem," Kellett admits. "Even if you're offering the hottest deal on the planet, [the venture fund managers] won't let you know that." Stumbling blocks include contracts offered by investors that place enough restrictions on entrepreneurs to "handcuff you to the desk," he says. Determining the value of the growing com-pany is a major source of disagreement, the entrepreneur adds. "You have to play the dilution game. Don't just raise money for the sake of raising money. The longer you can wait, the more value you can create, and the less you'll dilute your company. Today, I own a substantial amount of the company. Some [foun-ders] end up becoming just employees. It's easy to be really ex-cited because you're about to get funded, but you have to read the fine print. It's [a venture fund manager's] job to get the best deal for their shareholders."

Despite the negotiating difficulties, Kellett values venture capital money higher than other potential sources, such as Small Business Administration loans. The main reason: Along with cash, venture funds offer experienced business people who can spot holes in your strategy, identify potential sources for new growth, and open doors to other investors, accountants, and law-yers who are savvy about start ups. "Money is a commodity these days, so you have to evaluate investors according to what other value do they bring."

Kellett says negotiating with venture capitalists is "an art." He advises entrepreneurs to prepare themselves by anticipating any foreseeable question about the business strategy, the financial roadmap, a liquidity plan (a public stock offering or a merger strategy), and the commitment of the founders. Entrepreneurs need to prepare for these meetings in advance, like a political candidate preparing for a debate. Business managers also need to prepare a comprehensive operating plan with details about how they expect to meet their revenue goals. "You've got to have a business model that gets you profitable in 14 to 18 months," Kellett believes. "These days, investors don't want to see a lot of dollars spent on marketing. They want it spent on building an infrastructure."

At no time, however, should a business manager try to finesse an answer to a question he or she isn't prepared for. "[Venture capitalists] are really smart folks. If you don't have an answer, tell them you'll go get it and get back to them. Our business model actually evolved based on some of the objections we heard in the venture capital meetings. In every meeting, we took away something that's helped us, including the scalability of our company—we didn't have enough initially."

Kellett also says company managers have to know what can scare an investor away from a deal and remove those threats from the presentation. He rattles off a list of red flags that can alarm potential financing dealmakers. "If you change your story at all. If you've made big changes in your business strategy. Not meeting financial numbers." Playing the role of the appreciative entrepreneur doesn't hurt either, up to a point. "No matter how good your team is, you really have to go in those meetings with your hat in your hand. You can't be overzealous. Just make sure you don't get walked on either," Kellett says.

The strategy of focusing on local venture capital is paying off. In 1999, eAttorney received about $3.4 million from Frontier Capital, Imlay Investments, and Monarch Capital Partners (www.monarchpartners.com), all in Atlanta. In the fall of 2000, the company will use the commitments from local investment funds as ammunition for attracting $20 million from what Kellett calls the "halo firms" on Sand Hill Drive. "Having smart money behind us already will make that process easier," he believes.

PEOPLE NETWORKS ARE ESSENTIAL WHEN YOU'RE NOT A 'DOTCOM'

Peter Stasz, the founder of Dymedix Inc., St. Paul, MN, built his new company on a network: the kind consisting of important people connections.

His first foray into the entrepreneurial world came in 1983 when he invested $7,000 of his own money to launch Everest Medical, a Minnesota company that created bipolar surgical equipment, which uses radio-frequency energy to reduce bleeding during surgery. Although the technology was innovative and successful, Everest didn't enter its first funding round until 1986, partly because Stasz hadn't yet built a reputation around town as a business manager. "I had a good technical reputation in town, but I didn't have a reputation for management at a level that people thought I could pull off a start up," he recalls. "So I got a team together. The most critical one was marketing, someone who could explore the marketing area and our chances of penetrating the market. The other one was operations, to handle the financials."

Even with a management team in place, Everest needed the help of an area angel investor and a veteran of the medical-equipment industry to open doors into the conference rooms of investment bankers, angels, and local venture capitalists. Going it alone, Stasz says, is tough. "The doors never quite open until somebody opens them for you. I got into meetings with venture capital funds, but they have so many companies to consider, you need someone who can help separate you from the masses."

Stasz avoided Small Business Administration loans primarily because he felt the application paperwork is too time consuming for the potential return. "At the same time you're trying to get funding, you have to earn a living. I didn't have the money to pay somebody to get the SBA applications together, which can cost $5000 or more in filing fees. I was the only employee of my company." However, for real entrepreneurial disdain, nothing beats local banks, in Stasz's eyes. "They're worthless," he says. "They want collateral and other financial assurances. But when you're starting a new company, everything is iffy."

To guard against negative scrutiny of investors of any ilk, Stasz advises entrepreneurs to build their companies according to carefully unfolding strategy that doesn't subject the young idea to the cold cruel world too early. He says he mistakenly registered his first company too early—almost three years before he sought formal financing. During those years, Stasz slowly developed the business, but didn't yet create a revenue stream. In his mind, he was making progress while he was juggling other professional responsibilities. "It was important to me to have the idea and research its feasibility. See what the market potential is, then talk to the investment people. You've got to show them you know what you're talking about even if you don't have all the answers."

But to investors looking for fast-track profits, the three-year old company looked like it wasn't going anywhere. "When investors start looking at you, they ask, "What have you been doing the last three years?"

With his second company, Stasz's groundwork was already in place. He already had a track record as a start-up manager. He developed the business, Semiconductor NT International, a creator of fiber-optics for the process control industry, with three other business people, each of whom invested $25,000 of their own savings and added additional angel money using their individual business contacts. One partner, a veteran of the process control industry, became president, while Stasz became the technology czar.

Early on, the company earned consulting contracts from large corporations like Fuji Electric, which brought enough revenues into the business to sustain its initial development. Serendipitously, the founders discovered that the growing semiconductor industry needed a way to pump highly-corrosive chemicals through its manufacturing plants while maintaining the stringent "clean room" requirements necessary for making silicon products. "We fell into the semiconductor niche," Stasz admits. "We were using a lot of Teflon pipe to move liquids around. From this we developed temperature and flow monitors, and that took off."

The heavy investments of the founders jump started the young company, which grew in its early stages through consulting revenues. By the time the principals were ready to court outside financiers, they had a viable company with a good financial foundation. At first, Stasz and his partners cultivated the angels they had worked with on previous projects. In turn, the angels were able to open the doors to a local venture capital company, Capital Management, which kicked in cash and paved the way for additional backing from investment bankers and others. Even with the investment cash flowing, the founders considered themselves fortunate for not having to relinquish very much managerial control. "In both Everest and NT International, we didn't have any of those people sitting on the board. They visited, but they didn't have voting rights," Stasz says.

Today, he's in the beginning stages of creating Dymedix Corp., which is developing technology that will be used by medical researchers in sleep deprivation studies. The third time around the start-up track, Stasz is building the company steadily and methodically. "Even in today's environment, we wouldn't have any difficulty finding money if we had come up with an Internet company. But since we're in the medical field, people are not aware of the potential. Medical devices haven't been a big money maker. That means we had to get our first $100,000 through acquaintances to establish that the stuff works. Then there was a huge gap [in available funding] from $100,000 to $2 million. For the big boys, we weren't big enough. They prefer $5 million investments."

Thanks to their track record and methodology, Stasz and his partners are succeeding against all the Web competition. Step one was to build functioning prototypes of the technology. "My strategy is to keep dilution of the company to a minimum. I [build a prototype] to show the technology works, then go to big boys," he says, referring to venture capitalists. Investors "want to see and touch" a prototype," Stasz adds. "An idea you can't touch." His own savings paid for this launch stage.

Step two, once the prototypes were complete, was to file for and receive a patent, a key ingredient in any technology venture to validate the idea initially and later as a "barrier to entry" to block attempts by competitors to muscle in on the market once a commercial product hits the streets. The lack of a patent is an expensive sticking point when it's time for an entrepreneur to sit down with investors. "It will cost you; [investors] will want more shares," Stasz explains.

Step three, in April of 1998, was incorporation. At this point, he went for his first outside funding round, which netted $400,000 from angel investors. "I started with people I knew, who then brought in other people. One of the investors had a wife who had sleep problems, so he was aware of the issue."

Step four for Dymedix was to acquire a bridge loan, which Stasz made sure was convertible to company stock, not to cash. "From a legal point of view, a convertible loan gives you a quicker turnaround, you can use money sooner," he explains. "With a private placement memorandum, you have to wait to until you break the escrow limit."

Currently, the company has a small but measurable cash flow and the Dymedix founders are out talking to investment bankers for the next rounding of financing on the way to creating a commercial product line.

STAY LOOSE

All of the entrepreneurs agree that building a business is one of the hardest things they've done in their life, but, when markets and ideas click, it is also one of the most rewarding. Going through the process a second or third time can offer a chance for redemption from rookie mistakes first-time entrepreneurs inevitably suffer in their first meetings with angels and venture capitalists. But in a process as challenging as trying to get an investor to part with large sums of his or her financial resources, even experienced entrepreneurs must remain flexible enough to recover from missteps. In fact, O'Farrell, Kellet, and Stasz all benefited by learning from their mistakes and changing some of their original business ideas to attack a previously hidden opening in their market. In the end, the real message these business people have to offer new entrepreneurs isn't so much that nothing succeeds like success, but rather, nothing succeeds like open-mindedness.

VENTURE FUND DIRECTORY

Venture funds identified with a icon are those that use the Web to make it easy for entrepreneurs to electronically submit business ideas, executive summaries, or business plans. A 🌱 icon denotes funds that target young companies seeking investments of less than $1 million.

🌱

Abell Venture Fund

Focus: Baltimore-area companies in a variety of industries
Web Address: www.abell.org/venturef.htm

The fund manages a total of $25 million. Considers companies in any market as long as they are based in the Baltimore area. Looks for candidates that can reach sales of $30 million to $50 million over five years, especially through pioneering a new product or service. Typical investment amounts are $3 million or less. Fund managers participate in staff recruitment, follow-on fund raising, and formulating business strategies for companies that receive investment capital.

HOW TO APPLY:

Send a hard copy of the business plan to:

Abell Venture Fund
111 S. Calvert St. Suite 2300
Baltimore, MD 21202

ABN AMRO Private Equity

Focus: Business, outsourcing, communications, distribution, and health-care services; software, information technology, and specialty retail
Web Address: www.abnequity.com

Manages more than $70 million in fast-growth, private and select public companies. Seeks companies that can provide an investment return in seven years or less. Managerial talent is key consideration when evaluating investment candidates. Usually acts as a minority investor, although will sometimes take on a controlling-interest role. Typically invests between $1 million to $7 million per transaction. Participates as a member of the invested company's management board and contributes to strategic planning, acquisitions, future financings, underwriter selection and executive recruitment. Provides introductions to investment bankers, accountants, and attorneys. Will consider candidate companies at any stage of development, but prefers to work with companies that have attained $5 million to $100 million in revenues.

HOW TO APPLY:

Looks for reliable cash flow, high profit margins, and strong earnings potential. Encourages early conversations with a candidate's key manager. Contact the appropriate manager based on market specialty.

Business/Outsourcing Services: David Bogetz (312) 855-7079; Healthcare Services: Donna C.E. Williamson (312) 855-

6039; Telecommunications & Information Technology: Brian Hirsch (312) 855-7135.

ABN AMRO Private Equity
208 South LaSalle St., 10th Floor
Chicago, IL 60604-1003
(312) 855-7292
Fax: (312) 553-6648

ABS Capital Partners
Focus: Technology, business and financial services, media and communications, healthcare, and the Internet
Web Address: www.abscapital.com

Founded in 1993, now has more than $900 million in capital for management buyouts, expansion financings and recapitalizations. Doesn't typically back start ups, turnarounds or overseas businesses. Typically invests $10-30 million in each company. Looks for market leadership (real or potential) and managerial talent. Takes a board seat to help in management decisions and financial strategy.

HOW TO APPLY:
Complete electronic form at Web site or send funding proposals to the nearest office:

ABS Capital Partners
One South St., 25th Floor
Baltimore, MD 21202
(410) 895-4400
Fax: (410) 895-4380

ABS Capital Partners
Belle Meade Office Park
4515 Harding Road, Suite 100
Nashville, TN 37205
(615) 297-9079
Fax: (615) 297-8969

ABS Capital Partners
101 California St., 47th Floor
San Francisco, CA 94111
(415) 477-3297
(415) 477-3229

ABS Capital Partners
11921 Freedom Drive, Suite 550
Reston, VA 20190
(703) 736-8320
Fax: (703) 736-8321

Accel Partners
Focus: Communications, the Internet, and intranets
Web Address: www.accel.com

Previous communications investments funded video-conferencing, wide-area networking, and local-area networking technologies. Internet holdings have focused on electronic commerce, security, optical networking, voice-over-the-Net, and high-speed switching. Notable investments include UUNET, RealNetworks, and Arbor. Management partners include Mitch Kapor, founder of Lotus Development Corp. and designer of the spreadsheet program Lotus 1-2-3.

HOW TO APPLY:

Demonstrate technology expertise and a compatible business culture. Write to info@accel.com or call (650) 614-4800.

Accel Partners
428 University Ave.
Palo Alto, CA 94301
(650) 614-4800
Fax: (650) 614-4880

Advanced Technology Ventures
Focus: Information technology and health care
Web Address: www.atv.com

Founded in 1979. Focuses on start ups developing software and services; communications and computer hardware, communications services and electronics; medical diagnostics, health-care information systems and services, medical devices and pharmaceuticals. Advises funded companies in product development, business strategies, financial planning. Partners include executives with Sun Microsystems, Evans & Sutherland Computer Corp., and Xerox PARC (Palo Alto Research Center).

HOW TO APPLY:

Via the Web site or by calling (650) 321-8601 (Palo Alto, CA), or (781) 290-0707 (Waltham, MA).

Advanced Technology Ventures
8995 Westside Parkway, Suite 200
Alpharetta, GA 30004
Fax: (678) 336-2001

Advantage Capital
Focus: Communications, information processing, computer sciences, health care, life sciences
Web Address: www.advantagecap.com

Founded in 1992, the fund manages $125 million in investments. Participates in recapitalizations, management buyouts, and expansion capital for early-stage and middle-market companies. Shuns companies in oil and gas exploration, restaurants, real estate development, lending operations or licensed professional services. Usually invests $500,000 to $5 million, but can help provide investments of more than $10 million as part of a funding pool with other investors. Key criteria when reviewing candidates include managers' expertise, the candidate's product or market uniqueness, its potential to capture a sizable amount of a large and growing market over four to six years, a viable exit strategy, and current revenues. Participates in executive recruitment, business development, strategic planning, regulatory issues, debt financing, and marketing strategy development.

HOW TO APPLY:

Send business plan, financial history and forecasts, and managers' resumes to one of the addresses below. Positive reviews lead to meetings with key executives of the candidate company.

Advantage Capital
909 Poydras St., Suite 2230
New Orleans, LA 70112
(504) 522-4850
Fax: (504) 522-4950

Pierre Laclede Center
7733 Forsyth Boulevard, Suite 1850
St. Louis, MO 63105
(314) 725-0800
Fax: (314) 725-4265

One Penn Plaza
42nd Floor
New York, NY 10119
(212) 273-7250
Fax: (212) 273-7249

100 North Tampa St., Suite 2410
Tampa, FL 33602
(813) 221-8700
Fax: (813) 221-1606

Advent International
Focus: Cable TV and media, information technology, specialty chemicals, health care, consumer products and retailing
Web Address: www.adventinternational.com/

Manages $3.5 billion in funds through staff in 15 countries throughout Asia, Europe, Latin America, and North America. Backs approximately 100 new companies a year. Participates in minority equity investments, leveraged recapitalizations, and share purchases in businesses. Early-stage funding typically goes to product development or early revenue stages. Will selec-tively back companies with untested business models or products. Also funds mature, profitable entities. Prefers invest-ments of $20 million to $75 million, but provides for larger amounts through pool-ing efforts with other investors. Aims for a three- to five-year payout.

HOW TO APPLY:
Send proposal to

Advent International Corp.
75 State St.,
Boston, MA 02109
(617) 951-9400
Fax: (617) 951-0566

Aegis Capital
Focus: Computers and information systems
Web Address: www.aegis-capital.com

Offers early-stage and seed financing, and capital for acquisitions and buyouts. Will act as a sole, lead, co-lead, or syndicate in-vestor. Takes active role in financial, man-agement, technology development, and international business development activi-ties. Maintains Asia-Pacific operations for Pacific Rim opportunities.

Minimum investment: $250,000. Looks for candidates with experienced management and the potential for market growth.

HOW TO APPLY:

Send executive summary to:

Steve Kim
Chief Operating Officer
skim@aegis-capital.com

Aegis Capital
1001 4th Avenue Plaza, Suite 2310
Seattle, WA 98154
(206) 624-9254
Fax: (206) 624-9448

Agio Capital Partners
Focus: Manufacturing, production, distribution, and service companies
Web Address: www.agio-capital.com/

Provides investments ranging from $1 million to $5 million. Targets "noncyclical, noncommodity industries" and companies without past labor, legal, or environmental problems. Prefers management or family buyouts and corporate divestitures, but will consider start ups. Considers candidates from throughout the country, but focuses on firms in the Dakotas, Iowa, Minnesota, and Wisconsin. Typically takes a seat on a funded company's board.

HOW TO APPLY:

Demonstrate a positive earnings track record and predictable cash flow, and a management team with significant industry expertise. Send proposal to agiocap@aol.com.

or

Agio Capital Partners
US Bank Place, Suite 4600
601 Second Ave. South
Minneapolis, MN 55402
(612) 339-8408
Fax: (612) 349-4232

Alliance Technology Ventures
Focus: Early-stage information technology and life sciences
Web Address: www.atv.com/

Founded in 1994, manages over $110 million. Presently seeking telecommunications and Internet opportunities in the eastern half of the U.S., especially in Atlanta. Typically backs early-stage companies, but will consider other projects. Looks for clear market capable of achieving $250 million, proprietary technology, and executives with technology experience. Shuns retail, franchise, or distribution companies, real estate, oil and gas, financial services, or overseas projects. Investments usually range from $500,000 and $5 million. Acts of sole investor or syndicate member.

HOW TO APPLY:

Send business plans via UPS Document Exchange (not as unsolicited e-mail attachments) or forward plans to:

Alliance Technology Ventures
8995 Westside Parkway
Suite 200

Alpharetta, Georgia 30004
Fax: (678) 336-2001
info@atv.com

Alloy Ventures Inc.

Focus: Seed and early stage technology companies in information and life sciences
Web Address: www.alloyventures.com/

Manages more than $300 million in capital. Formerly, Asset Management Associates, Inc., continues to manage several of the AMA venture funds.

Alloy Ventures
480 Cowper St.
Palo Alto, California 94301
(650) 687-5000
Fax: (650) 687-5010
www.alloyventures.com

Alpha Capital Partners

Focus: Information technology, medical and healthcare, consumer businesses and manufacturing companies, mainly in the Midwest
Web Address: www.alphacapital.com

Actively investing $38.8 million from two open funds. Backs early-, expansion-, or mature-stage businesses, management buyouts, and recapitalizations. Typically invests $500,000 to $4 million. Often is a lead investor or in an investor partnership. Commits for three to seven years. Sits on board of directors. Participates in strategic and financial planning. Looks for managerial experience, market niche, growth potential, and exit strategy.

How to Apply:

Send business plan to:

A. Kalnow or **W. Oberholtzer**
Alpha Capital Partners
122 South Michigan Ave.
Suite 1700
Chicago, IL 60603
(312) 322-9800
Fax: (312) 322-9808
acp@alphacapital.com
or

O. Cook or C. Crocker
Alpha Capital Partners
310 West Monument Ave., Suite 400
Dayton, OH 45402
(937) 222-2006
Fax: (937) 228-0115
acp@alphcapital.com

Alpine Technology Ventures

Focus: Early-stage information technology, software, communications, telecommunications, computing technologies, multimedia, Internet, and semiconductor companies
Web Address: www.alpineventures.com

Focuses on California companies, particularly ones based in Silicon Valley. Maintains distribution networks to Asia and can help companies build strategic partnerships in the area. Typically invests $2 and $4 million per company from an investment pool of $72 million. Each fund partner works with six to seven companies. Partners become board members of backed companies.

HOW TO APPLY:

E-mail initial funding inquiries to kathryn@alpineventures.com. Follow up with an executive summary or business plan to:

Alpine Technology Ventures
20300 Stevens Creek Blvd, Suite 495
Cupertino, CA 95014
(408) 725-1810
Fax: (408) 725-1207

Alta Partners
Focus: Early-stage companies in telecommunications, traditional and wireless networks, on-line services, electronic commerce applications, medical devices, biopharmaceuticals, and developers of medical services delivery systems
Web Address: www.altapartners.com

Four-year-old Alta Partners is a successor to Burr, Egan, Deleage & Co. (see listing below). Manages more than $500 million in capital from U.S. and European investors. Typically invests between $2 million to $8 million in each portfolio company over five to ten years. Favors post-start up companies with growth potential. Typically acts as the primary investor and fills a seat on the company's management board.

HOW TO APPLY:

Demonstrate leadership potential in a high-growth market and a unique product or service. Managers should have a proven entrepreneurial track record and an understanding of the target market. Make initial contact via e-mail at alta@altapartners.com or telephone, at (415) 362-4022. Follow up with a business plan.

Alta Partners
One Embarcadero Center
Suite 4050
San Francisco, CA 94111

Altira Group
Focus: Technologies for the oil and gas industry
Web Address: www.altiragroup.com/

Focuses on seed and early-stage companies with investment usually between $250,000 and $4 million. Looks for experienced and highly motivated managers and proprietary technologies that provide competitive advantage.

HOW TO APPLY:

Demonstrate potential to deliver high margins and a technological niche. Send proposals to info@altiragroup.com

or

Altira Group
World Trade Center
1625 Broadway
Suite 2150
Denver, CO 80202-4727
(303) 825-1600
Fax: (303) 623-3525

Alternative Agricultural Research and Commercialization Corp.
Focus: Industrial uses of agricultural materials
Web Address: www.usda.gov/aarc/

Founded six years ago, this wholly-owned subsidiary of the U.S. Department of Agriculture has invested $135 million in venture funds for start ups that turn agricultural, forestry, and animal byproducts into industrial products. Prefers private companies or individuals with already marketable products prior to commercialization. An 11-person board of directors from the public and private sectors evaluates proposals and allocates funds. Initial investments average $300,000. In return for funding, takes an equity stake, a percentage of sales royalties, or both. Typical relationships last six to eight years. Candidates must match investment funds in a 1:1 ratio.

HOW TO APPLY:

Begin with a pre-proposal. Demonstrate suitability to the AARC mandate, viability of the technology, commercialization read-

iness, managerial expertise, and an ability of the technology to aid rural communities and the environment.

The Alternative Agricultural Research and Commercialization (AARC) Corporation
U.S. Department of Agriculture
0156 South Building
14th and Independence Avenue, S.W.
Washington, DC 20250-0401
(202) 690-1633
Fax: (202) 690-1655

Altos Ventures
Focus: Early-stage investments in business-to-business e-commerce, software, e-retailing, the Internet, networking, and communications
Web Address: www.altosvc.com

Currently managing Altos Ventures II, a $100 million fund for backing entrepreneurs with successful track records. Looks for projects in high-growth markets and unique products or services that offer ongoing competitive advantages. Will provide seed funding and consider late-stage opportunities on a case-by-case basis. Prefers to act as lead investor. Takes board seat. First funding rounds are typically $500,000 to $2 million, rising to $8 million in subsequent rounds.

Focuses on Northern California companies and those in other western states. Invests outside this geographical area only when there's a local lead investor.

HOW TO APPLY:

E-mail company profile to investments@altosvc.com. Demonstrate market potential, business innovation, and managerial expertise.

Altos Ventures
2882 Sand Hill Road, Suite 100
Menlo Park, CA 94025
(650) 234-9771
Fax: (650) 233-9821
info@altosvc.com

Ameritech Development Corp.
Focus: Communications and media companies
Web Address: www.ameritech.com/products/venture_rm/adc.html

Established in 1983, by communications provider Ameritech Corp. Invests in products a year or less from commercialization. Particular interests include communications technologies and services, network management applications, wireless communications, landline technologies, multimedia, technologies, electronic commerce, and the Internet. Typically funds early- and mid-stage companies with $500,000 to $3 million for three to five years. May co-invest with other funds and investors. Funded companies are assigned one or more Ameritech staff members from re-

lated markets. When appropriate, ADC uses Ameritech operations in Hungary, Poland, Norway and New Zealand to aid a funded company's global strategies. Seeks a board seat. Prefers to work with proven management teams.

HOW TO APPLY:

Demonstrate synergy with an Ameritech business unit, as well as the market potential and the expertise of the management team. Send business plan to:

Ameritech Development Corp.
Attn: Venture Capital
30 South Wacker Dr., Floor 37
Chicago, IL 60606
(312) 750-5083
Fax: (312) 609-0244

Ampersand Ventures
Focus: Specialty Materials and Chemicals (SMC) industry
Web Address: www.ampersandventures.com/

Founded in 1988, has funded more than 40 SMC companies. Manages $200 million in equity capital for early and expansion-stage companies. Will also provide funds for SMC acquisitions and recapitalizations, and for partial or total liquidity to existing owners. Offers funded companies managerial input and potential financial matchmaking with leading SMC companies.

How to Apply:

Send business plan to Caroline Marple at:

Ampersand Ventures
55 William St., Suite 240
Wellesley, MA 02481
Phone: (781) 239-0700
Fax: (781) 239-0824
info@ampersandventures.com

Angels' Forum Management Co.
Focus: New technologies from the greater San Francisco Bay area of California
Web Address: www.angelsforum.com

Past investments have funded companies in software, hardware, semiconductors, health care, telecommunications, chemical, biotechnology, consulting, and research. Focuses on very early stage companies with typical investments of $50,000 to $500,000. Investment strategy tuned to reflect a commitment to cultural and gender diversity. Frequently accepts a board position.

How to Apply:

Complete a questionnaire available at the Web site. In addition, in a Microsoft Word or Powerpoint file, send a short background summary, contact information, and two references for each of the key managers. List contact information for directors, law firms, accountants, and advisors associated with your company. List strategic customers, beta site, corporate, investor relationships, including contact in-formation. Provide a current capitalization table as is and fully diluted. List investors or employees with more than 1 percent ownership. Finally, create a Powerpoint slide page for each of the following topics: concept, market, customer benefit, management team, and competitive advantage.

Send package to *Plans@angelsforum.com*

or

The Angels' Forum LLC
P.O. Box 1605
Los Altos, CA 94023-1605
(650) 857-0700
Fax: (650) 857-0773

Apex Investment Partners
Focus: Telecommunications, software, information technology, specialty retail and consumer products
Web Address: www.apexvc.com/

Established in 1987, manages more than $130 million in venture capital. Most investments range from $1 million to $5 million for each company. Majority of investments are early-stage businesses. Key investment criterion: a skilled team of managers is onboard or able to be recruited. Most interested in large markets and those with high growth potential. Seeks young companies with proprietary products or services that offer a competitive advantage. Works side-by-side with funded companies to create a business strategy, cultivate additional funding sources, and develop the company's infrastructure. Provides introductions to distributors, possible customers, and technology alliances. Usually takes a board seat.

HOW TO APPLY:

To submit a business plan to:

Apex Investment Partners
233 South Wacker Drive,
Suite 9500
Chicago, IL 60606
(312) 258-0320
Fax: (312) 258-0592
apex@apexvc.com

Arbor Partners
Focus: Michigan-based technology, communications, software, and electronic commerce companies
Web Address: www.arborpartners.com

Looks for experienced executives and a business model that outlines a strategy for the company to become a top-two leader in the market. Participates as lead or co-investor. Will consider companies throughout the country.

HOW TO APPLY:

Send proposal to

Arbor Partners, LLC
130 South First St.
Ann Arbor, MI 48104
(734) 668-9000
Fax: (734) 669-4195
info@arborpartners.com

Artemis Ventures
Focus: Seed-stage business-to-business software, Internet software and services, e-commerce, outsourced services, customer relationship management, enterprise applications, and enabling technologies
Web Address: www.artemisventures.com/

Invests exclusively in seed-stage companies in California or Seattle. Follows up early growth phase funding with second round capital from other venture capital partners. Typically invests $500,000 to $1 million in the early round, using a fund that currently totals $22 million. Becomes a director, assists in sales, marketing, technology, and staff development.

HOW TO APPLY:

Fill out electronic screening application on Web site.

Artemis Ventures
207 Second St., Suite E (3rd Floor)
Sausalito, CA 94965
(415) 289-2500
Fax: (415) 289-1789
info@artemisventures.com

Arch Ventures
Focus: Seed and early-state investments in information technology, life sciences, and physical sciences
Web Address: www.archventure.com/

Traditionally funds new technologies developed inside healthcare organizations, universities and national laboratories, including Beth Israel Hospital, Massachusetts, and Institute of Technology, and Argonne National Laboratory. Web site offers a checklist to help entrepreneurs evaluate how closely their products match the fund's interests.

HOW TO APPLY:

If the checklist review reveals a possible fit, send a cover letter and business-plan summary (not a complete business plan) to info@archventure.com.

Arch Southwest
1155 University, S.E.
Albuquerque, NM 87106
(505) 843-4293
Fax: (505) 843-4294

Arch Midwest
8725 W. Higgins Road, Suite 290
Chicago, IL 60631
(773) 380-6600
Fax: (773) 380-6606

Arch Northeast
45 Rockefeller Plaza, Suite 2000
New York, NY 10020
(212) 332-3264
Fax: (212) 332-5054

Arch Northwest
1000 Second Ave., Suite 3700
Seattle, WA 98104

(206) 674-3028
Fax: (206) 674-3026

Aspen Ventures
Focus: Information technologies, early-stage companies only in the western United States
Web Address: www.aspenventures.com

Seeks technology applications that address large markets. Key executives must have previous success in creating a new technology company. Management should also present a clear product development strategy and analyses of the competition, distribution goals, and market trends.

HOW TO APPLY:

Start with a one- to four-page business plan summary. Include target market and its size and growth rate potential; concise descriptions of the product or service, as well as the appeal to the target market; competitive analysis; managers' resumes and expected additions of key personnel; distribution strategy; current status of product/service development, revenue, and capitalization; and three- to five-year financial projections. Feedback from fund managers often comes within two weeks.

E-mail executive summary to any of the partners or send it to the postal address below.

Alexander Cilento:
alex@aspenventures.com
E. David Crockett

dcrockett@aspenventures.com
Thad Whalen: twhalen@aspenventures.com

Aspen Ventures
1000 Fremont Avenue
Suite 200
Los Altos, CA 94024
(650) 917-5670
Fax: (650) 917-5677

Asset Management Company
Focus: Seed and early-stage companies in information and biological sciences
Web Address: www.assetman.com

Thirty-five years old with investments in more than 100 companies. Typically invests $100,000 to $2 million per company. Usually acts as lead investor, but will pool investments with other funds. Key market interests within information sciences include telecommunications, computer hardware and software, networking, Internet business applications and information services, mobile computing, databases, semi- and super-conductors. Life sciences interests include bio-pharmaceuticals, drug discovery services, drug delivery, diagnostics, research instrumentation, research and development software and analysis tools, clinical laboratory instrumentation, agricultural technology, and environmental technology.

HOW TO APPLY:
Send an executive summary or business plan and complete resumes of key foun-

ders. The documents should demonstrate how the product/service solves a relevant problem in a cost-effective way, how the technology is unique, realistic milestones for product/service rollout, competitive analysis, market potential of $100 million or more, a business strategy leading to profitability and market dominance, and the expertise of key managers.

E-mail: technology@assetman.com

or

medical@assetman.com

Asset Management Company Venture Capital
2275 E. Bayshore Road, Suite 150
Palo Alto, CA 94303
(650) 494-7400
Fax: (650) 856-1826

Associated Venture Investors
Focus: Convergence of information, communications, and entertainment technologies and services
Web Address: www.avicapital.com/

The Media Technology Ventures fund began in 1996 to back seed and start-up companies with $71 million in capital. Typically invests $750,000 to $2 million initially. Has invested as little as $50,000 to $100,000 for early technical and marketing development. Invests $2 million to $3 million over the life of the relationship. Frequently the first investor in the new company and usually acts as the lead investor. Prefers California-based companies.

The Media Technology Equity Partners fund, organized in 1998, targets early- and mid-stage companies with $155 million for convergence applications. Typically invests $4 million to $6 million (up to $10 million in some cases) per company. Usually funds expansion projects for companies with an established management team and a commercial product. Will evaluate nationwide and Western European investments.

HOW TO APPLY:
Send proposals to

Associated Venture Investors
One First St., Suite 2
Los Altos, CA 94022
(650) 949-9862
Fax: (650) 949-8510
vc@avicapital.com
vc@mtventures.com

Atlantic Medical Capital
Focus: Mid- and late-stage healthcare services companies, information systems, and databases
Web Address: www.sumnet.com/amc

Typically invests $3 to $15 million. Will consider larger stakes. Becomes sole, lead, or investor. Participates on boards to guide expansion, acquisitions, and asset divestitures. Looks for experienced management,

growth potential, market dominance, and solid earnings.

HOW TO APPLY:
Inquire at

Atlantic Medical Capital
156 West 56th St., Suite 1605
New York, NY 10019-3800
(212) 307-3580
Fax: (212) 957-1586
amc@atlanticmedcap.com

Atlas Venture
Focus: Transatlantic information technology and life sciences
Web Address: www.atlasventure.com

Maintains offices in Boston, Silicon Valley, and Europe. Seeks new companies in Europe and North America, but prefers those near Boston and Menlo Park, CA, or Benelux, France, Germany, Switzerland, or the United Kingdom. Specializes in expansions on both continents. Prime areas of interest currently are enterprise software, data and telecommunications, e-commerce businesses, and biopharmaceutical and medical device companies. Funds total more than $850 million, with initial investments ranging from $500,000 to $5 million. However, will consider seed investments under a half million dollars. Takes a board seat.

HOW TO APPLY:

Seeks a business plan complete with market, product, and management analysis; third-party market and product analysis; a two-year financial plan; a 12- to 18-month budget forecast; business references.

Boston Office

Atlas Venture
222 Berkeley St.
Boston, MA 02116
(617) 859-9290
Fax: (617) 859-9292
E-mail boston@atlasventure.com

Boston office contacts:

Information technology
Axel Bichara, abichara@atlasventure.com
Michael Feinstein,
mfeinstein@atlasventure.com
Barry Fidelman,
bfidelman@atlasventure.com
Ron Nordin, rnordin@atlasventure.com
Jeff Warren, jwarren@atlasventure.com

Life sciences

Marc Fogassa, mfogassa@atlasventure.com
Jean-Francois Formela,
jfformela@atlasventure.com

California Office

Atlas Venture
2420 Sand Hill Road, Suite 102
Menlo Park, CA 94025

(650) 926-0575
Fax: (650) 854 6907
E-mail menlopark@atlasventure.com

California office contact

Information Technology
Eric Archambeau,
earchambeau@atlasventure.com

Aurora Ventures Inc.
Focus: Life science and information science
Web Address: www.aurorafunds.com/

Invests primarily in the Southeastern United States. Targets emerging and high-growth companies in healthcare services, medical devices, diagnostic products, biotechnology and pharmaceuticals, medical information systems, application and system software, computer hardware systems and components, data-communications products and services, semiconductors, telecommunications products and services. Manages three funds (Aurora Ventures, LLC, Aurora Bright Fund, and Aurora Ventures II), which share advisory boards devoted to medical, engineering, and business issues. Typical investments range between $250,000 and $1.5 million over several rounds of financing. Investment relationships commonly last four to seven years. Typically acts as a lead or co-lead investor and takes a seat on the company's management board to participate in strategic and planning decisions.

HOW TO APPLY:

Send proposal to

The Aurora Funds, Inc.
2525 Meridian Parkway, Suite 220
Durham, NC 27713
(919) 484-0400
Fax: (919) 484-0444

Austin Ventures
Focus: E-commerce (business-to-business and business-to-consumer), communications, semiconductors
Web Address: www.austinventures.com

Targets companies based in Texas and the Southwestern U.S. Discourages proposals from companies focused on medical, industrial, consumer products, restaurant, real estate, energy, and entertainment industries. Founded in 1979, and now has almost $800 million under management. Typically provides $100,000 to $25 million for seed and early-stage companies. Provides introductions to high technology, services management, and financial sources. Offers a research staff to assist in business planning and market analysis. Typically, investment relationships last approximately five years, but in some cases have spanned ten years.

HOW TO APPLY:

Submit proposal to

Austin Ventures
114 West 7th St., Suite 1300
Austin, TX 78701
(512) 485-1900
Fax: (512) 476-3952
moreinfo@ausven.com

Avalon Investments
Focus: Emerging technology companies in the Midwest and California
Web Address: www.avaloninvest.com/

Looks for technology-based businesses success, experienced managers, products or services with market leadership, and an IPO strategy in three years or less. Requires significant investment by managers in the candidate company. Active board member. Typically invests $1 million to $6 million in late-stage companies, $1 million to $3 million in early-stage ventures.

HOW TO APPLY:

E-mail business summary to
bizplan@avaloninvest.com

Or send hard copies to

Avalon Investments, Inc.
First National Building
201 South Main St., 10th Floor
Ann Arbor, MI 48104
(734) 994-7000
Fax: (734) 994-4302

or

Avalon Investments, Inc.
1250 Fourth St., 5th Floor
Santa Monica, CA 90401
(310) 899-6225
Fax: (310) 899-6234

Bachow & Associates
Focus: Technology, communications, service businesses, manufacturing, and vertical software
Web Address: www.bachow.com

Formed in 1985, currently manages a $140 million fund. Seeks acquisitions or investments in established businesses. Considers projects outside focus industries, except those in retail, distribution, packaged goods, or real estate. Candidates should demonstrate current or near-term profitability.

HOW TO APPLY:

Send proposals to
info@bachow.com

Bachow & Associates, Inc.
Three Bala Plaza East, 5th Floor
Bala Cynwyd, PA 19004-3493
(610) 660-4900
Fax: (610) 660-4930

BancBoston Capital and BancBoston Ventures
Focus: Early-stage funding for information technology and healthcare companies; later-stage investments, mezzanine funding for buyouts, recapitalizations, and expansion funds for mid-size companies

Web Address: www.bancboscap.com

BancBoston Capital manages $1.5 billion for later-stage companies. BancBoston Ventures, a Small Business Investment Company (SBIC) licensee, courts emerging companies.

HOW TO APPLY:

Send proposal to

BancBoston Capital or BancBoston Ventures
175 Federal St., 10th Floor
Boston, MA 02110
(617) 434-2509
Fax: (617) 434-1153

The Barksdale Group
Focus: Internet services
Web Address: www.barksdalegroup.com/

Found by James Barksdale, former Chief Executive Officer of Internet browser developer Netscape Communications.

HOW TO APPLY:

E-mail business proposal to

ideas@barksdalegroup.com
The Barksdale Group
2730 Sand Hill Road
Suite 100
Menlo Park, CA 94025
(650) 234-5200
Fax: (650) 234-5201

Batterson Venture Partners
Focus: Electronics, software, telecommunications, advanced materials, biotech and other medical applications
Web Address: www.vcapital.com

Funds companies throughout the U.S. in seed, start-up, early, and late-stage development. Founded in 1995, manages approximately $100 million in investment capital. Investments typically total $500,000 to $5 million.

HOW TO APPLY:

Send proposals to Len Batterson, chairman and CEO, at

bvp@vcapital.com
Batterson Venture Partners
303 W. Madison St., Suite 1110
Chicago, IL 60606
(312) 269-0300
Fax: (312) 269-0021

Battery Ventures
Focus: Voice/data convergence technologies, software, the Internet, and e-commerce
Web Address: www.battery.com

Maintains offices in Wellesley, MA, San Mateo, CA. Operates six funds worth a total of $800 million. Focuses on U.S. companies in development stages ranging from seed-level to mezzanine and buyouts. Typical funding amounts span $5 million to $20 million, but will consider higher investments. Takes a board seat and participates in strategic decisions of the funded company.

HOW TO APPLY:

Send proposals for communications and networking companies to David Hartwig at the San Mateo office or to Morgan Jones in Wellesley, MA. Wireless and telecommunications companies should contact Hartwig or Sunil Dhaliwal, in Wellesley. Software companies should contact Dennis Phelps in San Mateo or Scott Tobin in Wellesley. Internet/online companies should contact Phelps or Michael Brown in Wellesley.

Battery Ventures, East Coast
20 William St., Suite 200
Wellesley, MA 02481
(781) 577-1000
Fax: (781) 577-1001

Battery Ventures, West Coast
901 Mariner's Island Blvd., Suite 475
San Mateo, CA 94404
(650) 372-3939
Fax: (650) 372-3930

Bay Partners
Focus: Early-stage companies in data networking, telecommunications infrastructure, hardware and software, and Internet markets
Web Site: www.baypartners.com/

Looks for projects backed by formal business plans or emerging companies in the process of developing the business model. Offers an entrepreneur-in-residence program to promote fledgling ideas and provide offices space. Typically invests $1 million to $5 million. Will consider seed rounds of less than $1 million. Participates as lead or co-investor. Backs companies from seed stage to post-IPO activities. Guides sales and marketing efforts and assists in developing business strategies. Will take a board seat and assist in finding additional funding. Looks for attractive market size, managerial talent, and a valid business model.

HOW TO APPLY:

Send proposals to

Bay Partners
10600 North De Anza Blvd., Suite 100
Cupertino, CA 95014-2031
(408) 725-2444
Fax: (408) 446-4502
partners@baypartners.com

BCI Partners
Focus: Media and entertainment, communications, business services, software, and the Internet
Web Address: www.bcipartners.com/

Founded in 1983, manages over $800 million in capital investments in more than 100 companies. Invests $5 million to $50 million for internal expansion, acquisi-

tions, and management led buyouts. Participates in developing corporate strategy and financial plans, analyzing new markets, targeting acquisitions, recruiting staff. Looks for candidates in large, rapidly growing markets or in high-profit niche markets. Prefers candidates that offer proprietary products and services.

HOW TO APPLY:

Demonstrate managerial leadership in the relevant market, along with a commercial product that is attracting growing revenues. Send a concise business plan with emphasis on company strategy, product/service overview, market analysis; historical and projected financials performance, management profiles.

BCI Partners, Inc.
Glenpointe Centre West
Mezzanine Level
Teaneck, NJ 07666
(201) 836-3900
Fax: (201) 836-6368
E-mail info@bcipartners.com

Beecken Petty & Company
Focus: Healthcare services
Web Address: www.beeckenpetty.com

Invests through a $150 million fund created by Healthcare Equity Partners. Targets service companies in healthcare industry. Considers emerging companies, consolidations, recapitalizations, and ownership changes.

HOW TO APPLY:

E-mail proposals to

Dave Beecken
Managing Director
dbeecken@bpcompany.com.

John Kneen
Managing Director
jkneen@bpcompany.com

Greg Moerschel
Managing Director
gregm@bpcompany.com

Ken O'Keefe
Managing Director
kokeefe@bpcompany.com

Bill Petty
Managing Director
bpetty@bpcompany.com

Beecken Petty & Company
901 Warrenville Road, Suite A
Lisle, IL 60532
(630) 435-0300
Fax: (630) 435-0370

BG Affiliates
Focus: Healthcare, financial services, real estate, furniture manufacturing, commercial laundries, janitorial, and building cleaning
Web Address: www.bgaffiliates.com

Typically invests from $2 million to $15 million for acquisitions and management buyouts. Invests growth capital in companies with a solid market niche, effective management, and demonstrable success. Considers opportunities in the U.S. and Canada.

HOW TO APPLY:

Send inquiries to BG Affiliates

Frank Apeseche, managing partner
frank.apeseche@berkshire-group.com
or
Matt Hills, senior partner
matt.hills@berkshire-group.com
1 Beacon St.
Suite 1500
Boston, MA 02108
(617) 556-1400
Fax: (617) 423-8916

Benchmark Capital
Focus: Consumer electronics, e-commerce, networking, semiconductors, and telecommunications
Web Address: www.benchmark.com

Makes investments in early-stage companies. Investments may total as much as $15 million over the span of a relationship, but initial amounts are usually $3 to $5 million. Works within a horizontal organization that minimizes bureaucratic delays when dealing with funded companies. Fund managers work as a six-person team for each investment. It participates in executive recruitment, corporate partnerships, and strategic planning. Offers a network of industry contacts for strategic partnerships, board representation, and managerial guidance.

HOW TO APPLY:

Send business plan to info@benchmark.com

or

Benchmark Capital
2480 Sand Hill Road, Suite 200
Menlo Park, CA 94025
(650) 854-8180
Fax: (650) 854-8183

Berkeley International Capital Corp.
Focus: Later-stage technology and medical companies
Web Address: www.berkeleyvc.com

Seeks $5 million to $15 million investments in companies in pre-launch stage of their product or service. Can commit within two weeks of initial contact. Will consider private equity funding for young public companies.

HOW TO APPLY:

Contact

Arthur I. Trueger or **Michael J. Mayer**
Berkeley International Capital Corp.
650 California St., Suite 2800
San Francisco, CA 94108-2609

(415) 249-0450
afoster@berkeleyvc.com

Berkshire Partners
Focus: Manufacturing, telecommunications, transportation, retail, and business services
Web Address: www.berkshirepartners.com/

Looks for growth potential, competitive advantages, managerial talent, company valuations up to $1 billion. Will invest up to $100 million per company. Backs leveraged buyouts, recapitalizations, privatizations, growth funding, and industry consolidations.

HOW TO APPLY:

Use form at Web site or write to:

Berkshire Partners LLC
One Boston Place, Suite 3300
Boston, MA 02108
(617) 227-0050
Fax: (617) 227-6105

Bessemer Venture Partners
Focus: E-commerce, communications, semiconductors and optical communications, healthcare
Web Address: www.bessemervp.com

Invests approximately $100 million a year in start ups and early-stage companies, as well as mature businesses with a viable "roll-up acquisition strategy." Looks for a compelling growth strategy with realistic cash-flow requirements. Shuns companies in that focus on natural resources, real estate, fashion/entertainment, commodity or highly capital intensive sectors. Looks for candidates with experienced managers, a niche in a growing market, and technology that can lead a market and overcome competitors. Investments normally span $1 million to $5 million, but will consider smaller investments under $1 million for the right start ups. Arranges co-funding partnerships with other venture-capital funds. Maintains offices in Menlo Park, CA, Wellesley Hills, MA, and Westbury, NY.

HOW TO APPLY:

Send your business plan, executive summary, and key executives' resumes to businessplan@bvp.com, or mail the package to

Bessemer Venture Partners
535 Middlefield Road
Menlo Park, CA 94025
(650) 853-7000
Fax: (650) 853-7001

83 Walnut Street
Wellesley Hills, MA 02481
(781) 237-6050
Fax: (781) 237-7576

1400 Old Country Road
Suite 407
Westbury, NY 11590
(516) 997-2300
Fax: (516) 997-2371

Blue Chip Venture Company
Focus: Health care, information technology, retail/consumer products, and communications
Web Address: www.bcvc.com

Founded in 1991, serves entrepreneurs in the Cincinnati area, as well as the greater Midwest region. Will also consider investments in companies in other U.S. regions and Canada. Maintains ties to Procter & Gamble, the consumer-products corporation that's based in Cincinnati. Manages $200 million in capital. Targets companies with managers that demonstrate previous success in the target market or in a comparable industry. Usually requires at least $1 million in annual revenues and near-term profitability. Will consider mezzanine or bridge loans. Typically invests $3 million to $6 million per company in multiple funding rounds. Considers investments of $1 million for early-stage ventures. Seeks returns within five years.

HOW TO APPLY:

Send proposals to

info@bcvc.com

or

Blue Chip Venture Company
1100 Chiquita Center
250 East Fifth St.
Cincinnati, OH 45202
(513) 723-2300
Fax: (513) 723-2306

Boston Capital Ventures
Focus: Software, communications, service-based companies
Web Address: www.bcv.com/

Founded in 1982. Focuses on Northeastern U.S. companies, but will consider those in other regions. Targets early-stage, growth-oriented companies with strategies for near-term revenues. Often, such candidates have prototype or shipping stage products or services. Key investment criteria: a skilled management team that is willing to accept input from the fund managers. Also the candidate should demonstrates the potential to deliver a return on investment of 10 times, or revenue projections of $50 million in five years. Looks to recoup investments in three to seven years. Typically invests $2 to $7 million per company. Seeks a board seat. Participates in strategic planning, executive recruitment, and development of financial relationships.

HOW TO APPLY:

Craft business plan with a focus on management expertise, market analysis, and the business model. Demonstrate that your market is large enough for significant growth potential, and discuss your company's relative strengths and weaknesses against the competition. Follow-up communications, if warranted, usually include a presentation by the candidate to Boston Capital partners and a visit by Boston Capital to the candidate's offices.

Submit the materials to:

Johan von der Goltz, general partner; **Jack Shields,** general partner; **Alex von der Goltz,** principal; or **Alexander Wilmerding,** principal, all at info@bcv.com, or at

Boston Capital Ventures
Old City Hall
45 School St.
Boston, MA 02108
(617) 227-6550
Fax: (617) 227-3847

Boston Millennia Partners
Focus: Telecommunications, information technology, healthcare and life sciences
Web Address: www.millenniapartners.com/

Founded in 1979, manages $250 million in capital. Usually acts as the lead investor, but will consider being part of a funding syndicate. Generally takes a board seat, but avoids day-to-day management decisions in favor of participation in business and financial strategies, follow on financing activities, and merger and acquisition plans. Provides funding for stages ranging from first-round capital to late-stage expansions. Looks for managers with successful track records and a product or service that offers the potential for ongoing competitive advantages. First-round investment usually are between $3 million and $7 million, with total capitalizations up to about $15 million in any one company. In special instances, has agreed to initial funding of $1 million and up to $10 million.

HOW TO APPLY:

Use form at
http://www.millenniapartners.com/
contact_email.html or send a proposal to:

Boston Millennia Partners
30 Rowes Wharf, Suite 330
Boston, MA 02110
(617) 428-5150
Fax: (617) 428-5160

or

Boston Millennia Partners
20 Valley Stream Parkway, Suite 265
Malvern, PA 19355-1457
(610) 993-8727
Fax: (610) 695-2517

Brand Equity Ventures
Focus: E-commerce, restaurants, niche products, retailing, direct response, consumer services
Web Address: www.brand-equity.com/

Looks for companies with potential to build strong brand names. Prefers early-stage companies that have proved their product or service concept but may not be profitable yet. Will also invest in later-stage, pre-IPO companies seeking recapitalization or a management buyout. Considers projects throughout the United States. Typically invests $5 million to $10 million, with first rounds as low as $1 million. Will syndicate to attract additional funding. Takes a board seat.

HOW TO APPLY:

Fax or e-mail an executive summary, follow up with a phone call. Send summaries to info@brand-equity.com or www.brand-equity.com

Equity Ventures
Three Pickwick Plaza
Greenwich, CT 06830
(203) 862-5500
Fax: (203) 629-2019

Brown, McMillan & Co
Focus: Healthcare, media, and business services
Web Address: www.brownmcmillan.com

Founded in 1996, considers opportunities throughout the U.S. Invests $3 million to $15 million per company. Targets markets with potential for start ups to benefit from regulatory, demographic, or competitive changes. Prefers managers with industry-specific experience. Typically takes a board seat and acts as financial advisor. Acts as sole or co-investor.

HOW TO APPLY:

Send proposals to

Cabot Brown, cabot@brownmcmillan.com
Peter McMillan,
peter@brownmcmillan.com

Brown, McMillan & Co., LLC
930 Montgomery St., Suite 301
San Francisco, CA 94133

(415) 273-7160
Fax: (415) 273-7171

Burr, Egan, Deleage & Co.
Focus: Information technology, life sciences, communications
Web Address: www.venus.co.uk/homes/AMills/talks/roth/bed/docs/index.htm

Twenty-years old, has invested more than $600 million in companies throughout North America. Investments usually range between $1.5 million to $10 million. Primarily backs start ups, but will consider funding for business expansions and acquisitions. Expects a seat.

HOW TO APPLY:

The fund maintains offices in Boston and San Francisco. Call the San Francisco office at (415) 362-4022 to gauge interest. Follow up with a business plan.

Burr, Egan, Deleage & Co.
West Coast Office:
One Embarcadero Center, Suite 4050
San Francisco, CA 94111
E-mail: info@bedco.com

East Coast Office:
One Post Office Square, Suite 3800
Boston, MA 02109
(617) 482-8020

Brentwood Venture Capital
Focus: Computer networks, enterprise software, healthcare, the Internet

Web Address: www.brentwoodvc.com

Twenty six years old, with offices in Menlo Park, Los Angeles and Orange County, CA. Targets start ups, early-stage, and emerging companies. Manages $400 million in capital invested in more than 300 companies. Participates in business strategy development and planning, staff recruiting, and follow on financing strategies. Provides introductions to executives in technology, medical, and financial markets. Looks for experience managers able to build teams. Candidates should be involved in a solid market capable of generating company revenues of more than $50 million in five years. Fund will also consider companies in niche markets or opportunities where a new technology can achieve dominance. The proposed product or service should have clear competitive advantages and customer benefits.

HOW TO APPLY:

Submit business plan to busplan@brentwoodvc.com or to

Brentwood Venture Capital
3000 Sand Hill Road
Bldg. 1, Suite 260
Menlo Park, CA 94025
(650) 854-7691
Fax: (650) 854-9513

11150 Santa Monica Blvd., Suite 1200
Los Angeles, CA 90025
(310) 477-7678
Fax: (310) 312-1868

1920 Main St.
Suite 820
Irvine, CA 92614
(949) 251-1010
Fax: (949) 251-1011

C3 Holdings

Focus: Midwestern buyouts, acquisitions, and expansions
Web Address: www.c3holdings.com

Funds buyouts, exit projects, acquisitions, and growth plans. Looks for competitive advantage, a unique product or distribution channel, market penetration, and a solid business strategy. Prefers companies in the Midwest.

HOW TO APPLY:

E-mail proposals to businessdevelopment@c3holdings.com or use the electronic form at the Web site, or contact

C3 Holdings

4520 Main St., Suite 1600
Kansas City, MO 64111
(816) 756-2225
Fax: (816) 756-5552

C3 Holdings

233 South Wacker Drive

Sears Tower
Suite 5330
Chicago, IL 60606
(312) 655-5990

Fax: (312) 655-5999

C3 Holdings

5005 LBJ Freeway
LB 119
Dallas, TX 75244
(972) 233-8778
Fax: (972) 233-0112

Calvert Ventures

Focus: Healthcare, education, the environment, and energy
Web Address: http://www.calvertventures.com/

Targets early-stage, socially responsible ventures with the potential for economic and social gains. Projects may be short or long term involving companies of any size. Backs candidates with the "promise of creating a more healthy, peaceful and productive world through the very nature of their products, services and methods of business." Seeks early-stage companies looking for initial funding after a product prototype. Prefers being lead investor. Generally invests $50,000 and $250,000, but will consider funding up to $500,000. Can act as a board member to help develop strategic plans, follow on financing sources, and connections to industry executives and service professionals, such as accountants and attorneys.

HOW TO APPLY:

Contact John May, managing partner, or Steve Moody, associate portfolio manager, via e-mail at calven2000@aol.com, or at

Calvert Ventures
402 Maple Ave. West, Suite C
Vienna, VA 22180
(301) 718-4272
Fax: (301) 656-4421

The Cambria Group
Focus: Manufacturing, processing, distribution, transportation, resource or service businesses
Web Address: www.cambriagroup.com/

Founded in 1996, acquires and invests in established small and mid-sized businesses. Targets companies that normally aren't attractive to venture-fund managers because they aren't in high-growth markets. Focuses on companies with revenues under $40 million. Fund managers provide most of the investment equity. Looks for candidates with found business fundamentals and skilled managers. Usually invests from $250,00 to $3 million for a controlling interest. Works closely with company managers to develop business strategies. Takes a board seat.

HOW TO APPLY:
Submit proposals to proposals@cambriagroup.com (send as a document attachment in Microsoft Word or Corel WordPerfect format), or to

The Cambria Group
724 Oak Grove Ave., Suite 120
Menlo Park, CA 94025
(650) 329-8600
Fax: (650) 329-8601

Cambridge Technology Capital Fund
Focus: Enterprise software, e-commerce, customer management systems, knowledge management systems, interactive media, supply chain management, strategic consulting, services, and money management and trading
Web Address: www.ctc.ctp.com/html/ctc-mission.html

A subsidiary of technology consultant Cambridge Technology Partners. Generally provides between $500,000 to $2 million in capital, sometimes over a number of rounds. Seeks companies with potential to lead development of growing markets. The most attractive candidates offer a product or service compatible with Cambridge's strengths, such as marketing, distribution, and deployment. Analyzes prospective projects for market potential and managerial strength. Then chooses candidates that are ready for marketing and delivery assistance. Requires investment participation by a minimum of one large venture capital fund. Makes introductions to other financial sources, possible customers, industry consultants, and other appropriate executives. Takes board seats. Prefers to be part of an investment pool rather than being the lead investor. Typically owns less than a 20-percent stake in its investment companies.

HOW TO APPLY:

E-mail business plan to:
ctc-prospects@ctp.com or send to

Cambridge Technology Capital Fund
11512 El Camino Real, Suite 215
San Diego, CA 92130
(619) 259-7869
Fax: (619) 259-7909

Canaan Partners
Focus: Information technology, healthcare, medical
Web Address: www.canaan.com/

Will consider companies throughout the U.S. in any industry segment and in any stage of development from early to expansion levels. Investments have backed more than 100 companies. Also evaluates investments in public companies, management buyouts, and recapitalizations. Funding amounts can be as low as $500,000 or $15 million and higher. Looks for young companies with potential for long-term revenue and profit growth, or mature companies with substantial equity. Seeks out strong management teams. Prefers a board seat. Helps funded companies develop business strategies, employee recruitment, strategic alliances, and industry contacts.

HOW TO APPLY:

E-mail proposals to John D. Lambrech at jlambrech@canaan.com, or send via the postal service to:

Canaan Partners
105 Rowayton Ave.
Rowayton, CT 06853
(203) 855-0400
Fax: (203) 854-9117

2884 Sand Hill Road, Suite 115
Menlo Park, CA 94025
(650) 854-8092
Fax: (650) 854-8127

Capital Insights
Focus: Companies in the Carolinas
Web Address: 207.144.96.6/ci-home.nsf/pages/CapitalInsights

Seeks companies able to provide a return on investments in five years with a market value greater than $50 million. Looks for marketing plans based on a proprietary product or service, a substantial base of mainstream customers, and a viable distribution channel. Candidates should possess expert leadership and demonstrate a strategy for product improvements and evolution, including ways to defend against moves by competitors. Recruiting and training talent should be a priority of the candidate.

How to Apply:

Contact John Warner at

Capital Insights
P. O. Box 27162
Greenville, SC 29616-2162
(864) 242-6832

Capital Resource Partners
Focus: Manufacturing, specialty retail, consumer products, and manufacturing, financial, business, health care and consumer services
Web Address: www.crp.com/

Founded in 1988, manages more than $900 million in capital. Specializes in funding structured as mezzanine debt for roll-ups, acquisitions, buyouts, recapitalization, and expansion. Funds middle-market companies throughout the U.S. with sales between $10 million and $200 million. Each year, invests between $100 million to $150 million in approximately a dozen companies. Typically invests $8 million to $20 million in each entity, with $10 million the average. Makes introductions to other financial sources, business consultants, and management experts. Looks for candidates that were profitable for the two most recent fiscal years, that hold an established position in their market, and can demonstrate

predictable cash flow. Also analyses managerial skill and market growth potential.

How to Apply:

E-mail a partner listed at the Web site or submit a proposal to

Capital Resource Partners
85 Merrimac St.
Boston, MA 02114
(617) 723-9000
Fax: (617) 723-9819

Capital Southwest Corp.
Focus: Manufacturing, technology, healthcare, specialty retailing
Web Address: www.capitalsouthwest.com/

Established in 1961, focuses on small and medium-sized across the U.S. Manages $300 million in capital. Individual investments usually range from $1 million to $6 million, but will participate in financing pools for companies requiring higher amounts. Also considers follow on financing. Targets early-stage investments, expansion financings, management buyouts, recapitalizations, and industry consolidations. Looks for high growth potential, managers with successful track records, companies with the potential to become long-term leaders in their markets. Doesn't insist on a formal exit strategy. In some cases maintains financial relationships with funded companies for 20 or 30 years. Provides introductions to relevant venture capitalists, bankers, asset-based lenders, and investment bankers.

HOW TO APPLY:

E-mail a summary of the business plan to info@capitalsouthwest.com or initiate a contact through a phone call or a letter to

Capital Southwest Corporation
12900 Preston Road, Suite 700
Dallas, TX 75230
(972) 233-8242
Fax: (972) 233-7362

Capstone Ventures
Focus: E-commerce, health care and out-sourced business services
http://www.capstonevc.com/

Generally invests between $1 million and $2 million as an initial investment, going up to a total of approximately $5 million per company. Often acts as lead investor, but partners with other venture capital funds for follow-on investments. Seeks a board seat. Targets companies with existing products that use established technology in new service model. Customers of the funded company often have an Internet tie-in.

HOW TO APPLY:

Complete electronic survey at www.capstonevc.com/contact/

companyInfoForm.asp. If the fund managers see a potential fit based on the survey information, candidates will be asked to send a business plan.

Capstone Ventures
3000 Sand Hill Road
Building 1, Suite 290
Menlo Park, CA 94025
(650) 854-2523
Fax: (650) 854-9010

Dain Rauscher Plaza
60 South Sixth St.
Minneapolis, MN 55402
(612) 371-7733
Fax: (612) 371-2837

The Carlyle Group
Focus: Aerospace, defense, environmental services, healthcare, information technology, Internet, real estate, and telecommunications
Web Address: www.thecarlylegroup.com

Acts as lead investor for growth funding, management-led buyouts, consolidations, and other strategies. Founded in 1987, now has more than $5 billion under management. Offers global partner network.

HOW TO APPLY:

Send proposals to

The Carlyle Group
1001 Pennsylvania Avenue, NW

Suite 220 South
Washington, DC 20004-2505
(202) 347-2626
Fax: (202) 347-1818

or

The Carlyle Group
520 Madison Avenue, 41st Floor
New York, New York 10022
(212) 381-4900
Fax: (212) 381-4901

Castile Ventures
Focus: Data networking, telecommunications, and the Internet
Web Address: http://www.castileventures.com

Manages $50 million in investment capital available to candidates along the Eastern Seaboard. Targets companies developing products or services to capitalize on infrastructure changes within the telecommunications industry, including Web-based business applications and voice and data delivery systems. Focuses on seed and early-stage investments. Seeks companies with proprietary technology, products, or services with the potential to become a market leader in some aspect of the telecommunications industry. Looks to recoup investments payoff within three to seven years. Typically invests a total of from $3 million to $5 million over multiple investment rounds. Supports follow-on and pooled investments from other venture capital funds and corporate investors. Pro-

vides introductions to telecommunications industry executives and trade associations to help fund companies with product/service positioning, marketing, product development, and sales strategies. Works with funded companies to recruit executives and key talent. Seeks a board seat and involves itself with strategic planning.

HOW TO APPLY:
Send proposals to
Nina F. Saberi, general partner, at
nina@castileventures.com or mail to

Castile Ventures
890 Winter St., Suite 140
Waltham, MA 02451
(781) 890-0060
Fax: (781) 890-0065

CCG Venture Partners
Focus: Internet and e-business businesses
Web Address: www.ccgvp.com/

Prefers seed-stage start ups and early-stage ventures. Helps formulate the young company's business infrastructure. Looks for unique business idea, desire to expand the business nationwide, ROI potential, including short-term gains, and a company strategy for quickly reaching revenues of $10 million. Management should demonstrate past business successes and the ability to collaborate with an outside investor. Should have a clear mission statement, a five-year growth plan, and annual interim plans.

HOW TO APPLY:

Contact Rick Davis (rdavis@ccgvp.com) or John Kiltz (jkiltz@ccgvp.com).

CCG Venture Partners, LLC
14450 T.C. Jester, Suite 170
Houston, TX 77014
(281) 893-8331
Fax: (281) 893-2420

CeBourn Ltd.
Focus: Internet, e-commerce, software networking, telecommunications, and basic-industry companies in or near Colorado
Web Address: www.cebourn.com

Looks for talented managers, a large target market, and a unique product. Often invests with other funds. Requires seat on board or on a technical advisory board.

HOW TO APPLY:

E-mail business plans to assistant@cebourn.com. Note: the company only responds to proposals it's interested in pursuing. Managers ask that candidates don't follow up by phone to check status.

CeBourn, Ltd.
One Norwest Center
1700 Lincoln St., Suite 3700
Denver, CO 80203-4537
(303) 832-8220

Fax: (303) 832-8232

The Centennial Funds
Focus: Computer networking, electronic media, telecommications
Web Address: www.centennial.com/

Founded in 1981, now manages $724 million from offices in Denver and Houston. Targets communications outsourcing companies, Internet-based private and commercial communications providers, high-speed access providers for residential and business applications, and developers of virtual network software.

Focuses on early- and late-stage companies. Typical investments range from $250,000 to $500,000 for seed-stage companies, and $5 million for early or late-stage projects. Maximum investment is $20 million. Seeks a board seat. Assists in strategic planning, executive recruitment and training, international expansion, and other operational tasks.

HOW TO APPLY:

Usually meets candidates through referrals. Accepts opportunities after reviewing a business plan and meeting with key managers. Approval process may take several months, although sometimes provides a small seed investment.

Send business plans and financial proposals to

The Centennial Funds
1428 Fifteenth St.
Denver, CO 80202-1318
(303) 405-7500

CenterPoint Ventures
Focus: Texas-based companies selling software, Web-based services, the Internet, intranets, data communications, computer hardware, telecommunications, and semiconductors
Web Address: www.centerpointvp.com/

Founded in 1996, current funding resources total $100 million. Seeks early-stage companies headquartered in Texas, although will consider candidates from other regions depending on business orientation. Shuns non-U.S.-based companies, entertainment businesses, or biotech firms. Typically acts as a first-round or second-round investor. Prefers to limit total investments in a single project to $3 million to $5 million, invested over two or three rounds. Looks for the potential to achieve annual revenues of at least $50 million within five years.

How to Apply:

Send a business plan or summary to *businessplans@cpventures.com,* or write to

CenterPoint Ventures
Two Galleria Tower
13455 Noel Road, Suite 1670
Dallas TX 75240

(972) 702-1101
Fax: (972) 702-1103

8920 Business Park Drive, Suite 100
Austin TX 78759-7405
(512) 231-1670
Fax: (512) 651-6266

Charles River Ventures
Focus: Communications, software, and information services industries.
Web Address: www.crv.com/

Founded in 1970, and based in Boston, this organization manages nine different funds valued collectively at $565 million. The most recent fund, Charles River Partnership IX, has $175 million in capital resources. Targets early stage companies with the potential to reach $50 million or more in revenues in five to seven years. Candidates should be in markets valued at $250 million per year. Prefers companies in the northeastern U.S. from Boston to Washington, D.C. Generally acts as lead investor and seeks a board seat. First round investments typically range from $1 million to $5 million, with totals for multiple financing rounds averaging $3 million to $10 million per company. Will consider supplying seed financing to back the evolution of a business concept, and will even help select entrepreneurs develop a business concept before Charles River makes a financial commitment. Reports that half of its current investments were made when the funded companies had less than 10 employees. Helps arrange follow-on financing from other venture capitalists, corporate and private investors, banks, and venture leasing firms.

HOW TO APPLY:

Inquiries usually receive a reply within three weeks. Before committing capital, fund managers meet with founders and arrange for follow-on meetings between founders and executives within Charles River's business network.

E-mail proposals to principals listed at Web site or to

Charles River Ventures
Bay Colony Corporate Center
1000 Winter St., Suite 3300
Waltham, MA 02451
(781) 487-7060
Fax: (781) 487-7065

Charter Ventures
Focus: Data networking, telecommunications, enterprise software, systems and peripherals, Internet software, and electronic commerce; life sciences, including biotechnology, medical devices, diagnostics, pharmaceuticals, and health care services.
Web Address: www.charterventures.com

Manages two funds: Charter Venture Capital, which targets seed- and early-stage technology companies, and Charter Growth Capital, which provides late-stage and expansion financing. Together, the funds have backed 300 companies with more than $325 million.

Charter Venture backs private companies from the initial idea to mezzanine equity and debt transactions. Funding ranges from $250,000 to $5 million or more. The fund prefers to be the lead investor. Seeks candidates that can achieve annual revenues of $50 million in five years. Also values strong leadership and proprietary technologies with high profit margin potential.

Charter Growth Capital focuses on companies that have developed a commercial product and are generating revenue. Particular interests are companies selling enterprise software and services, communications products, electronic commerce applications, and health-care services. Funding amounts are generally $2 million to $5 million. Fund managers offer contacts in Hong Kong, Mainland China, and Japan for companies that target Asian markets.

Looks for a technology or product that offers a sustainable competitive advantage, a market with growth potential, and skilled management.

HOW TO APPLY:
Send proposals to

info@charterventures.com

or

Charter Ventures
525 University Ave., Suite 1400
Palo Alto, CA 94301
(650) 325-6953
Fax: (650) 325-4762

Chase Capital Partners
Focus: Broad range of industries and geographic areas
Web Address: www.chasecapital.com

The Chase Manhattan Corp., parent of Chase Manhattan Bank, is the main limited partner. The fund invests growth and mezzanine capital for private and public ventures. Will back a company through all life cycles. Now has $15.9 billion under management. Founded in 1984. May invest $5 million to $200 million, depending on the opportunity and the type of financing being sought. Acts as lead or co-investor. Usually takes a board seat. CCP will lead transactions or partner with other investors. CCP is generally represented on the board of directors of its portfolio companies, but does not expect to have involvement in the day-to-day operations.

HOW TO APPLY:

E-mail business plan to
chasecapital@chase.com, or send it to

Chase Capital Partners
380 Madison Ave., 12th Floor
New York, NY 10017

(212) 622-3100

Chase Capital Partners
50 California St., 29th Floor
San Francisco, CA 94111
(415) 591-1200
Fax: (415) 591-1205

Chase Capital Partners
108 South Frontage Road West, Suite 307
Vail, CO 81657
(970) 476-7700
Fax: (970) 476-7900

Chinavest
Focus: Business selling in or with China, Hong Kong and Taiwan; includes distributors, fast-food restaurants, light-manufacturing companies, and high technology firms.
Web Address: www.chinavest.com/

Invested more than $200 million in the area since founding in 1985. Provides regional contacts and offers strategic guidance for doing business in the region. Seeks experienced entrepreneurs with personal investments in their companies. Targets market leaders in the U.S. that want to expand in China. Typically invests $2 million to $12 million over three to six years. Frequently takes a board seat.

HOW TO APPLY:

Demonstrate high commitment and integrity of the managers. Show past financial performance and future growth assumptions. Also, analyze the overall target market and competitive environment.

Chinavest

160 Sansome St., Suite 1800
San Francisco, CA 94104
(415) 276-8888
Fax: (415) 276-8885

Chisholm Private Capital Partners

Focus: Oklahoma, Texas and adjacent-state manufacturing companies, or those selling information technologies, life sciences products and services
Web Address: www.chisholmvc.com/

Manages $23 million. Typically invests $500,000 to $1.5 million in financial relationships that last from three- to five-year periods. Seeks a board seat. Aids in executive and director recruitment. Insists on influence over financial, compensation, and strategic decisions. Prefers early-stage companies but will consider investments in businesses at any development stage. Prefers candidates in large markets with growth potential, especially in emerging sectors where the candidate can become a leader. Also values companies with the potential to attract business from established competitors. Shuns lifestyle businesses and those with significant regulatory risk. Acts as lead investor in funding pools. Typically invests $1 for every $6 invested by pool sources. Looks to recoup investments in three to five years.

HOW TO APPLY:

Submit a short business plan that addresses customer purchase decisions and sales cycles. Detail the strengths of the management team. Finally, provide a competitive analysis.

Send the plan in Microsoft Word format to jfrick@chisholmvc.com or to

Chisholm Private Capital Partners, LP

Towne Center
10830 E 45th St., Suite 307
Tulsa, OK 74146
(918) 663-2500
Fax: (918) 663-1140

Chisholm Private Capital Partners, LP

211 N Robinson, Suite 210
Oklahoma City, OK 73102
(405) 848-8014 or (405) 416-1033
Fax: (405) 416-1035

CID Equity Partners

Focus: Midwest companies in information technology, telecommunications, medical technology and services, manufacturing technology, and financial services
Web Address: www.cidequity.com/

Offers mezzanine financing and venture capital for start-up, early-stage, and middle-market companies. Formed in 1981, the group's venture capital funding projects typically range between $1 million and $5 million per company. Looks for growth markets with potential to reach $500 million. Candidates should demonstrate a competitive advantage through a unique technology or strategy. Mezzanine funding typically ranges from $3 million to $10 million. Successful candidates usually have revenues of $10 million to $200 million.

HOW TO APPLY:

Complete the electronic questionnaire at the Web site.

CID Equity Partners
One American Square
Suite 2850, Box 82074
Indianapolis, IN 46282
(317) 269-2350
Fax: (317) 269-2355

CID Equity Partners
41 South High St., Suite 3650
Columbus, OH 43215
(614) 222-8185
Fax: (614) 222-8190

CID Equity Partners
2 North LaSalle St., Suite 1705
Chicago, IL 60602
(312) 578-5350
Fax: (312) 578-5358

CID Equity Partners
312 Elm St., Suite 2600
Cincinnati, OH 45202
(513) 381-4748
Fax: (317) 269-2355

CMEA Ventures
Focus: Computer software and hardware, communications, E-commerce, the Internet, agriculture, electronic-bioindustry applications, healthcare, genomics, bioinformatics, and proteomics
Web Address: www.cmeaventures.com/

Targets early-stage technology companies, but will consider more mature candidates. Originally an affiliate of New Enterprise Associates, and, while independent since 1998, continues to co-invest in a number of companies. Manages $130 million in capital. Typically provides $500,000 to $3 million in capital to each funded company. Looks for strong information technology companies in high-growth markets with skilled management teams.

HOW TO APPLY:

For information-technology proposals, contact

Thomas R. Baruch, General Partner
(415) 352-1520 ext. 18
tom@cmeaventures.com

Gordon D. Hull, General Partner
(415) 352-1520 ext. 17
gordon@cmeaventures.com,

David B. Tuckerman, Partner
(415) 352-1520 ext. 19
david@cmeaventures.com

or

Vlad Dabija, Vice President
(415) 352-1520 ext. 14
vlad@cmeaventures.com

For life-sciences proposals, contact

Thomas R. Baruch, General Partner
(415) 352-1520 ext. 18
tom@cmeaventures.com

Gordon D. Hull, General Partner
(415) 352-1520 ext. 17
gordon@cmeaventures.com

Christine B. Cordaro, General Partner
(415) 391-8950 ext. 11
cbc1@viridiancapital.com

or

Karl D. Handelsman, Vice President
(415) 352-1520 ext. 23
karl@cmeaventures.com

CMEA Ventures
235 Montgomery St., Suite 920
San Francisco, CA 94104

Coastal Enterprises Inc.
Focus: Maine people and communities, particularly those with low incomes
Web Address: http://www.ceimaine.org/

With $5 million under mangement, .CEI's Coastal Ventures Limited Partnership (CVLP) invests between $50,000 and $500,000 in Maine businesses. Typical funding amounts range from $10,000 to $25,000. Previous funding recipients have included women-owned businesses, low-income and minority entrepreneurs, child care services, and small manufacturers. Candidates should demonstrate the potential for above-average equity returns in seven years or less. Offers help in strategic planning, follow-on financing, and in established key industry contacts. Usually takes a board seat. Looks for candidates with strong management teams with track records relevant to the target market. Candidates should be new or refocused companies with solid growth and profit potential. Will consider candidates in any industry sector. Prefers companies with a competitive edge based on a unique technology, distribution system, or other advantage. Targets companies that create jobs for low-income workers and requires funded companies to sign an agreement committing the company to low-income hiring. Also interested in projects with social benefits.

HOW TO APPLY:
Send proposal to

Nathaniel V. Henshaw, president, at nvh@ceimaine.org
or
Coastal Enterprises Inc.
Two Portland Fish Pier, Suite 302
Portland, ME 04101
(207) 772-5356
Fax: (207) 772-5503

Collinson Howe & Lennox
Focus: Biotechnology, pharmaceuticals, genomics, drug delivery technology, medical and diagnostic devices, and health care services
Web Address: www.chlmedical.com/

Established in 1981, has invested in more than 100 companies. Targets seed and start up investments in the medical industry. Manages more than $100 million in capital resources. Current fund is valued at $60 million. Typical investments range from $100,000 to $5 million. Often becomes the lead investor. Seeks a board seat.

HOW TO APPLY:
Submit proposals to

Collinson Howe & Lennox
1055 Washington Blvd.
Stamford, CT 06901
(203) 324-7700
Fax: (203) 324-3636

Columbia Capital Corp.
Focus: Communications and information technology companies
Web Address: www.colcap.com

Manages more than $100 million in capital investments. Arranges debt and equity financing and offers financial advice. Usually acts as lead investor, but participates in investment pools for large-scale funding projects. Usually funds companies with internal capital from the corporation's partners. Participates in strategic planning of funded companies. Partners sometimes fill temporary vacancies on funded-company management teams.

HOW TO APPLY:
Submit proposals to info@colcap.com
or

Columbia Capital Corp.
201 North Union St., Suite 300
Alexandria, Virginia 22314-2642
(703) 519-3581
Fax: (703) 519-3904

Comdisco Ventures
Focus: The Internet, software, computer services, communications, networking, hardware, semiconductors/EDA, biotech, medical devices and services, mass media
Web Address: www.comdisco.com/products/ventures/

Founded in 1987, has invested $1.5 million in more than 600 companies. Invests in companies ranging from seed-stage to mezzanine and pre-IPO. Offers customized financing options, including leasing, subordinated debt, secured debt (lines of credit, working capital), bridge loans, expansion loans, landlord guarantees, convertible debt, and equity. Provides discounts for new and reconditioned equipment through its parent company.

HOW TO APPLY:

Submit proposals to

Comdisco Ventures
6111 N. River Road
Rosemont, IL 60018
(847) 698-3000
www.comdisco.com

Commerce Capital
Focus: Healthcare, manufacturing, environmental products, communications
Web Address: www.commercecap.com/

A Small Business Investment Companies (SBIC) licensed by the Small Business Administration. Focuses on small businesses worth no more than $18 million with average after tax income of $6 million in a three-year period. Established in 1994, focuses on loans to companies in the southeastern U.S. Typically invests in established businesses seeking to expand, but will consider funding early-stage companies. Limits funding to debt transactions and requires involvement of founders in funded companies. Also requires an exit strategy outlining a payout within five years.

HOW TO APPLY:

Complete the questionnaire at www.commercecap.com/question.html.

Candidates usually receive feedback within a week. If Commerce Capital is interested in pursuing a relationship, candidates are asked to send a business plan outline, a loan request summary, and the credit information release.

Commerce Capital, L.P.
611 Commerce St., Suite 2602
Nashville, TN 37203
(615) 244-1432
Fax: (615) 242-1407

Commonwealth Capital Ventures
Focus: Technology, healthcare, and other high-growth opportunities in New England
Web Address: www.ccvlp.com/

Manages $145 million in capital resources. Has invested in more than 90 companies. Looks for strong management teams with successful track records. Typically invests $500,000 for seed financing to $6 million for more mature companies. Will consider investments for a variety of business needs, including start ups, early-stage developing companies, business expansions, acquisition financings, and buyout transactions. Participates as sole investor or as a member of an investment pool.

HOW TO APPLY:

Submit proposals to

Commonwealth Capital Ventures L.P.
20 William St.
Wellesley, MA 02481

(781) 237-7373
Fax: (781) 235-8627

Community Technology Fund (CTF)
Focus: Communications and networking, Internet and enterprise software, computer systems and components, healthcare information systems, medical devices, clinical diagnostics, biotechnology, pharmaceuticals, and drug delivery systems
Web Address: http://www.bu.edu/ctf/

Part of Boston University, invests in early-stage private companies and some later-stage businesses.

HOW TO APPLY:

Send inquiries or proposals to
Roger Kitterman, director of New Ventures Community Technology Fund
Boston Unviersity
108 Bay State Road
Boston, MA 02215
(617) 353-4550

The Community Development Ventures, Inc. (CDVI)
Focus: Companies near Baltimore's Empowerment and Enterprise Zones
Web Address: www.mmggroup.com/

Funds growth or start up candidates that currently or after expansion will hire part of their staff from the empowerment or enterprise zones. Investments generally range from $100,000 to $500,000. Looks for ex-

isting, viable businesses. CDVI also offers loans, management advice, and technical expertise.

HOW TO APPLY:

E-mail your name, the business's name, market, and address, and the project to msbdfa@mmggroup.com

Community Development Ventures, Inc.
826 E. Baltimore St.
Baltimore, MD 21202
(410) 333-2550
Fax: (410) 333-2552

ComVentures
Focus: Early-stage communications and networking companies
Web Address: http://www.comven.com/

Backs communications companies near the end of their R&D stage and ready to create a prototype product or service within a year. Will work with companies without a full management team on board. Assists in executive recruitment. Typically invests $200,000 to $5 million in a seed- or first-round projects, with a total of $6 million to $10 million committed per company over the life of the relationship.

HOW TO APPLY:

Inquire at

ComVentures
505 Hamilton Ave., Suite 305
Palo Alto, CA 94301
(650) 325-9600
Fax: (650) 325-9608
info@comven.com

Conning & Co.
Focus: Insurance, financial services and healthcare companies
Web Address: www.conning.com

Founded in 1985, investments to date total more than $346 million. Takes a board seat to assist in business planning, fund raising, and acquisitions for the companies it backs. Works as the lead investor and seeks projects with paybacks in four to seven years. Looks for managerial experience, the ability of principle to work with investors, and business proposals that define a competitive advantage in a growing market segment. Submit business plans to:

John B. Clinton, Senior Vice President
or
Steven F. Piaker, Senior Vice President

Conning & Company
CityPlace II, 185 Asylum St.
Hartford, CT 06103
Fax: (860) 520-1299
jclinton@conning.com
spiaker@conning.com

Cordova Ventures
Focus: Telecommunications, financial services, healthcare, medical devices and services, environmental, and information technology
Web Address: www.cordovaventures.com

Formed in 1989, now has more than $160 million in capital. Backs companies in start up through later-growth stages. Candidates typically are generating or close to generating revenues. Targets ventures in the Southeast with the capability to go national and product a 30 to 40 percent compounded annual return on the investment. Investments range from $500,000 to $4 million. Looks for experienced managers who have a stake in the company. A roadmap for a public offering or exit plan should be in place. Seeks paybacks in three to five years.

How to Apply:

Contact the following partners, depending on industry specialty:

Financial services:

Gerald (Jerry) F. Schmidt, President
js@cordovaventures.com
or
Ralph R. Wright, Jr.
rw@cordovaventures.com

Information technology:

Frank X. Dalton
fd@cordovaventures.com

Ralph R. Wright, Jr.
rw@cordovaventures.com

Healthcare services:

T. Forcht Dagi, MD
td@cordovaventures.com

John R. Runningen
jr@cordovaventures.com

Charles E. Adair
ea@cordovaventures.com

Telecommunications:

Gerald (Jerry) F. Schmidt, President
js@cordovaventures.com

Ralph R. Wright, Jr.
rw@cordovaventures.com

Biotechnology/medical devices or other sectors:

Cordova Ventures
Three NorthWinds Center
2500 NorthWinds Parkway, Suite 475
Alpharetta, GA 30004
(678) 942-0300
Fax: (678) 942-0301

Cornerstone Equity Investors
Focus: Healthcare service providers, data-communications and telecommunications business services
Web Address: www.cornerstone-equity. com/

Current venture fund totals $550 million. Typically invests $5 million to $50 million in early-stage Internet, datacom, and telecom companies. Also backs growth-oriented later-stage companies, management-led buyouts, and recapitalizations. Candidates should be able to achieve revenues of $75 million to $150 million with three to five years. Targets companies with commercialized products or services, backed by seasoned managers, with current or near-term profit potential. Considers managerial talent and expertise the primary selection criterion. Takes a board seat. Advises companies on financing, acquisitions, and public offerings.

HOW TO APPLY:
Send inquiries to the following partners, based on industry specialty:

Technology, retail, and consumer products
Mark Rossi,
Mrossi@Cornerstone-equity.com

Business Services and Healthcare
Dana J. O'Brien,
Dobrien@Cornerstone-equity.com

Telecommunications and business services
Robert H. Getz,
Rgetz@Cornerstone-equity.com

Stephen L. Larson,
Slarson@Cornerstone-equity.com

Cornerstone Equity Investors, L.L.C.
717 Fifth Ave., Suite 1100

New York, NY 10022
(212) 753-0901
Fax: (212) 826-6798
Tdowner@Cornerstone-equity.com

Crescendo Ventures
Focus: Information technology, communication services and health care
Web Address: www.crescendoventures.com/

Targets early stage companies with almost $500 million under management. Maintains partnerships in Europe. Looks for high-growth, high-profit potential and a talented managerial staff. Initial investments may be thousands of dollars to help create a business plan or early R&D. Typically invests $3 million to $15 million per company over multiple rounds. Serves as lead investor and member of funding syndicates. Usually takes a board seat.

HOW TO APPLY:
For information technology and communications, contact

Subra Narayan, Principal,
snarayan@crescendoventures.com

R. David Spreng,
Managing General Partner,
dspreng@crescendoventures.com
or
Anthony Daffer, General Partner,
adaffer@crescendoventures.com

For healthcare, contact
Jeffrey R. Tollefson, General Partner,
jtollefson@crescendoventures.com
or
Jay Schmelter, Principal,
jschmelter@crescendoventures.com

For software, contact
Lorraine Fox, general partner,
lfox@crescendoventures.com

For communications and technology services, contact
Roeland Boonstoppel, general partner,
rboonstoppel@crescendoventures.com

Crescendo Ventures
800 LaSalle Ave., Suite 2250
Minneapolis, MN 55402
(612) 607-2800
Fax: (612) 607-2801

Crescendo Ventures
480 Cowper St., Suite 300
Palo Alto, CA 94301
(650) 470-1200
Fax: (650) 470-1201

Crosslink Capital
Focus: Internet, education and training, human resources, media, business marketplaces, infrastructure, semiconductors, and e-health
Web Address: //www.omegaventures.com/

Formerly Omega Venture Partners, Crosslink backs companies from early stages to initial public offerings. Usually acts as the lead investor. Investments range from $4 million to $12 million.

HOW TO APPLY:

Contact
Jason Sanders,
jsanders@CrosslinkCapital.com,

or

Jason Duckworth,
jduckworth@CrosslinkCapital.com, for inquiries regarding the Internet, education and training, human resources, and media.

Contact **Stephen Perkins,**
sperkins@CrosslinkCapital.com, for business marketplaces, infrastructure, semiconductors, e-health, and other industries.

Crosslink Capital, Inc.
555 California St., Suite 2350
San Francisco, CA 94104
(415) 693-3355
Fax: (415) 676-2556

Crosspoint Venture Partners
Focus: E-business services, software, next-generation telecommunications carriers
Web Address: www.crosspointvc.com

HOW TO APPLY:

Send business plan as a Microsoft Word e-mail attachment to partner@cpvp.com, or fax executive summaries up to five pages to the northern California office, (650) 851-7661, or the southern California office, (949) 852-9804.

Crosspoint Venture Partners
The Pioneer Hotel Building
2925 Woodside Road
Woodside, CA 94062

Crosspoint Venture Partners
18552 MacArthur Blvd., Suite 400
Irvine, CA 92612

Davis, Tuttle Venture Partners
Focus: Diversified by industry, growth stage, and geography
www.davistuttle.com/

Backs early stage, expansion, and buyout/acquisition projects, with a bias toward expansion situations. Demonstrate growth-industry market and positive financials for buyout and acquisition consideration. In all proposals, consider managerial talent and experience as key criteria. Also looks for high growth and capital appreciation opportunities, competitive market advantages, a well defined business plan, and modern technology underpinning to the product or service. Typically invests $500,000 to $5 million, but may contribute up to $20 million in special cases. Acts as lead investor or partners with other venture funds.

HOW TO APPLY:

Submit business plan to

Davis, Tuttle Venture Partners, L. P.
320 South Boston, Suite 1000

Tulsa, OK 74103-3703
(918) 584-7272
Fax: (918) 582-3404

or

Davis, Tuttle Venture Partners, L. P.
8 Greenway Plaza, Suite 1020
Houston, TX 77046
(713) 993-0440
Fax: (713) 621-2297

Dawntreader LP
Focus: Seed and early-stage Internet businesses
Web Address: www.dawntreaderlp.com

Founded in 1998, targets e-commerce (business-to-business and business-to-consumer) companies and opportunities in software and services for the digital economy. Backs companies with potential to reach revenues of $50 million in five years. Assists companies through all growth stages from product definition to exit strategy. Actively participates on the board of directors. Also participates in developing strategic partnerships for funded companies, as well as hiring executive talent. Helps create business and marketing plans and develop additional funding sources. Looks for candidates in large markets and those with a variety of revenue sources. Shuns capital-intensive endeavors with high fixed costs and staffing requirements.

HOW TO APPLY:

Demonstrate product or service uniqueness, competitive advantage, and high entry barriers. First, complete electronic company information form at the Web site. Then send an executive summary to info@dawntreaderlp.com. Follow up with a business plan to

Dawntreader
c/o Wit Capital
826 Broadway, 7th Floor
New York, NY 10003
(646) 654-2600

DigitalVentures
Focus: E-commerce and financial services.
Web Address: www.dtpnet.com

Formerly Digital Technology Partners, invests in early stage companies and acts as an incubator for business-to-business Internet ventures. Becomes active in daily business decisions of funded companies. Assists in forging partnerships, recruiting managers and directors, and formulating business strategies. Also offers public relations and legal services, as well as physical space.

HOW TO APPLY:

Send a business plan, including references, to

DigitalVentures
50 California St., Suite 850

San Francisco, CA 94111
(415) 354-6200

Doll Capital Management
Focus: Communications, networking, and Internet services
Web Address: www.dollcap.com

Targets start ups, but will consider older or international companies. Seeks long-term, managerial relationships. Seed-money investments typically are less than $1 million. Total funding usually ranges from $2 million to $6 million per company.

HOW TO APPLY:
Submit a business plan to

Doll Capital Management
3000 Sand Hill Road
Bldg. 3, Suite 225
Menlo Park, CA 94025
(650) 233-1400
Fax: (650) 854-9159

Dolphin Communications
Focus: Private communications companies
http://www.dolphinfund.com/

Founded in 1990, counts more than $160 million in committed capital. Targets communication companies in North America. Typically invests $5 million to $20 million in each venture. Co-invests with other funds in commitments to $100 million and higher. Fund managers have experience in a variety of communications sub-markets, including telephony, the Internet, wireless, broadcasting, cable television, and media content.

HOW TO APPLY:
Send proposals to

Richard J. Brekka, Senior Managing Director
(212) 446-1601
richard.brekka@dolphinfund.com
or
Barry W. Stewart, Managing Director
(212) 446-1602
barry.stewart@dolphinfund.com

Dolphin Communications
750 Lexington Ave., 16th Floor
New York, NY 10022
(212) 446-1600
Fax: (212) 446-1638

Domain Associates
Focus: Healthcare
Web Address: www.domainvc.com/

Founded in 1985, invests $30 million to $40 million each year. Often works as the lead investor. Will join other investment funds. Commits to early-stage ventures during conceptualization and commercialization stages. Targets biopharmaceuticals, drug discovery services, medical devices, instrumentation, diagnostics, healthcare information systems, e-health, healthcare services, and advanced materials.

HOW TO APPLY:

Send inquiries to domain@domainvc.com

or

Domain Associates
One Palmer Square
Princeton, NJ 08542
(609) 683-5656
Fax: (609) 683-9789

or

Domain Associates
28202 Cabot Road, Suite 200
Laguna Niguel, CA 92677
(949) 347-2446
Fax: (949) 347-9720

Draper Fisher Jurvetson
Focus: Software, communications, electronic information, and electronics
Web Address: www.drapervc.com

Participates in executive recruitment, financial strategy development, and exit planning. Seeks a board seat and preferred stock. Key selection criteria include managerial strength, a strong, high-gross-margin-oriented business model, and product uniqueness. Looks for companies that have the potential to attain $100 million in value in five years.

HOW TO APPLY:

Send a hard copy business plan and detailed resumes of top executives to address below (discourages e-mail submissions). Review process typically takes up to three weeks.

Draper Fisher Jurvetson
400 Seaport Ct., Suite 250
Redwood City, CA 94063
(650) 599-9000
Fax: (650) 599-9726

Dougery Ventures
Focus: Internet, data communications, client/server software, networking software, electronic design automation, and telephony software
Web Address: www.dougery.com

Takes board seat. Assists in financial planning, hiring executives, and formulating business strategies.

HOW TO APPLY:

Send business plan and resumes of managers to

Dougery Ventures
165 Santa Ana Ave.
San Francisco, CA 94127
(415) 566-5220
Fax: (415) 566-5757
dougeryven@aol.com

Draper International

Focus: India-based companies and U.S. ventures that market information technology and telecommunications in the country
Web Address: www.draperintl.com/

Shuns medical, industrial, or consumer product companies. Invests $2 million or less in early-stage and start up companies. Also backs some later-stage ventures. Takes a board seat. Assists in business strategy, executive recruitment, and follow-on funding.

HOW TO APPLY:

Demonstrate managerial talent and expertise. Also show company's competitive advantages, growth opportunities, and technology strengths. Send a business plan and comprehensive managers' resumes to Robin Donohoe at

Draper International
50 California St., Suite 2925
San Francisco, CA 94111
(415) 616-4050
Fax: (415) 616-4060
mail@draperintl.com

Note: the domestic investment arm of Draper International is Draper Richards L.P. It backs early-stage ventures in their first funding round. E-mail the fund at www.draperrichards.com/ or write to the street address above.

DynaFund Ventures
Focus: Early-stage Internet services and e-commerce, software, communications, electronics, and photonics
Web Address: www.dynafundventures.com/

Backs companies that use the Internet as a strategic tool to market internationally or those companies that develop software and communications systems that promote the business use of the Internet. Usually invests $1 million to $4 million per funding cycle in each company. Typically works as the lead investor. Will join funding syndicates.

HOW TO APPLY:

Submit business plan with an executive summary (up to three pages) to

DynaFund Ventures
21311 Hawthorne Blvd.
Suite 300
Torrance, CA 90503
Attn: Christine Gray
(310) 792-4929
Fax: (310) 543-8733
info@dynafundventures.com

Early Stage Enterprises
Focus: Early-stage, mid-Atlantic companies in information technology, computer software, Internet software and services, medical devices and diagnostics, life sciences, and healthcare services
Web Address: www.esevc.com

A Small Business Investment Company (SBIC) licensee with a capital pool of $44 million. Targets ventures often with less than $3 million in revenues but demonstrate high growth opportunities. Companies generally seek $250,000 to $2 million. Typically acts as the first institutional investor for the funded company. Seeks companies with unique product or service, with potential for large market, and an experienced executive staff.

HOW TO APPLY:

Mail or e-mail an executive summary.

Early Stage Enterprises, LP
995 Route 518
Skillman, NJ 08558
(609) 921-8896
Fax: (609) 921-8703
partners@esevc.com

East/West Capital Associates
Focus: Technologies, applications, and services for next-generation of communications, information, commerce, and entertainment companies
Web Address: www.ewcapital.com

Seeks early-stage opportunities in the convergence of video, audio, voice, images, text, data, and transactions. Co-manager with Wasserstein, Perella of a $135 million fund.

HOW TO APPLY:

Does not encourage unsolicited business plans or inquiries.

10900 Wilshire Blvd., Suite 950
Los Angeles, CA 90024

Fax: (310) 209-6160
ravin@ercapital.com

Edelson Technology Partners
Focus: International technology companies
Web Address: www.edelsontech.com

Manages more than $100 million for start up, second-round, and mezzanine financings. Considers all types of technology opportunities in North American, Asia, and Europe. Typically invests $300,000 to $1.5 million. Aids U.S. portfolio companies with international expansion strategies. Looks for experienced managers, a viable financial strategy, revenue potential of $50 million or more, unique technology, and competitive advantage.

HOW TO APPLY:

Submit proposals to

webmaster@edelsontech.com

Edelson Technology Partners
300 Tice Blvd.
Woodcliff Lake, NJ 07675
(201) 930-9898
Fax: (201) 930-8899

Edison Venture Fund
Focus: Mid-Atlantic software, communications, and electronics companies
Web Address: www.edisonventure.com/

Targets expansion-stage companies with $2 million to $15 million in revenues, and the chance to attain $25 million in revenues in five years. Typically invests $1 million to $5 million as sole or lead investor. Provides follow on funding to $6 million. Looks for managerial talent, proprietary products or services, and fast-growth markets. Will consider highly attractive start-ups and later-stage companies as well as opportunities outside the mid-Atlantic region.

HOW TO APPLY:

Call or send written inquiry to gauge interest in a full business plan. E-mail

deals@edisonventure.com

Egan-Managed Capital
Focus: Early-stage technology companies based in New England.
Web Address: www.egancapital.com/

A $33 million venture fund with an emphasis on New England technology ventures. Usually invests $250,000 to $2 million as a lead investor or as part of a syndicate. Assists in attracting management and follow-on financing.

HOW TO APPLY:

Submit inquires to

Egan-Managed Capital
30 Federal St.
Boston, MA 02110
(617) 695-2600
Fax: (617) 695-2699

www.egancapital.com,

El Dorado Ventures
Focus: Early-stage, West Coast technology companies in enterprise software, Internet software and services, communications, and semiconductors
Web Address: www.eldoradoventures.com/

Assists in introductions to Silicon Valley technical and financial resources.

HOW TO APPLY:

Send inquiries to

El Dorado Ventures
2400 Sand Hill Road
Suite 100
Menlo Park, CA 94025
(650) 854-1200
Fax: (650) 854-1202

Encompass Ventures
Focus: Western U.S. and Canadian companies in electronic commerce, Internet/ intranet, digital audio and video, embedded systems, home computing, and healthcare
Web Address: www.encompassventures.com

Prefers start ups but considers ventures in any growth stage with an Asian or European growth strategy. Invests $200,000 to $3 million per company. Assists in international funding, marketing, and distribution.

HOW TO APPLY:

E-mail queries to info@evpartners.com

EnCompass Ventures
777 108th Avenue NE
Suite 2300
Bellevue, WA 98004
(425) 468-3900
Fax: (425) 468-3901

EnerTech Capital Partners
Focus: Utility, telecommunications, data communications, security, Internet access, and energy industries.
Web Address: www.enertechcapital.com/

Founded in 1996, currently manage a $50 million investment fund.

HOW TO APPLY:

E-mail or fax an executive summary to srice@enertechcapital.com
Fax: (610) 254-4188

or send business plan to

EnerTech Capital Partners
435 Devon Park Drive
700 Building
Wayne, PA 19087

Eno River Capital
Focus: Bioscience companies in North Carolina
Web Address: www.enorivercapital.com/

Backs emerging ventures with funding of $500,000 to $2 million. Assists in product development.

HOW TO APPLY:

Contact
Dr. Charles Hamner or **Tom Laundon**
North Carolina Biotechnology Center
(919) 541-9366

or

Paul Jones or **Daniel Egger**
Eno River Capital (919) 419-1284

Enterprise Partners
Focus: Information technology, communications, healthcare, and select consumer products and services
Web Address: www.ent.com

Focuses on early-stage and emerging growth ventures based in California. Investments include seed-stage and start up companies. Manages about $745 million in capital. Invests up to $20 million per company . Looks for liquidity in four to seven years.

HOW TO APPLY:

Fill out electronic application at the company's Web site, or send an executive summary (five pages maximum) to

Enterprise Partners
7979 Ivanhoe Ave., Suite 550
La Jolla, CA 92037-4543
(858) 454-2489

EOS Partners
Focus: Business, consumer, healthcare, and technology services, and value-added distribution and energy
Web Address: www.eospartners.com/

Founded in 1994, now has $350 million under management. Targets industries with high long-term growth potential and companies with $20 million to $200 million in revenues. Focuses on small and mid-market companies involved in management buyouts, consolidations, recapitalizations, and growth investments. Looks for significant investment in the candidate company by managers. Takes a board seat. Assists in managing growth. Considers projects through the U.S. and Canada.

HOW TO APPLY:

Inquire at

Eos Partners, L.P.
320 Park Ave., 22nd Floor
New York, NY 10022
(212) 832-5800
Fax: (212) 832-5815
mfirst@eospartners.com

Equus Capital Management Corp.
Focus: All sectors except high-technology, financial, and real estate

Web Address: www.equuscap.com/

Founded in 1983, looks for candidates with before-tax earnings of $1.5 million to $7.5 million. Will consider companies outside that range on an individual basis. High growth not a requirement. In general, the companies Equus backs have a market value of $10 million to $80 million. Initial investments typically are $3 million to $8 million. Biased toward company acquisitions in consolidating industries. Looks for investment payoffs in five to seven years. Requires that company managers have a significant stake in the venture. Values established businesses with a three-year or more history of stable cash flow. Takes a board seat.

HOW TO APPLY:

Start with a phone call to gauge interest.

Equus
2929 Allen Parkway, Suite 2500
Houston, TX 77019-2120
(713) 529-0900
(800) 856-0901

Euclid Partners
Focus: Information systems, communications, and healthcare
Web Address: www.euclidpartners.com/

Founded in 1970, targets early-stage companies involved in product development and commercialization. Evaluates managerial talent, market potential, the uniqueness of the product or business strategy, and

ROI. Looks for companies that can reach revenues of $50 million to $100 million in five years. Assists in staff recruitment, financial planning, negotiating manufacturing and marketing relationships, and public offerings.

HOW TO APPLY:

Send business plan to

Euclid Partners
45 Rockefeller Plaza
Suite 907
New York, NY 10111
(212) 218-6880
Fax: (212) 218-6877

Evanston Business Investment Corporation
Focus: Early-stage ventures in the Chicago area, particularly those in Evanston, IL, or affiliates of Northwestern University
Web Address: www.ebic.com/

Established in 1986 as a seed fund. Three quarters of the companies it backs are in Evanston or plan to relocate there. Only considers ventures with high-growth potential. Typically invests $100,000 to $150,000 in each company. Takes a board seat.

HOW TO APPLY:

Send inquiries to

Thomas E. Parkinson, Executive Director

Evanston Business Investment Corporation
1840 Oak Ave.
Evanston, IL 60201
(847) 866-1840
Fax: (847) 866-1808
parkinson@nwu.edu

Exelon Capital Partners
Focus: Retail energy, energy services, energy logistics, infrastructure management, and communications
Web Address: www.exeloncapitalpartners. com

Part of the PECO Energy Company, the fund designates $45 million annually for new ventures. Prefers growth-round companies with a commercial product and sales of $5 million or more. Will consider companies in other growth stages. Seeks high-growth ventures. Looks for experienced managers, a valid business model, and a competitive advantage. Candidates should demonstrate the potential to reach market valuation of $100 million or more in five years.

HOW TO APPLY:

Contact Andrea F. Kramer
principal@exeloncapitalpartners.com
or complete the online form at the Web site.

FBR Technology Venture Partners
Focus: Early, middle-, and late-stage electronic commerce, telecommunications, and

Internet/Intranet software and services companies
Web Address: www.fbrcorp.com

A $50 million fund that targets technology companies near Washington, D.C., and the mid-Atlantic. Also considers projects in California and New England. An affiliate of the investment bank Friedman, Billings, Ramsey & Co. Participates in staff development, honing business strategies, and building strategic partnerships. Offers global contacts. Usually invests $1 million to $3 million per round. Looks for companies that can benefit from a competitive advantage over time and can generate higher than average margins.

How to Apply:
Send executive summary or business plan to

Gene Riechers, Hooks Johnston, Scott Frederick or Harry Weller
FBR Technology Venture Partners
1001 Nineteenth Street North
Arlington, VA 22209
griechers@fbr.com
hooks@fbr.com
sfrederick@fbr.com
hweller@fbr.com.

Fidelity Ventures
Focus: Healthcare, software, communications, employer services, and education

Web Address: www.fidelityventures.com

The venture capital arm of mutual-fund giant Fidelity Investments. Invests more than $100 million each year. Considers seed stage through mezzanine and leveraged buyout opportunities. Typical initial investments range from $1 million for start ups to $20 million for buyouts. Currently targets for-profit education, including public charter schools, and employer services. Also manages funds specializing in telecommunications, Pacific Rim start ups, and healthcare. Recently launched Healthcare Venture Partnership (HVP), an incubator. Evaluates prospects for managerial talent and experience. Takes a board seat.

How to Apply:
Send a business plan to

Fidelity Ventures
82 Devonshire St., R25C
Boston, MA 02109-3614
(617) 563-9160
Fax: (617) 476-5015
ventures@fmr.com

First Analysis Venture Capital
Focus: Information technology, outsourced services, and infrastructure industries
Web Address: www.facvc.com/

Manages more than $500 million in investments. Considers early-stage, emerging-growth, expansion, and buyout opportunities. Investments typically are $1 million to $10 million total per company. Acts as sole or lead institutional investor and actively participates in corporate strategy development, building strategic alliances, recruiting key staff, and locating follow on financing.

HOW TO APPLY:

Use online form at the Web site to send business plans and other relevant information.

First Analysis Venture Capital
The Sears Tower, Suite 9500
233 South Wacker Drive
Chicago, IL 60606
(312) 258-1400
Fax: (312) 258-0334

First Capital Group
Focus: Texas and Southwest companies in communications, electronics, energy, environmental systems, healthcare, medical technology, manufacturing systems, and services
Web Address: www.firstcapitalgroup.com/

A Small Business Investment Company licensee. Considers early- and expansion-stage opportunities as well as management buyouts. Looks for a successful management team with a financial stake in the company. Also seeks ventures with a competitive edge in a large market.

HOW TO APPLY:

Send proposals to

Jeffrey P. Blanchard
P.O. Box 15616
750 E. Mulberry, Suite 305
San Antonio, TX 78212
(210) 736-4233
Fax: (210) 736-5449
jpb@texas.net

Wm. Ward Greenwood
P.O. Box 50587 (78763)
100 Congress Ave., Suite 730
Austin, TX 78701
(512) 494-9754
Fax: (512) 494-9756
wwg@texas.net

or

Steven D. Arnold
5433 Westheimer, Suite 405
Houston, TX 77056
(713) 623-6538
Fax: (713) 623-6609
sda@texas.net

First Chicago Equity Capital
Focus: Management buyouts, acquisitions, growth strategies
Web Site: www.imdr.com

Can provide equity for transactions up to $150 million. For management buyouts, targets companies with revenues of $20 million to $250 million. Looks for liquidity in four to seven years.

How to Apply:

Call Lauren R. Cislak at (317) 236-2159 or send e-mail to cislak@imdr.com.

First Chicago Equity Capital
One American Square, Box 82001
Indianapolis, IN 46282-0002
(317) 236-2100
Fax: (317) 236-2219

First Chicago Equity Capital
135 S. LaSalle St., Suite 4100
Chicago, IL 60603
(312) 726-1567
Fax: (312) 641-6263

First Chicago Equity Capital
6430 Norwood
Mission Hills, MO 66208
(913) 403-8788
Fax: (317) 592-5403

First Chicago Equity Capital
211 W. Washington St., Suite 2420
South Bend, IN 46601
(219) 234-7955
Fax: (219) 234-7965

Flatiron Partners
Focus: Internet companies specializing in content, commerce, and communications, primarily in the New York City region
Web Address: www.flatironpartners.com/

Founded in 1996, affiliated with Chase Capital Partners (CCP), the supplier of the $300 million under management. Fund includes $50 million for ventures in the convergence of the consumer electronics, wireless technologies, and the Web. Seeks opportunities that still require significant business development. Typically, these are first-round fundings after a revenue stream has already been established. Actively funding Internet ventures in Asia and Latin America.

How to Apply:

Send a printed copy of the business plan to

Flatiron Partners
257 Park Avenue South, 12th Floor
New York, NY 10010
(212) 228-3800
Fax: (212) 228-0552

Fluke Venture partners
Focus: Unique products, technologies, services, or market ventures
Web Address: www.flukecapital.com/

Founded in 1976, now has over $100 million under management. Looks for growing ventures in the Pacific Northwest. Prefers a minority equity position. Investments range from $500,000 to $2 million per round. Will consider lower minimum investments. Prefers to co-invest with other venture funds. Seeks liquidity within five years. Evaluates prospects for managerial strength, size and growth potential of the target market, and the uniqueness of the product or service.

HOW TO APPLY:

Call to gauge interest. Prefers complete business plan to executive summary when following up. Include current organization chart and comprehensive resumes and charts for the next two years. Detail plans to fill key positions. Also, discuss capital requirements under best-case and worst-case scenarios. Finally, provide a complete competitive analysis.

Contact Dennis Weston (weston@flukecapital.com) or Kevin Gabelein (gabelein@flukecapital.com).

Fluke Venture Partners
11400 S.E. 6th St., Suite 230
Bellevue, WA 98004-6423
(425) 453-4590
Fax: (425) 453-4675

FMC Capital Markets
Focus: Early- and late-stage funding opportunities
Web Address: www.fmccapital.com

Targets initial and secondary public offerings, bridge and mezzanine financing, and public and private debt financing. Looks for start ups with the potential to attain $50 million to $100 million in market value in five years.

HOW TO APPLY:

Detail past experience of company managers, including appropriate professional references. Show competitive strength of product or service, and growth potential of the market.

FMC Capital Markets
201 8th Street South, Suite 306
Naples, FL 34102
(941) 434-8405
Fax: (941) 643-6670
info@fmccapital.com

Flynn Ventures
Focus: Retail, lifestyle, e-commerce, the Web, information technology, telecommunications and restaurant chains
Web Address: www.flynnventures.com/

Targets early-stage companies in the western U.S. and western Canada. Typically invests $200,000 to $1 million in each enterprise.

HOW TO APPLY:

Send business plans to

Flynn Ventures
One Flynn Center
825 Van Ness Ave.
San Francisco, CA 94109

Forward Ventures
Focus: Early-stage biotechnology and healthcare companies
Web Address: www.forwardventures.com/

Targets seed and start up ventures, primarily in southern California. Manages $55 million in capital. Frequently signs on before the business plan is written. Helps develop the business strategy. Prefers to be the first venture fund investor. Invests $500,000 to $1.5 million initially, with total investments up to $3 million.

HOW TO APPLY:

Send a brief business plan or executive summary to

Forward Ventures
Attention: Julia Reynolds
9255 Towne Centre Drive, Suite 300
San Diego, CA 92121
(858) 677-6077, x3107
Fax: (858) 452-8799
reynolds@forwardventures.com

Foundation Capital
Focus: Consumer e-commerce, e-business, Internet infrastructure, telecommunications, and networking
Web Address: www.foundationcapital.com/

Targets seed- and start up stage companies. Typically invests $1 million to $5 million in first round. Acts as lead investors. Takes a board seat.

HOW TO APPLY:

Call or send idea or formal business plan to

Foundation Capital
70 Willow Rd., Suite 200
Menlo Park, CA 94025
(650) 614-0500
Fax: (650) 614-0505

Frazier & Co.
Focus: Healthcare
Web Address: www.frazierco.com

Founded in 1991, targets emerging growth companies. Manages more than $350 million. Usually invests in mid to later-stage companies, although is now considering more early-stage ventures.

HOW TO APPLY:

Call to gauge interest. Follow up with a business plan.

Frazier & Co.
Two Union Square
Suite 3300
Seattle, WA 98101
(206) 621-7200
Fax: (206) 621-1848

Frontenac Company

Focus: Consumer and business services, information technology and telecommunications services, and manufacturing
Web Address: www.frontenac.com/

Current fund totals $300 million. Weighs management experience heavily in the evaluation process.

HOW TO APPLY:

Send inquiries to

Frontenac Company
135 South LaSalle St., Suite 3800
Chicago, IL 60603
(312) 368-0044
Fax: (312) 368-9520
info@frontenac.com

Fusient Media Ventures,
Focus: Programming for the Internet
Web Address: www.fusient.com

Seeks early-stage ventures backed by experienced managers. Will also provide later-stage growth funding.

HOW TO APPLY:

E-mail send business plans to newbiz@fusient.com

or contact

John Murphy or Jim Bolen at mPRm Public Relations

(212) 268-3080
jmurphy@mPRm.com
jbolen@mPRm.com

JK&B Capital
Focus: Telecommunications, software and information technologies
Web Address: www.jkbcapital.com/

Founded in 1995, the fund manages $220 million. Has ties to computer software giant Computer Associates. Looks for prospects with proprietary products or services that is able to reach $75 million or more in market value in five years. First-round investment typically are $2 million to $5 million, with investments over time reaching $5 million to $15 million per company. Usually acts as the lead investor. Takes a board seat. Past investments have been U.S. companies, but will consider international opportunities.

HOW TO APPLY:

Send an investment proposal and a business plan to

JK&B Capital
205 N. Michigan Ave., Suite 808
Chicago, IL 60601
(312) 946-1200
Fax: (312) 946-1103
info@jkbcapital.com

JMI Equity Fund
Focus: Software and information services
Web Address: www.jmi-inc.com/

Begun 1992, the fund provides $1 million to $10 million for start ups, expansion projects, recapitalizations, and buyouts.

HOW TO APPLY:

Send proposals to the nearest office.

JMI, Inc.
1119 St. Paul St.
Baltimore, MD 21202
(410) 385-2691
Fax: (410) 385-2641

Harry S. Gruner, General Partner,
hgruner@jmi-inc.com

Bradford D. Woloson, General Partner,
bwoloson@jmi-inc.com

JMI, Inc.
12680 High Bluff Drive, 2nd Floor
San Diego, CA 92130
(858) 259-2500
Fax: (858) 259-4843

Paul V. Barber, General Partner,
pbarber@jmi-inc.com

Charles E. Noell, General Partner,
cnoell@jmi-inc.com

JMI, Inc.
100 Anchor Drive, Suite 376
Key Largo, FL 33037
(305) 367-8886
Fax: (305) 367-3882

Robert J. Sywolski, General Partner,
bsywolski@jmi-inc.com

Kansas City Equity Partners
Focus: Information technology, telecommunications, retail, consumer products, and industrial manufacturing in the Midwest
Web Address: www.kcep.com/

This Small Business Investment Company licensee manages $75 million for companies throughout Kansas, Missouri, Illinois, Iowa, Nebraska, Colorado, and Oklahoma. Considers companies in all developmental stages as long as they are high-growth candidates. Minimum investment is $500,000. Looks for managerial expertise, a clear product or service idea, competitive advantage, and an established market. Assists in staff development and introductions to other strategic business resources.

HOW TO APPLY:

Submit a business plan to info@kcep.com
or
Investment Manager
Kansas City Equity Partners
233 West 47th St.
Kansas City, MO 64112
(816) 960-1771
Fax: (816) 960-1777

KB Partners
Focus: Start up and early stage Internet products and services, information technol-

ogy, computer hardware and software, telecommunications, medical devices and healthcare products, industrial and engineering technology, and analytical instrumentation
Web Address: www.kbpartners.com/

Provides $500,000 to $3 million for seed-, first-, or second-round funding. Looks for start ups distinguished by a compelling product, technology, or leader. Also targets private-company acquisitions.

HOW TO APPLY:
Complete the electronic funding request form at the Web site or send proposal to:

KB Partners, LLC
500 Skokie Blvd., Suite 446
Northbrook, IL 60062
(847) 714-0444
Fax: (847) 714-0445

Keith D. Bank, keith@kbpartners.com

Byron A. Denenberg,
byron@kbpartners.com

Robert A. Garber, robert@kbpartners.com

Kestrel Venture Management
Focus: New England-based Basic manufacturing, healthcare, software, computer devices, service companies, media communications, and food products.
Web Address: www.kestrelvm.com

Prefers early-stage companies with a working business model, but will also consider seed fundings, management buyouts, and other development stages. Managerial strength and a viable business plan are the two primary investment criteria. Invests up to $4 million per company.

HOW TO APPLY:
Send a business idea or formal business plan.

Kestrel Venture Management
31 Milk St.
Boston, MA 02109-5400
(617) 451-6722
Fax: (617) 451-3322
msilva@kestrelvm.com

Keystone Venture Capital
Focus: Mid-Atlantic information technology, consumer, and outsourcing companies
Web Address: keystoneventures.com/

Founded in 1982, manages $150 million in capital. Targets high-growth companies with a market tested business model and past the seed or start up phase. Looks for managerial talent, commercial products or services, a viable marketing strategy, market growth, and an existing revenue stream. Takes a board seat. Works as sole investor or leader of an investment group. Typically invest $1 million to $4 million per company.

HOW TO APPLY:

Send inquiries to info@keystonevc.com or to

Keystone Venture Capital
1601 Market St., Suite 2500
Philadelphia, PA 19103
(215) 241-1200
Fax: (215) 241-1211

Kleiner, Perkins, Caufield, & Byers
Focus: Information and life sciences
Web Address: www.kpcb.com/

An influencial venture-capital force since 1972, it has raised more than $1.2 billion in capital. Participates in an "keiretsu" style network of shared intelligence with hundreds of companies and thousand of executives to help managers of new companies.

HOW TO APPLY:

Inquire at

Kleiner, Perkins, Caufield, & Byers
2750 Sand Hill Road
Menlo Park, CA 94025
(650) 233-2750
Fax: (650) 233-0300
or
Kleiner, Perkins, Caufield, & Byers
Four Embarcadero Center
Suite 1880
San Francisco, CA 94111
(415) 421-3110
Fax: (415) 421-3128

Kline Hawkes & Co.,

Focus: Information technology and healthcare
Web Address: www.klinehawkes.com/

A Small Business Investment Corp. licensee with $112 million in capital. Targets later-stage ventures and consolidations primarily in California (will consider projects elsewhere). Typically invests $3 million to $6 million. Evaluates proposals according to high-growth potential, managerial strength, and the size of the target market.

HOW TO APPLY:

Send proposals to

Kline Hawkes & Co.
11726 San Vicente Blvd., Suite 300
Los Angeles, CA 90049
(310) 442-4700
Fax: (310) 442-4707
Info@klinehawkes.com

Leonard Kramer & Associates
Focus: Early-stage and growing companies
Web Address: www.lkcapital.com

Typical candidates are early-stage companies or established businesses with $3 million to $100 million in sales. Usually provides $2 million to $25 million in funding. Also fund recapitalizations prior to a management buyout, internal expansion project, or industry consolidation. Provides $5 million to $100 million for these initiatives. Backs companies headquartered in the United States and Canada with significant growth potential. Doesn't usually back start ups.

HOW TO APPLY:

Call to discuss your proposal and gauge interest. Follow up with an executive summary. If using E-mail, don't send the summary as an attachment; integrate it into the main body of the message. The fund can help write the business plan.

Leonard Kramer & Associates
621 Bernardston Road
Greenfield, MA 01301
(413) 774-4245
Fax: (413) 774-4342
equity@lkcapital.com

Levy Trajman Management Investment Inc.
Focus: Software companies with high, international growth potential
Web Address: www.ltmi.com

Targets software developers based in Boston, Silicon Valley, Israel, or India that have a post-prototype product with the commercial potential to reach $500 million in sales in five years. The software should display prospects for long-time growth and strength against competition. Managers should demonstrate abilities to guide the company through its growth.

HOW TO APPLY:

Send proposals to

Levy Trajman Management Investment Inc.

67 South Bedford St., 400W
Burlington, MA 01803
(781) 229-5818
Fax: (781) 229-1808
info@ltmi.com

Lewis Hollingsworth
Focus: Startup and later-stage ventures
www.lewispartners.com/

Founded in 1987, specializes in leveraged buyouts, growth funding, recapitalizations, and industry consolidations. Actively contributes to strategic and financial initiatives. Also acts as a merchant banker for some portfolio companies.

HOW TO APPLY:

Inquire at

Lewis Hollingsworth LP
One Galleria Tower
13355 Noel Rd., Stuite 2210
Dallas, TX 75240
(972) 702-7390
Fax: (972) 702-7391
drangel@lewispartners.com

The Long Island Venture Fund
Focus: Information technology and life sciences
Web Address: www.livf.com/

Established in 1994, targets seed- and early-stage ventures in emerging-technology companies based on Long Island. A partner with the Long Island Research Institute, a not-for-profit development company backed by New York national laboratories and universities. Typically invests $500,000 to $1.5 million per venture. Will consider later-stage manufacturing and retail candidates. Looks for skilled entrepreneurs. Works as lead investor in the Northeast or a co-investor for young domestic or international companies.

HOW TO APPLY:

Use the electronic form at the Web site to send an executive summary or forward a business plan to plans @Livf.com.

The Long Island Venture Fund
123 Hofstra University
Business Development Center
Axinn Library, West Wing, Suite 213
Hempstead, NY 11550-1090
(516) 463-3662
Fax: (516) 463-3667

Lucent Venture Partners, Inc.,
Focus: Early-stage ventures in high-growth communications technologies, including wireless communications, data networking, semiconductors, communications software, and professional services.
Web Address: www.lucentventurepartners.com

A venture capital arm of Lucent Technologies, Murray Hill, NJ. Formed in 1998, to supports business relationships between Lucent and private companies in related markets. Currently manages a $100 million fund. Typically invests $500,000 to $5 million per venture. Seeks early-stage technologies that complement Lucent's R&D. Usually invests in East Coast and West Coast companies, by considers candidates from all over the world.

HOW TO APPLY:

E-mail proposals to
info@lucentventurepartners.com

Lucent Venture Partners
3180 Porter Drive
Palo Alto, CA 94304-1226
(650) 565-7400
Fax: (650) 565-7401

Madison Dearborn Partners
Focus: Communications, natural resources, consumer, healthcare, financial services, industrial, and basic industries
Web Address: www.mdcp.com/

Targets management buyouts, growth initiatives, recapitalizations, and acquisitions for start-up and early-stage companies. Evaluates candidates according to managerial strength and long-term growth potential of the company. Invests $30 million to $400 million when it's the lead investor. Seeks pay out in five to ten years. Manages a total fund of $4 billion.

How to Apply:

Send proposal to

Madison Dearborn Partners
Three First National Plaza
Suite 3800
Chicago, IL 60602
(312) 895-1000
Fax: (312) 895-1001
info@mdcp.com

Marathon Investment Partners
Focus: Manufacturers, distributors, specialty
retailers, technical and service companies
Web Address: www.marathoninvestment.
com

Targets small and middle market ventures
in growth or later stages. Usually invests $1
million to $3 million. Can act as lead or co-
investor. Looks for candidates in growing
markets that are building market share and
have predictable cash flow. Managerial expertise weighs heavily in evaluation of new
candidates.

How to Apply:

Forward a comprehensive business plan, including three years of financial statements
and a five-year projection, to mark-
ham@marathoninvestment.com.

Marathon Investment Partners
10 Post Office Square, Suite 1225
Boston, MA 02109
(617) 423-2494
Fax: (617) 423-2719

Mason Wells
Focus: Paper, packaging, printing, industrial
products and materials, business services,
and software
Web Address: www2.masonwells.com/

Founded in 1982, manages more than $350
million. Assists executives in devising
growth and operations strategies.

How to Apply:

Send a business plan to

Mason Wells
770 North Water Street
Milwaukee, WI 53202
(414) 765-7800
Fax: (414) 765-7850
info@masonwells.com

**Massachusetts Technology Development
Corporation**
Focus: Start up and expansion of early-stage
technology companies operating in Massa-
chusetts.
Web Address: www.mtdc.com/

Typically invests $100,000 to $300,000,
sometimes up to $500,000. Ventures must
be based in, or relocate to the state. Candidates should have exhausted conventional
capital sources before applying. Looks for
technology products with a competitive advantage. Expansion projects must have potential to significantly increase employment.

How to Apply:

Mail hard copy of a comprehensive business plan, including projected employment impact to

John F. Hodgman, President
MTDC
148 State St.
Boston, MA 02109
(617) 723-4920
Note: MTDC does not accept business plans sent via the Internet or fax

Matrix Partners
Focus: Software, networking equipment, semiconductors, computers, storage, the Internet, and e-business applications
Web Address: www.matrixpartners.com/

Typically invests $100,000 to $300,000 for seed ventures. Will consider early-stage investments of $10 million or more over a number of rounds.

How to Apply:

Send inquiries to info@matrixlp.com

Matrix Partners
Bay Colony Corporate Center
1000 Winter St., Suite 4500
Waltham, MA 02451
(781) 890-2244
Fax: (781) 890-2288

or

Matrix Partners

2500 Sand Hill Road, Suite 113
Menlo Park, CA 94025
(650) 854-3131
Fax: (650) 854-3296

Maveron
Focus: Companies with products or services for domestic and foreign growth
Web Address: www.maveron.com/

Established in 1998. targets ventures with national or international growth potential.

How to Apply:

Send an executive summary to

Maveron LLC
800 Fifth Ave., Suite 4100
Seattle, WA 98104
(206) 447-1300
Fax: (206) 470-1150
info@maveron.com

Mayfield Fund
Focus: Healthcare and information technologies, software, and semiconductors
Web Address: www.mayfield.com

Founded in 1969, now has $1 billion under management. Looks for ventures with the potential to achieve market value of $200 million in five years. Targets seed- to second-round financing stages. Typically invests $2 million to $5 million per company, but has supplied as little as $50,000 and as much as $10 million in the past. Usually acts as lead investor. Prefers companies that supply software-based middleware, tools, applications, on-line services, as well as Internet-based education and consumer entertainment projects. Will act as incubator for fledgling companies. Assists in recruiting and developing staff.

HOW TO APPLY:

Send business plan, if available. Will assist in creating a plan.

Mayfield Fund
2800 Sand Hill Road
Menlo Park, CA 94025
(650) 854-5560
Fax: (650) 854-5712
info@mayfield.com

M/C Venture Partners
Focus: High-growth communications and IT services
Web Address: www.mcventurepartners.com/

Focuses on early-stage ventures. Manages a $250 million fund. Typically invests $5 million to $40 million per company. Works actively with managers on business strategy, follow on funding, and recruitment. Usually takes a lead investor role. in structuring and assembling any additional financing needed to execute a business plan by establishing management's credibility with lenders and underwriters. Current investments include data carriers/ISPs, broadband networks, wireless systems, outsourcing services, net-work integrators, and applications hosting companies. Will consider selective offshore proposals.

HOW TO APPLY:

Send proposals to

M/C Venture Partners
75 State St., Suite 2500
Boston, MA 02109
(617) 345-7200
Fax: (617) 345-7201
contact@mcventurepartners.com

Medicus Venture Partners
Focus: Early stage medical and biotechnology companies based in the western U.S.
Web Address: http://www.medicusvc.com/

Actively seeking prospects for medical and diagnostic devices, drug delivery systems, biopharmaceuticals, genomics, healthcare information systems; medical instruments, and healthcare services. Usually invests $35,000 to $3 million to start, or up to $5 million over multiple funding rounds. Looks for companies with potential for $100 million in sales, a competitive advantage, managerial talent, and proprietary technology.

HOW TO APPLY:

Send proposals to

Medicus Venture Partners

12930 Saratoga Ave., Suite D8
Saratoga, CA 95070
(408) 447-8600
Fax: (408) 447-8599
fred@medicusvc.com

or

Medicus Venture Partners
800 Airport Blvd., Suite 508
Burlingame, CA 94010
(650) 375-0200
Fax: (650) 375-0230
john@medicusvc.com

Menlo Ventures
Focus: Communications, software, and healthcare technology
Web Address: www.menloventures.com/

Manages a total of $1.2 billion for all developmental stages from start ups to mezzanine funding. Looks for management expertise and unique products or services. Usually invests $4 million to $10 million over multiple rounds. Frequently takes a board seat.

HOW TO APPLY:
Send proposals to

Menlo Ventures
3000 Sand Hill Road
Building 4, Suite 100
Menlo Park, CA 94025
(650) 854-8540
Fax: (650) 854-7059
info@menloventures.com

Mentor Capital Partners, Ltd.
Focus: Pennsylvania, New Jersey, or Mid-Atlantic companies in business services, consumer markets, distribution, financial services, healthcare, industrial technology, and information technology
Web Address: www.mentorcapitalpartners.com/

Looks for private and public companies with revenues between $5 million and $100 million. Key criterion is managerial expertise.

HOW TO APPLY:
Inquire at

Edward F. Sager, Jr.
Mentor Capital Partners, Ltd.
P.O. Box 560
Yardley, PA 19067
Phone and Fax: (215) 736-8882
sager@mentorcapitalpartners.com

or

George P. Stasen
Mentor Capital Partners, Ltd.
1354 Hainesport Road
Mt. Laurel, NJ 08054
(609) 802-1788
Fax: (609) 802-1791
stasen@mentorcapitalpartners.com

Millennium Three Venture Group
Focus: Manufacturing, service, and distribution companies in Phoenix, Reno, Las Vegas, Sacramento, and Stockton/Modesto, CA

Web Address: www.m3vg.com/

Looks for ventures in a solid niche market, with high-growth potential, and with $5 million or more in revenues. Other key criteria: Stable cash flow, managerial expertise, and ability to weather down markets. Targets non-commodity markets not threatened by technological change. Shuns ventures with potential environmental or labor problems.

HOW TO APPLY:

Inquiry at

Millennium Three Venture Group
6880 S. McCarran Blvd., Suite A-11
Reno, NV 89509
(775) 954-2020
Fax: (775) 854-2023
rsmith@m3vg.com

Mitsui USA Private Equity Group
Focus: Information technology and healthcare
Web Address: www.mitsuipe.com/

A subsidiary of the multinational corporation Mitsui, the group early-stage companies in North America with capital and introduction to Asian and other international companies. Initial investments are typically $2 million or less. May not always take a board seat.

HOW TO APPLY:

Send business plan to

Private Equity Department
Mitsui & Co. (U.S.A.), Inc.
200 Park Ave., 36th Floor
New York, NY 10166-0130
(212) 878-4066
Fax: (212) 878-4070
MitsuiPE@nyc.mitsui.com

MMG Ventures, L.P
Focus: Communications and computer, information, and healthcare services companies in Delaware, Maryland, New Jersey, Pennsylvania, Virginia, and Washington, D.C.
Web Address: www.mmggroup.com/

Targets businesses with majority control by a socially or economically disadvantaged person or group. Company should also have high growth potential, a solid marketplace niche, managers with successful track records, the ability to create jobs for minorities, and lucrative ROI outlook. Will consider a small number of investments outside the Mid-Atlantic region. Typically invests $500,000 to $1.5 million per company.

HOW TO APPLY:

Send a detailed business plan and investment proposal (including projected economic impact on the local business community).

MMG Ventures, LP
826 E. Baltimore St.
Baltimore, MD 21202
(410) 659-7850
Fax: (410) 333-2552
msbdfa@mmggroup.com

Mohr, Davidow Ventures
Focus: Early-stage companies
Web Address: www.mdv.com/

Looks for entrepreneurial talent with well defined business models. Takes an active role in recruiting and developing staff, creating business strategies, marketing and promotion, and making introductions for strategic relationships.

HOW TO APPLY:
Send business idea or business plan to

Mohr, Davidow Ventures
2775 Sand Hill Road, Suite 240
Menlo Park, CA 94025
(650) 854-7236
Fax: (650) 854-7365

Montreux Equity Partners
Focus: Early-stage technology and healthcare ventures
Web Address: www.montreuxequity.com/

Founded in 1993, considers investments as small as $100,000 up to $3 million. Usually invests 500,000 to $1 million in the first round up to $2 million to $3 million total per company over multiple rounds. Acts as lead or co-investor.

HOW TO APPLY:
Forward business plans to information@montreuxep.com.

Montreux Equity Partners
2700 Sand Hill Road
Menlo Park, CA 94025
(650) 234-1200
Fax: (650) 234-1250

Morgan Stanley Dean Witter Venture Partners
Focus: Later-stage, high-growth ventures in information technology and healthcare
Web Address: www.msdw.com/institutional/venturepartners/

Founded in 1985, it is currently making investments from a $275 million fund. Typically invests $5 million to $25 million per company. Doesn't require a controlling interest in portfolio companies, but expects a significant ownership stakes. Assists in business planning and strategy, including buyouts and consolidations. Helps negotiate favorable rates for essential services such as telephone service, insurance, payroll processing, and credit cards. Expected life of each investment is three to five years. Usually takes a board seat.

HOW TO APPLY:

Send a business plan to the nearest office or e-mail to msventures@ms.com.
Morgan Stanley Dean Witter
Venture Partners
1221 Avenue of the Americas
33rd Floor
New York, NY 10020
(212) 762-7900
Fax: (212) 762-8424

or

3000 Sand Hill Road
Building 4, Suite 250
Menlo Park, CA 94025
(650) 233-2600
Fax: (650) 233-2626

Morgenthaler

Focus: Early stage information technology and healthcare companies, as well as management buyouts, expansions, and recapitalizations
Web Address: www.morgenthaler.com/

An active venture-capital source since1968, assists in executive recruiting, acquisitions, establishing corporate partnerships, and cultivating additional funding. Usually provides $2 million to $8 million in investment funding, or $25 million to $200 million for buyouts. Considers candidates from throughout the country.

HOW TO APPLY:

Submit an executive summary or business plan to:

Morgenthaler

2730 Sand Hill Road, Suite 280
Menlo Park, CA 94025
(650) 388-7600
Fax: (650) 388-7601

MPM Capital Advisors

Focus: Healthcare and life sciences
Web Address: www.mpmcapital.com/

Provides investments and merchant banking services. Backs expansions, acquisitions, and buyouts for emerging technologies. Manages BioVentures, a $230 million suite of funds dedicated to U.S. and European healthcare companies. Seeks managerial talent in ventures capable of leading a market. About 80 percent of the fund will go to biotechnology firms, the remainder to medical device and pharmaceutical service ventures. Three-quarters of the investment are earmarked for U.S. companies. Each investment will range from $5 million to $20 million total per company.

HOW TO APPLY:

Send proposals to:

MPM Capital Advisors

One Cambridge Center
9th Floor
Cambridge, MA 02142
(617) 225-7054
Fax: (617) 225-2210

or

601 Gateway Blvd., Suite 360
South San Francisco, CA 94080

(650) 829-5820
Fax: (650) 829-5828

Mustang Ventures
Focus: Early-stage companies in data and communications networking, applications, and services
Web Address: www.mustangventures.com

Created by Siemens Information and Communication Networks Group 1998 to provide seed-, first-, and second-round funding. Headquartered in Santa Clara, CA, with affiliate offices in Munich, Germany. Assists in business and financial development. Sometimes takes a board seat.

How to Apply:

Inquire at

Mustang Ventures
4900 Old Ironsides Drive
Santa Clara, CA 95054
(408) 492-6953
Fax: (408) 492-3614
mary.stradner@icn.siemens.com

Nassau Capital
Focus: Communications, health care, and real estate
Web Address: www.nassau.com/

Manages about $2 billion worth of Princeton University's endowment. Targets management buyouts, growth equity financings, recapitalizations, industry consolidations,

and ventures. Selectively backs early-stage ventures. Typically provides $10 million to $30 million per investment for companies valued between $25 million to $250 million. Has access to the university's network of investors and alumni. Also maintains relationships with private-equity and real-estate investment companies.

How to Apply:

Contact Curtis Glovier, cglovier@nassau.com or Jonathan Sweemer, jsweemer@nassau.com

Nassau Capital, L.L.C.
22 Chambers St.
Princeton, NJ 08542
(609) 924-3555
Fax: (609) 924-8887

NCIC Capital Fund
Focus: Early-stage technology ventures
Web Address: www.ncicfund.org

The National Center for Industrial Competitiveness is a non-profit economic development company that backs companies based in Ohio or Indiana. Candidates must have a full management team with a background in starting companies. Managers also should have a financial commitment to the venture and an established exit path. Targets companies with existing customers or a product ready for commercialization. Considers investments of $200,000 to

$750,000 for initial financing rounds, up to $1.5 million total. Seeks an exit within two years.

How to Apply:

Mail a completed funding application form and a release and indemnification form (both available at the site) along with three copies of a comprehensive business plan. Include a discussion of how the economy of the region, as well as employees, could benefit from the proposed venture. Note: The NCIC discourages electronic submissions.

NCIC
3155 Research Blvd., Suite 203
Dayton, OH 45420
(937) 253-1777
Fax: (937) 253-2634

New Enterprise Associates
Focus: Early stage companies in information technology, medical and life sciences, healthcare services, medical devices, instrumentation and information management
Web Address: www.nea.com/

Founded in 1978, invests $500,000 to $6 million in U.S. technology companies. Total investments can range up to a maximum of $15 million. Looks for a unique product or service, high-growth potential, and managerial expertise.

How to Apply:

Contact the nearest office.

New Enterprise Associates
One Freedom Square
11951 Freedom Drive
Suite 1240
Reston, VA 20190
Attn: Anne Miller

New Enterprise Associates
1119 St. Paul St.
Baltimore, MD 21202
Attn: Ryan Drant

New Enterprise Associates
2490 Sand Hill Road
Menlo Park, CA 94025
Attn: Beth Reed

New Vista Capital
Focus: Early-stage information technology ventures
Web Address: www.nvcap.com/

Founded in 1997, the company is a Small Business Investment Company licensee. Manages $50 million for young technology companies run by women and minorities. Funding typically is $250,000 to $1 million initially, and $2 million total. Looks for entrepreneurs driven to become market leaders and a growth plan that leads to an IPO or acquisition in five years or less. Assists in developing business strategies, staff development, distribution sources, and follow on funding.

HOW TO APPLY:

Send proposals to Roger Barry, rbarry@nvcap.com, or Frank Greene, fgreene@nvcap.com.

New Vista Capital
540 Cowper St., Suite 200
Palo Alto, CA 94301
(650) 329-9333
Fax: (650) 328-9434

Nippon Investment & Finance Co. Ltd
Focus: Overseas companies, especially in Japan and the rest of Asia, devoted to distribution, healthcare, industrial waste treatment, leisure and entertainment, retirees, and multimedia.
Web Address: www.nif.co.jp/

Founded in 1982, the company is part of Daiwa Securities Group. Manages more than $860 million in capital. Assists in staff recruiting and development, joint ventures, mergers, and acquisitions. U.S. investments center on technology ventures, especially those marketing multimedia products or services. Targets small- and medium-sized companies seeking Mezzanine funding. Looks for managerial expertise, market potential, and a near-term public offering.

HOW TO APPLY:
Contact

Yuzuru Miyamoto, President

NIF Ventures USA, Inc.
First Market Tower
525 Market St., Suite 3420
San Francisco, CA 94105
miyamoto@nifusa.com

Nokia Ventures
Focus: Early-stage, information technology companies
Web Address: www.nokia.com/inbrief/units/nvcf.html

The $100 million fund backs start ups and technologies outside of the companies usual endeavors. Looks for high-growth potential, experienced managers, and an ongoing competitive advantage. Investments typically go to pre-Mezzanine ventures needing $1 million to $5 million. Assists in management development, strategic planning, and introductions to business and technical experts.

HOW TO APPLY:
Send a business plan to:

Nokia Ventures
545 Middlefield Road, Suite 210
Menlo Park, CA 94025
Attention: Gina Bauman

Noro-Moseley Partners
Focus: Information technology and healthcare ventures
Web Address: www.noro-moseley.com/

Founded in 1983, manages four funds worth $260 million. All but 10 percent of its investments go to companies in the Southeast. Targets small to medium-sized companies. Will consider firms in business services and consumer products in addition to its core focus. Evaluates proposals according to management strength, market size, and the potential to become a market leader. Typically provides $2 million to $5 million initially, up to a maximum of $10 million over multiple funding rounds.

HOW TO APPLY:

Call to gauge interest.

Noro-Moseley Partners

9 North Parkway Square
4200 Northside Parkway, N.W.
Atlanta, GA 30327
(404) 233-1966
Fax: (404) 239-9280
info@.noro-moseley.com

North Atlantic Capital Corporation

Focus: Computer products, financial services, healthcare, information services, the Internet, e-commerce, materials technology, software, telecommunications, and waste and environmental management
Web Address: www.northatlanticcapital. com/

Manages $85 million in investment capital. Seeks ventures in the Northeast U.S. that can attain annual growth of 20 percent. Usually invests $1 million to $4 million. Targets companies with $3 to $30 million. Considers management strength a high priority. Investment projects include internal

growth, acquisitions, recapitalizations, and buyouts.

HOW TO APPLY:

Send an executive summary and full business plan.

North Atlantic Capital Corporation

Seventy Center St.
Portland, ME 04101
(207) 772-4470
Fax: (207) 772-3257
info@northatlanticcapital.com

North Bridge Venture Partners

Focus: Healthcare, software, and data communications
Web Address: www.nbvp.com/

Targets early-stage ventures, including seed stages, with minimum investments of $100,000 to $200,000. Offers office space for incubation. Maximum funding goes up to $20 million over multiple rounds. capital fund based in the Boston, Massachusetts area

HOW TO APPLY:

E-mail business plans to bph@nbvp.com or to

North Bridge Venture Partners

950 Winter St., Suite 4600

Waltham, MA 02451
(781) 290-0004
Fax: (781) 290-0999

North Coast Technology Investors, LP
Focus: Early-stage enterprise software, manufacturing, distribution, and materials science companies in Indiana, Michigan, and Ohio
Web Address: www.northcoastvc.com/

Targets young companies, including those in the seed stage, with a technology focus. Typically invests $500,000 to $4 million over multiple rounds. Will consider investments as low as $100,000. Looks for niche products or services with a chance to expand into wider markets. Partners with other investors. Assists in developing business strategies and recruiting staff. Seeks a 20 percent stake in companies and an exit within five years.

HOW TO APPLY:
Submit a hard copy of the business plan to either address below, or send an executive summary of up to five pages as a Microsoft Word attachment to partners@northcoastvc.com.

North Coast Technology Investors, LP
300 Rodd St., Suite 201
Midland, MI 48640-6596
(517) 832-2300
Fax: (517) 832-2301

North Coast Technology Investors, LP
206 S. Fifth Ave., Suite 550
Ann Arbor, MI 48104-2229
(734) 662-7667
Fax: (734) 662-6261

North Carolina Enterprise Fund, L.P
Focus: Small to medium-sized North Carolina-based companies
Web Address: www.ncef.com/

A total of $28 million of capital for growth companies in the state. Usually invests $500,000 to $3 million over multiple rounds. Typically backs early-stage companies, but will consider mezzanine fundings and leveraged or management buyouts. Besides the geographic requirements, candidates should have annual revenues of $40 million or less. Also looks for sound management, a product or service with market demand, and a viable business model. Looks for liquidity in four to seven years.

HOW TO APPLY:
Send a business plan to

The North Carolina Enterprise Corp.
P. O. Box 20429
Raleigh, NC 27619
(919) 781-2691
Fax: (919) 783-9195

North Dakota Development Fund
Focus: Businesses expanding or relocating to the state

Web Address: www.growingnd.com/

Targets manufacturing, food processing, and exported service businesses. Invests up to $300,000. Candidates should demonstrate an increase in area employment within 24 months of the funding the project under consideration.

HOW TO APPLY:

Send proposals to

Sheila Auch, Administrative Assistant
Economic Development and Finance
1833 East Bismarck Expressway
Bismarck, ND 58504
(701) 328-5310
Fax: (701) 328-5320
sauch@state.nd.us

North Hill Ventures, L.P.
Focus: Financial services, telecommunications services, information technology, and direct consumer marketing
Web Address: www.northhillventures.com/
An affiliate of Capital One Financial, a multi-billion dollar financial services and telecommunications company. Manages $40 million in capital.

HOW TO APPLY:

Send proposals to

Brett Rome, Managing Director
North Hill Ventures, L.P.
One Boston Place, Suite 3705
Boston, MA 02108

(617) 788-2112
Fax: (617) 367-8007

Northwood Ventures
Focus: Telecommunications, manufacturing, retailing, broadcasting, financial services, healthcare, the Internet and service businesses
Web Address: www.northwoodventures. com/

Founded in 1983, targets growth funding for early- to later-stage ventures, management buyouts and industry consolidations. More than $200 million under management. Shuns the real estate, energy, software, or hardware companies. Looks for managerial excellence, preferable with a track record in other businesses. Typically invests $2 million to $5 million. May contribute up to $10 million over subsequent rounds. Looks for a four to seven-year exit.

HOW TO APPLY:

Send an executive summary to

Northwood Ventures
485 Underhill Blvd., Suite 205
Syosset, NY 11791
(516) 364-5544
Fax: (516) 364-0879

or

Northwood Ventures
485 Madison Ave., 20th Floor
New York, NY 10022
(212) 935-4595
Fax: (212) 826-1093

Norwest Venture Partners
Focus: Enterprise software, communications systems, and communications services
Web Address: www.norwestvp.com/

Founded in 1961, manages more than $1 billion in capital. Assists in establishing contacts with business and financial resources and recruiting staff. Backs seed-, early-, and expansion-stage ventures. Typically invests $10 million to $15 million over multiple rounds. Initial investments may be as low as $1.5 million. Often works as the lead investor, will also partner with other capital sources. Evaluates candidates according to managerial experience, market potential, technology strength, and product or service appeal.

How to Apply:
Fax or e-mail an executive summary to

Promod Haque or George J. Still, Jr.
Norwest Venture Partners
245 Lytton Ave., Suite 250
Palo Alto, CA 94301
(650) 321-8000
Fax: (650) 321-8010

or

Norwest Venture Partners
Ernest C. Parizeau or Blair P. Whitaker
Wellesley Office Park
40 William St., Suite 305
Wellesley, MA 02481
(781) 237-5870

Fax: (781) 237-6270

Novak Biddle Venture Partners
Focus: Information technology
Web Address: www.novakbiddle.com/

Founded in 1997, backs ventures with a unique technology or competitive advantage and strong management. Looks for liquidity in five to seven years. Considers very early stage and first round ventures, as well as later stage companies and spinouts. Invests $100,000 to $3 million, or more when partnering with other funds.

How to Apply:
Send proposals to

Novak Biddle Venture Partners
1750 Tysons Blvd., Suite 1190
McLean, VA 22102
(703) 847-3770
Fax: (703) 847-3771
info@novakbiddle.com

Nth Power Technologies, Inc.
Focus: Energy companies
Web Address: www.nthfund.com

Established in 1992, backs opportunities brought about by deregulation in the energy industry. Manages more than $60 million in capital. Offers business and financial contacts throughout the energy industry. Prefers companies beyond the seed stage and ready to launch a commercial product. Invests $500,000 to $2 million, not including follow on funding. Evaluates proposals according to management expertise, the viability of the business plan, competitive strength, and ability to provide a profitable exit in three to five years.

How to Apply:

Send queries via the electronic form at the Web site or write to

Nth Power Technologies, Inc.
100 Spear St., Suite 1450
San Francisco, CA 94105
(415) 974-1668
Fax: (415) 974-0608
wkoenig@nthfund.com

Novell Ventures
Focus: Networking
Web Address: http://developer.novell.com/ventures/

Formed in 1997, offers $50 million for ventures that can help grow Novell Directory Services (NDS) technology and other Novell products. Targets development-stage companies seekingr first or second round financing. Invests $1million to $3 million per company. Looks for a strategic fit with Novell, strong managers, prototype or later networking or distributed-computing soft-

ware, a solid business plan, and strong financial projections. Novell seeks a 20 percent annual return on investment.

How to Apply:

Send an executive summary of five pages or less to ventures@novell.com.

Oak Investment Partners
Focus: Communication equipment and services, Internet infrastructure, and enterprise and consumer services
Web Address: www.oakinv.com

Formed in 1978, backs early and later stage ventures with $8 million to $15 million over several rounds. Often co-invests with other funds.

How to Apply:

Prefers referrals from portfolio companies, partners or affiliated individuals rather than unsolicited business plans.

Oak Investment Partners
525 University Ave., Suite 1300
Palo Alto, CA 94301
(650) 614-3700
Fax: (650) 328-6345

Oak Investment Partners
One Gorham Island
Westport, CT 06880
(203) 226-8346
Fax: (203) 227-0372

Oak Investment Partners

4550 Norwest Center
90 South Seventh St.
Minneapolis, MN 55402
(612) 339-9322
Fax: (612) 337-8017

Ohana Ventures
Focus: Internet and telecommunications
Web Address: www.ohanaventures.com/

Typically invests $1 million to $3 million in the first round, up to a total of $6 million. Seeks a 25 percent share of the portfolio company. Usually takes a board seat. Backs seed-stage through mezzanine ventures.

HOW TO APPLY:
Inquire to chrisa@ohanaventures.com

Olympic Ventures
Focus: Software, life sciences, Internet, communications and healthcare ventures in the Western U.S.
Web Address: www.ovp.com

The latest fund, formed in 1997, currently has $63.8 million in capital.

HOW TO APPLY:
Send a business plan, preferably after an introduction by a third party familiar to Olympic Ventures, to info@ovp.com or to the nearest office.

Olympic Venture Partners
2420 Carillon Point

Kirkland, WA 98033
(425) 889-9192
Fax: 425-889-0152

Olympic Venture Partners
340 Oswego Pointe Drive, Suite 200
Lake Oswego, OR 97034
(503) 697-8766
Fax: (503) 697-8863

OneLiberty Ventures
Focus: Information and medical technologies and telecommunications
Web Address: www.oneliberty.com/

Targets ventures with talented managers and unique products or services. Typically invests $1 million to $3 million (less if required by a seed venture).

HOW TO APPLY:
Send business ideas or proposals to

OneLiberty Ventures
150 Cambridge Park Drive
Cambridge, MA 02140

Onset Ventures
Focus: Software and Internet products and services, communications, networking, and medical technology
Web Address: www.onset.com/

Targets seed and early-stage ventures and incubator opportunities. Focuses on Northern California companies. Contributes hundreds of thousands of dollars to $4 million, depending on the development stage. Typical investment is $5 million over multiple funding rounds.

HOW TO APPLY:

Send business idea in a two to five page summary or business plan. Also complete the electronic questionnaire at the Web site.

Onset Ventures

2400 Sand Hill Road
Suite 150
Menlo Park, CA 94025
(650) 529-0700
Fax: (650) 529-0777
menlopark@onset.com

Opus Capital

Focus: Communications, software, and medical equipment
Web Address: www.opuscapital.com

Targets small-cap companies with a revenue stream, solid market niche, and growth potential. Offers worldwide business and financial contacts.

HOW TO APPLY:

Opus Capital

1113 Spruce St.
Boulder, CO 80302
(303) 443-1023

Fax: (303) 443-0986
dheidrich@opuscapital.com

Orchid Group Holdings

Focus: Internet and e-commerce
Web Address: www.orchidholdings.com

Prefers early-stage ventures. Assists in strategic planning, management recruitment, and follow on financing.direction, helping assemble a winning management team, and providing guidance on future financings.

HOW TO APPLY:

Send proposals to *inquiries@orchidholdings.com.*

Orchid Group Holdings

555 California St., Suite 5180
San Francisco, CA 94104-1716
(415) 781-2200
Fax: (415) 781-2189

Pacific Horizon Ventures

Focus: Life science and healthcare
Web Address: www.pacifichorizon.com/

Backs early-, expansion-, and late-stage North American companies. Especially interested in biotechnology/pharmaceutical, medical devices, healthcare services and medical information technology.

HOW TO APPLY:

Send proposal to

Pacific Horizon Ventures:

1001 Fourth Avenue Plaza, Suite 4105

Seattle, WA 98154
(206) 682-1181
Fax: (206) 682-8077
phv@pacifichorizon.com

Pacific Venture Group
Focus: Healthcare and information systems
Web Address: www.pacven.com

Manages $178 million in capital. Considers start ups and early-stage ventures as well as buyouts, consolidations, and public companies.

HOW TO APPLY:
Complete electronic form at the Web site.

Pacific Venture Group
16830 Ventura Blvd., Suite 244
Encino, CA 91436
(818) 990-4141
Fax: (818) 990-6556
lcrouch@pacven.com
ekurtin@pacven.com

Pacific Venture Group
555 California St., Suite 3130
San Francisco, CA 94104
(415) 397-5730
Fax: (415) 989-5108
abianchi@wpgvp.com

Pacific Venture Group
15635 Alton Parkway, Suite 230
Irvine, CA 92618
(949) 753-0490
Fax: (949) 753-8932
rsabin@pacven.com

Palomar Ventures
Focus: Data- and telecommunications, broadband, e-business software, business-to-business and business-to-consumer applications
Web Address: www.palomarventures.com/

Founded in 1999, targets early-stage ventures. Assists in business strategy, recruiting, and introductions to outside resources. Palomar Ventures does not require a minimum investment. Typical investments are $1 to $5 million with Palomar acting as a lead investor on a $5- to $10-million first round. Because many young companies require multiple rounds of financing, Palomar Ventures also provides assistance in raising follow-on rounds of capital.

HOW TO APPLY:
Send an executive summary of three to five pages to proposals@palomarventures.com or to the nearest office.

Palomar Ventures
100 Wilshire Blvd., Suite 400
Santa Monica, CA 90401
(310) 260-6050
Fax: (310) 656-4150

Palomar Ventures
18881 Von Karman Ave., Suite 960
Irvine, CA 92612
(949) 475-9455
Fax: (949) 475-9456

Paradigm Capital Partners
Focus: Biotechnology, business-to-business e-commerce, education, healthcare, recreation and leisure, and service businesses
Web Address: www.paradigmcp.com

Targets early-stage or "angel" projects. Will consider later-stage companies. Usually acts as the lead investor. Contributes $1 million to $5 million per company. Looks for managerial talent, a comprehensive business plan, and high growth potential.

HOW TO APPLY:
Send three copies of the business plan as hard copy or electronically in Adobe Acrobat or Microsoft Word formats to plans@paradigmcp.com

Paradigm Capital Partners, LLC
6410 Poplar Ave., Suite 395
Memphis, TN 38119

Patricof & Co. Ventures, Inc.
Focus: Computer hardware and software, consumer-goods and services, business and financial services, healthcare, industrial goods and services, the Internet, semiconductors and electronics, retail, and telecommunications
Web Address: www.patricof.com/

Manages more than $5.5 billion for early-stage and later-stage ventures, including growth and buyouts. Acts as a lead investor or sole investor. Assists in strategic planning, staff recruitment, and business introductions. Has affiliates in the United Kingdom, France, Germany, Israel, Spain, and Switzerland. Invests $5 million to $25 million in relationships that typically last three to seven years.

HOW TO APPLY:
Query with a phone call or e-mail or send business plan to

Patricof & Co. Ventures, Inc.
445 Park Ave.
New York, NY 10022
(212) 753-6300
Fax: (212) 319-6155

Patricof & Co. Ventures, Inc.
2100 Geng Road, Suite 150
Palo Alto, CA 94303
(650) 494-9944
Fax: (650) 494-6751

Patricof & Co. Ventures, Inc.
Executive Terrace Building
455 South Gulph Road, Suite 410
King of Prussia, PA 19406
(610) 265-0286
Fax: (610) 265-4959

PNC Equity Management
Focus: Telecommunications, healthcare services, education and training, business services, and niche manufacturing industries
Web Address: www.pncequity.com/

Based in Pittsburgh, manages $1 billion in capital. Typically invests $3 million to $20 million. Targets expansions, mezzanine funding, and buyouts. Investments range from $3 million to $15 million. Takes a board seat. Shuns investments in biotechnology, medical devices, software, or high technology.

How to Apply:

Send proposals using the electronic form at www.pncequity.com/contact.eml

Polaris Venture Partners
Focus: Internet software, e-commerce, networking, computer systems, medical devices, pharmaceuticals, genomics, and healthcare
Web Address: www.polarisventures.com/

Targets fast-growing, high profits ventures. Backs seed-stage and early-stage companies. Initial investment range from $250,000 to $6 million. Contributes a maximum of $10 million over multiple rounds. Offers offices and infrastructure to seed companies.

How to Apply:

Send proposal to the nearest office.

Polaris Venture Partners
1000 Winter St., Suite 3350
Waltham, MA 02451-1215
(781) 290-0770
Fax: (781) 290-0880

Polaris Venture Partners
Bank of America Tower

701 Fifth Ave., Suite 6850
Seattle, WA 98104
(206) 652-4555
Fax: (206) 652-4666

Polaris Venture Partners
2305 Barton Creek Blvd., #44
Austin, TX 78735
(512) 347-1162
Fax: (512) 347-1163

Primedia Ventures
Focus: Early-stage Internet software and services companies
Web Address: www.primediaventures.com/

Targets commerce services, enterprise software applications, distance learning and advertising-related ventures. Candidates should show potential to become leaders in large, $1 billion+ markets. Typically invests $1 million to $3 million.

How to Apply:

Send inquiries or business plans to

Primedia Ventures
745 Fifth Ave., 21st Floor
New York, NY, 10151
(212) 745-1203
Fax: (212) 610-9422
busplans@primediaventures.com

Primus Venture Partners
Focus: The Internet, e-commerce, telecommunications, financial services, for-profit education, outsourcing, and medical services and devices

Web Address: www.primusventure.com/

Established in 1983, currently manages more than $340 million in capital. Targets talented managers in high-growth markets. Typically invests $5 million to $10 million.

HOW TO APPLY:

Send a business plan, with an executive summary to

Primus Venture Partners, Inc.
5900 Landerbrook Drive, Suite 200
Cleveland, OH 44124-4020
(440) 684-7300
Fax: (440) 684-7342
info@primusventure.com

Prism Venture Partners
Focus: Healthcare, telecommunications, and information systems
Web Address: www.prismventure.com/

Backs start ups through growth-stage companies that exploit a high-growth, under-serviced market. Candidates should have potential to reach $50 million to $100 million in revenues in five years.

HOW TO APPLY:

Send a business plan with three- to five-year outlook and founders' resumes to Joy Rocci at jrocci@PrismVenture.com

Prism Venture Partners
100 Lowder Brook Drive, Suite 2500
Westwood, MA 02090

(781) 302-4000
Fax: (781) 302-4040

Quantum Capital Partners
Focus: Technology, retail and wholesale distribution, manufacturing, service and hospitality industries primarily in the Southeast
Web Address: www.quantumcapitalpartners. com/

Assists in strategic planning, financial forecasts and business plan development, staff recruitment, and information technology systems. Takes a board seat. Looks for management expertise, 25 percent per year growth potential, and companies based in Southeastern U.S.

HOW TO APPLY:

Send a business plan to

Quantum Capital Partners
One Tampa City Center
Tampa, FL 33602
(813) 221-3306
Fax: (813) 221-3206
info@quantumcapitalpartners.com

Rader Reinfrank & Co.
Focus: Communications, telecommunications, media, and electronic commerce
Web Address: www.rrco.com/

Manages a $100 million fund based in Los Angeles. Targets emerging technology ventures with talented managers. Typically invests $5 million to $20 million. Backs ventures at a variety of developmental stages, including post start ups to established firms. Assists in business and financial planning. Takes a board seat.

How to Apply:

Send business plan to business-plans@rrco.com

Rader Reinfrank & Co., LLC

9465 Wilshire Blvd., Suite 950
Beverly Hills, CA 90212-2617
info@rrco.com
(310) 246-2977
Fax: (310) 246-2988

Ravenswood Capital

Focus: The Internet, e-commerce, direct marketing, and educational services
Web Address: www.ravenswoodcapital.com/

Backs early-stage ventures with investments and introductions to business and financial resources. Assists in developing business strategies, recruiting staff, and cultivating follow on funding. Typically invests $500,000 to $4 million.

How to Apply:

Send proposals to

Dan Kanter: (312) 443-5243
dkanter@ravenswoodcapital.com

David Abraham: (312) 443-5242
dabraham@ravenswoodcapital.com

Ravenswood Capital Corp.

225 West Washington St., Suite 1650
Chicago, IL 60606
Fax: (312) 368-9015

Redleaf Venture Management

Focus: Silicon Valley companies developing Web-enabled corporation applications
Web Address: www.redleaf.com

Targets early-stage and later-stage companies. Assists in coaching entrepreneurs in how to growth their businesses.

How to Apply:

Send inquiries to

Redleaf

14395 Saratoga Ave.
Suite 130
Saratoga, CA 95070
(408) 868-0800
Fax: (408) 868-0810
info@redleaf.com

Redpoint Ventures

Focus: Broadband, the Internet, digital TV, and digital media
Web Address: www.redpointventures.com/

Formed by a combination of managers at two existing funds, IVP and Brentwood Venture Capital. Targets Internet ventures. Manages $600 million.

HOW TO APPLY:

Send proposals to the nearest office.

Redpoint Ventures
3000 Sand Hill Road
Building 2, Suite 290
Menlo Park, CA 94025
(650) 926-5600
Fax: (650) 854-5762

Redpoint Ventures
11150 Santa Monica Blvd., Suite 1200
Los Angeles, CA 90025
(310) 477-7678
Fax: (310) 312-1868

Red Rock Ventures
Focus: Early-stage information technology
Web Address: www.redrockventures.com/

Manages $130 million in capital for seed and first-round financing. Targets business-to-business applications, Internet software, and e-commerce ventures with the potential to capture large market shares. Candidates must be based in the Western U.S.

HOW TO APPLY:

Send a business plan or executive summary by fax or e-mail.

Red Rock Ventures
180 Lytton Ave.
Palo Alto, CA 94301
(650) 325-3111

Fax: (650) 853-7044
info@redrockventures.com

Rein Capital
Focus: Data- and telecommunications, software, and information services
Web Address: www.reincapital.com/

Focuses on seed and growth opportunities, leveraged buyouts, and joint venture agreements. Assists in developing business plans, forming strategic alliances, and providing business advice.

HOW TO APPLY:

Inquire at

Rein Capital
150 Airport Road,
Lakewood, NJ 08701
(732) 367-3300
Fax: (732) 367-8948

Richards L.L.C.
Focus: Early-stage and established companies
Web Address: www.richardsco.com/

Targets companies with $10 million to $100 million in annual revenues with a talented management team. Will consider a small number of early-stage investments for a unique product or service. Shuns oil and gas exploration, commercial banking, high technology research and development, real estate and bankruptcy reorganizations.

HOW TO APPLY:

Inquire at

Richards L.L.C.
303 Peachtree St., N.E., Suite 4100
Atlanta, GA 30308
(404) 572-7200
Fax 404-572-7227
info@richardsco.com

Ricoh Silicon Valley
Focus: Communications, computer hardware, office services, electronics, electronic commerce, information technologies, media, and software
Web Address: www.rsv.ricoh.com

An affiliate of Ricoh Company, Ltd., a multinational office automation company. Targets ventures that dovetail with the parent company's products. Manages $10 million in capital. Typically invests $250,000 to $2 million. Prefers first- and second-stage investments.

HOW TO APPLY:

Send proposals to

Ricoh Silicon Valley
2882 Sand Hill Road, Suite 115
Menlo Park, CA 94025-7022
(650) 496-5700
Fax: (650) 854-8740
contact@rsv.ricoh.com

Ridgewood Capital
Focus: Business-to-business e-commerce
Web Address: www.ridgewoodcapital.com/

Will consider ventures in markets outside its core focus. Advises in financial, technology, intellectual property, and management issues.

HOW TO APPLY:

Send inquires to the nearest office.

Ridgewood Capital Management LLC
Ridgewood Commons
947 Linwood Ave.
Ridgewood, NJ 07450
(201) 447-9000

Ridgewood Capital Management LLC
540 Cowper St., Suite 200
Palo Alto, CA 94301
(650) 208-4015

River Cities Capital
Focus: Healthcare, manufacturing, technology and software, telecom and communications primarily in the Midwest and Southeast
Web Address: www.rccf.com/

Invests $1.5 million to $6 million. Doesn't back start ups, only companies with revenues from an existing commercial product.

HOW TO APPLY:

Prefers introductions from a familiar third party. Initiate discussions with a phone call or executive summary.

River Cities Capital Fund
221 East Fourth St., Suite 1900

Cincinnati, OH 45202
(513) 621-9700
Fax: (513) 579-8939
www.rccf.com

Roser Ventures
Focus: Capital equipment and services, communications, distribution, electronics, medical medical products, software, specialty chemicals and manufacturing
Web Address: www.roserventures.com/

Looks for potential for superior long-term returns in early-stage companies. Majority of investments are within Colorado, and is diversified across a broad range of industries.Usually invest $250,000 to $3 million. Key selection criterion is managerial expertise. Looks for an exits in three to seven years.

HOW TO APPLY:
Send a business plan to

Donna Befus
Roser Ventures, LLC
1105 Spruce St.
Boulder, CO 80302
(303) 443-6436
Fax: (303) 443-1885
roserventures@roserventures.com

Rosewood Capital
Focus: Small to medium-size businesses in Internet, e-commerce, and other direct-to-consumer markets

Web Address: www.rosewoodvc.com/

Founded in 1985, looks for seasoned managers, the potential for the company to become a market lead, growth potential, and a solid economic model. Usually invests $5 million to $15 million over multiple rounds.

HOW TO APPLY:
Send proposals to

Rosewood Capital
One Maritime Plaza, Suite 1330
San Francisco, CA, 94111-3503
(415) 362-5526
Fax: (415) 362-1192

RRE Ventures
Focus: E-commerce, software, communications and related enterprises
Web Address: www.rre.com/

Manages $350 million in capital. Usually invests $4 million to $7 million in early-stage ventures. Does not back seed companies. Looks for rapid growth potential, seasoned managers, market leadership, lack of regulatory risk.

HOW TO APPLY:
Send a hard copy of a comprehensive business plan, including executive summary to

Ilana Graf
RRE Ventures,
126 East 56th St.

New York, NY 10022
(212) 418-5110
Fax: (212) 355-0330
info@rre.com

Salix Ventures
Focus: Early-stage health care services
Web Address: www.salixventures.com/

Targets first-round financing opportunities. Invests a maximum of $5 million over multiple rounds. Prefers to be a co-investor rather than the sole capital source. Takes a board seat. Considers managerial strength a key criteria when evaluating prospects.

HOW TO APPLY:
Contact the nearest office.

Chris Grant:
cgrant@salixventures.com

David Ward:
dward@salixventures.com

Marty Felsenthal:
mfelsenthal@salixventures.com

Salix Ventures
30 Burton Hills Blvd., Suite 370
Nashville, TN 37215
(615) 665-1409
Fax: (615) 665-2912
or

Mark Donovan:
mdonovan@salixventures.com
Salix Ventures

350 Townsend St., Suite 405
San Francisco, CA 94107
(415) 369-9626
Fax: (415) 369-9624

Sanderling Ventures
Focus: Biomedical companies
Web Address: www.sanderling.com/

Backs innovative technologies and experienced entrepreneurs in seed and early-stage ventures. Helps develop long-term business strategies and cultivating funding syndicates for follow-on finances.

HOW TO APPLY:
Send proposals to

Sanderling Ventures
2730 Sand Hill Road, Suite 200
Menlo Park, CA 94025-7067
(650) 854-9855
Fax: (650) 854-3648
info@sanderling.com

Sand Hill Group
Focus: Enterprise technology
Web Address: www.sandhill.com/

Founded in 1996, offers capital and business expertise to start ups and high-growth established companies. Counts managerial talent as a key factor in evaluating candidates (typically backs one venture for every 100 considered). Takes a board seat and becomes active in the portfolio company's organization. Helps cultivate sources for follow on funding.

HOW TO APPLY:

Prefers introductions from familiar third parties. Will consider inquiries sent via e-mail to info@sandhill.com.

Scripps Ventures
Focus: Early-stage Internet, consumer, and business-to-business ventures
Web Address: www.scrippsventures.com/

Founded in 1996, backs companies with capital and with advice on developing staff, building alliances, and honing business strategies.

HOW TO APPLY:

Send an executive summary or business plan to

Scripps Ventures
200 Madison Ave.
New York, NY 10016
(212) 293-8700
Fax: (212) 293-8717
buildvalue@scrippsventures.com

Seaflower Ventures
Focus: Early-stage biomedical firms
Web Address: www.seaflower.com/

Targets seed- and first-round funding for biotechnology, medical devices, healthcare

information technology, and healthcare services. Backs ventures in New England and the Great Lakes region. Usually invests $250,000 to $1.25 million. Takes a board seat, often becoming chairman. Management talent and commitment a must in funded companies.

HOW TO APPLY:

Send proposals to

Alexander Moot
Bay Colony Corporate Center
1000 Winter St., Suite 1000
Waltham, MA 02451-1248
(781) 466-9552
Fax: (781) 466-9553
moot@seaflower.com

or

Christine Gibbons
5170 Nicholson Rd.
P.O. Box 474
Fowlerville, MI 48836
(517) 223-3335
Fax: (517) 223-3337
gibbons@seaflower.com

Selby Venture Partners,
Focus: Seed and early-stage technology and Internet ventures in Silicon Valley
Web Address: www.selbyventures.com/

A $30 million fund targeting seed and incubation stage start ups. Provides capital, business advice, and introductions to business and resources. Usually invests $500,000 to $1.5 million.

HOW TO APPLY:

Send inquiries to

Selby Venture Partners
2460 Sand Hill Road—Suite 200
Menlo Park, CA 94025
(650) 854-7399
Fax: (650) 854-7039
info@selbyventures.com

Sentinel Capital Partners
Focus: Consumer businesses, business-to-business services, and outsourced manufacturing
Web Address: www.sentinelpartners.com

Manages $200 million in capital. Looks for fast growth potential and talented management teams. Will consider investment of up to $30 million. Funds leveraged buyouts, recapitalizations, corporate divestitures, growth strategies, industry consolidations, and restructurings. Requires existing revenues of $4 million or more, company value of up to $150 million.

HOW TO APPLY:

Send business ideas or proposals to info@sentinelpartners.com.

Sentinel Capital Partners
777 Third Ave., 32nd Floor
New York, NY 10017

(212) 688-3100
Fax: (212) 688-6513

Sequel Venture Partners
Focus: Early-stage healthcare, information technology, and telecommunications companies in the Rocky Mountain states
Web Address: www.sequelvc.com/

Manages a total of $66 million in capital. Backs seed and early-stage ventures. Takes a board seat. Invests an average of $3 million in early stage companies.

HOW TO APPLY:

Submit an executive summary or business plan to

Sequel Venture Partners
4430 Arapahoe Ave., Suite 220
Boulder, CO 80303
(303) 546-0400

Sevin Rosen Funds
Focus: Data communications, telecommunications, semiconductors, software and information services
Web Address: www.srfunds.com/

Founded in 1981, now making investments from a $175 million fund. Prefers start up or first-round projects and welcomes seed and incubation ventures. Usually invests $4 million to $5 million over multiple rounds.

Frequently provides less than $100,000 for seed and incubation opportunities. Looks for market potential, management talent, a viable business model, ongoing competitive advantage, and a chance for the candidate to reach $100 million or more in market value in five to seven years.

How to Apply:

Send a concise, comprehensive business plan to

Jon Bayless
jbayless@srfunds.com

John Jaggers
jjaggers@srfunds.com

Charles Phipps
cphipps@srfunds.com

Two Galleria Tower
13455 Noel Road, Suite 1670
Dallas, TX 75240
(972) 702-1100
Fax: (972) 702-1103

or

Steve Domenik
steved@srfunds.com

Steve Dow
sdow@srfunds.com

Jennifer Gill Roberts
jgill@srfunds.com
169 University Avenue
Palo Alto, CA 94301

Fax: (650) 326-0707

SGI Capital
Focus: Healthcare, information technology, commercial, industrial, and manufacturing companies
Web Address: www.sgicapital.com/

Targets growing companies with $5 million or more in revenues, experienced managers, and a compelling growth strategy. Invests $2 million to $10 million. Assists in staff deveopment and follow on financing.

How to Apply:

Send a complete business plan to Thomas M. Balderston or Richard W. Stewart:

SGI Capital, LLC
3 Radnor Corporate Center, Suite 400
Radnor, PA 19087
(610) 964-2000
Fax: (610) 964-2001
info@superior-group.com

Sequoia Capital
Focus: Start ups in information technology and healthcare
Web Address: www.sequoiacap.com/

Targets very early stage companies in new and rapidly growing markets. Backs companies on the West Coast, Boston, and Austin, TX, or will consider established companies nationwide. Invests $50,000 to $10 million.

HOW TO APPLY:

E-mail Sequoia at businessplans@ sequoiacap.com and include the following as attachments: A 15-20 page Microsoft PowerPoint presentation outlining the business and an executive summary.

Sequoia Capital
3000 Sand Hill Road
Bldg. 4, Suite 280
Menlo Park, CA 94025
(650) 854-3927
Fax: (650) 854-2977

Shawmut Capital Partners, Inc.
Focus: Financial services
Web Address: www.shawmutcapital.com

Manages $108 million for financial services companies needing $3 million to $12 million for Internet and e-business strategies, transaction processing, creating new distribution channels, outsourcing service, and related ventures.

HOW TO APPLY:

Contact

Joel B. Alvord, President and Managing Director, at jalvord@shawmutcapital.com

Shawmut Capital Partners, Inc.
75 Federal St., 18th Floor
Boston, MA 02110
(617) 368-4900
Fax: (617) 368-4910

Siemens Venture Capital (SVC)
Focus: Information technology, telecommunications, medical engineering, and microelectronics
Web Address: www.siemens.com/svc/

Global fund that backs seed and early-stage technology ventures. Assists with creating international distribution channels and business and technology expertise.

HOW TO APPLY:

Send inquiries to

Siemens Venture Capital
4900 Old Ironsides Drive
P.O. Box 58075
Mail Stop 999
Santa Clara, CA 95052-8075
Penne.Stockinger@icn.siemens.com

The Shepherd Group
Focus: Communications, consumer products, Internet commerce and media, traditional media, niche manufacturing, software and technology
Web Address: www.tsgequity.com/

Targets early-stage, growth, and acquisition funding projects for venture and middle-market companies. Looks for fast growth possibilities in ventures that are beyond the conceptualization stage. Prefers New England companies, but will consider prospects in other locations. Invests $500,000 to $2 million per company.

HOW TO APPLY:

Send a business plan to Sean Marsh at

The Shepherd Group
636 Great Road
Stow, MA 01775
(978) 461-9900
Fax: (978) 461-9909
shepherd@tsgequity.com

Sierra Ventures
Focus: Early stage healthcare, information technology, and service businesses
Web Address: www.sierraven.com/

Acts as lead investor using an ongoing $250 million fund. Assists in honing business strategies, staff recruitment, and finding follow-on funding. Expects relationship to last five to seven years.

HOW TO APPLY:

Submit an executive summary or full business plan to

Sierra Ventures
3000 Sand Hill Road
Building 4, Suite 210
Menlo Park, CA 94025
(650) 854-1000
Fax: (650) 854-5593
funding@sierraven.com

Sigma Partners

Focus: Technology companies
Web Address: www.sigmapartners.com/

Founded in 1984, target high-growth companies using four funds worth $300 million. Typically backs companies developing products or services in computers, electronics, software, and communications, but will consider select non-technology candidates.

HOW TO APPLY:

Send proposals to

Sigma Partners
2884 Sand Hill Road, Suite 121
Menlo Park, CA 94025
(650) 854-1300
Fax: (650) 854-1323

or

Sigma Partners
20 Custom House St., Suite 830
Boston, MA 02110
(617) 330-7872
Fax: (617) 330-7975
info@sigmapartners.com

Signature Capital
Focus: Early-stage software, computer, electronic equipment, semiconductors, telecommunications, medical and healthcare products
Web Address: www.signaturecapital.com/

Seeks companies unique product or service on track to achieve annual revenues of $100 million. Talented managers a must. Should be ready for an IPO in two to three years.

How to Apply:

Send proposals to William Sick, wsick@sigcap.com, or William Turner, wturner@sigcap.com.

Signature Capital, L.L.C
712 Fifth Ave., 11th Floor
New York, NY 10019
(212) 765-4700
Fax: (212) 765-3843

Silver Lake Partners
Focus: Growth-stage technology companies
Web Address: www.slpartners.com/

In addition to backing venture candidates, the firm also looks for spinoffs and acquisitions of select public companies.

How to Apply:

Inquire at

Silver Lake Partners
2800 Sand Hill Road
Menlo Park, CA 94025
(650) 233-8120
Fax: (650) 233-8125

or

Silver Lake Partners
320 Park Ave., 33rd Floor
New York, NY 10022
(212) 981-5600
info@slpartners.com

Skywood Ventures
Focus: Early-stage information technology and healthcare companies

Web Address: www.skywood.com

Helps develop business strategies and staff. Targets high-growth ideas and companies with exceptional management teams.

How to Apply:

E-mail inquiries to info@skywood.com

Skywood Ventures
3000 Sand Hill Road
Building 3, Suite 100
Menlo Park, CA 94025

Sloan Ventures
Focus: Early-stage technology companies
Web Address: www.sloanenterprises.com

Helps in prototype creation, marketing strategies, funding, and preparing the business plan. Targets products or technologies with a patent. Invests $500,000 to $2 million per company. Helps cultivate follow on funding.

How to Apply:

Send inquiries to: sloanmail@aol.com

Sloan Ventures
312 George St.
Birmingham, MI 48009
(248) 540-9660

or

Sloan Ventures

Santa Monica, California
(310) 458-9334

SOFTBANK Venture Capital
Focus: Internet companies
Web Address: www.sbvc.com/

Prefers acting as lead investor. Current early-stage fund is capitalized at $636 million; a later-stage fund offers $1.2 billion in total capital. Manages HotBank, an incubator which supports entrepreneurs with recruiting, financial services, technology support, and other fundamental resources. Invests $500,000 to $10 million or more, depending on the development stage of the venture. The majority of investments are in California, with the remainder in other western states as well as New York and Boston.

HOW TO APPLY:

Submit an executive summary (one to two pages in length) to plans@sbvc.com.

SOFTBANK Venture Capital
200 West Evelyn Ave., Suite 200
Mountain View, CA 94043
(650) 962-2000

South Atlantic Venture Funds

Focus: Communications, healthcare, technology, manufacturing, consumer products, and specialty retail
Web Address: www.southatlantic.com/

Targets ventures in Florida, Texas, and the Southeast. Invests $1.5 million to $7.5 million, and will help cultivate follow on capital. Backs expansions, acquisitions, management buyouts, and recapitalizations.

HOW TO APPLY:

Send business plan to the closest office.

South Atlantic Capital, Inc.
614 West Bay St.
Tampa, FL 33606-2704
(813) 253-2500
Fax: (813) 253-2360
www.southatlantic.com/

South Atlantic Capital, Inc.
Terremark Center, Suite 1147
2601 South Bayshore Drive
Miami, FL 33133
(305) 250-4681
Fax: (305) 250-4682

South Atlantic Capital, Inc.
102 Marseille Place
Cary, NC 27511
(919) 461-0803
Fax: (919) 319-0026

South Atlantic Capital, Inc.
1239 O. G. Skinner Drive
West Point, GA 31833

(706) 645-8758
Fax: (706) 643-5067

Southeast InteractiveTechnology Funds
Focus: Early-stage telecommunications, enterprise management, Internet infrastructure, bandwidth services, and e-commerce ventures
Web Address: www.se-interactive.com/

Acts as sole or co-investor. Provides business and strategy advice. Looks for a management team with a range of business expertise.

HOW TO APPLY:
Send a business plan to stephanie@seinteractive.com.

Southeast InteractiveTechnology Funds
630 Davis Dr., Suite 220
Morrisville, NC 27713
(919) 558-8324
Fax: (919) 558-2025

Southeastern Technology Fund
Focus: Early-stage companies in the Internet, information technology, and communications
Web Address: www.setfund.com/

Targets ventures in the Southeastern U.S.; will consider prospects outside the region. Backs first and second round companies with investments of $250,000 to $1.5 million. Prefers companies with annual revenues of $250,000 to $7 million. Requires candidates go through a "disciplined financial analysis" to gauge ROI potential. Seeks prospects capable of a positive cash flow within a year of the investment.

HOW TO APPLY:
E-mail an executive summary to Emerson Fann, fanne@setfund.com.

Southeastern Technology Fund
4035 Chris Drive, Suite C
Huntsville, AL 35802
(256) 883-8711
Fax: (256) 883-8558

SpaceVest
Focus: Space-related applications, telecommunications, Internet infrastructure and software
Web Address: www.spacevest.com

Founded in 1991, maintains a close relationship with NASA. Currently invests from a $138 million fund that targets appropriate information technology ventures.

HOW TO APPLY:
Send a business plan along with complete contact information to

SpaceVest
11911 Freedom Drive, Suite 500
Reston, VA 20190
(703) 904-9800

Sparkventures

Focus: Early-stage New England companies developing smart materials, Internet applications, and software
Web Address: www.sparkventures.com/

Invests an average of $1.5 million to post-Angel, early-stage ventures with a unique technology. Assists in recruiting managers and developing business strategies.

HOW TO APPLY:

E-mail business plans to:
mail@sparkventures.com

Sparkventures

44 Pleasant St., Suite 210
Watertown, MA 02472
(617) 314-8735
Fax: (617) 314-8737

Spectrum Equity Investors

Focus: Communications services, networking infrastructure, electronic commerce, and media industries
Web Address: www.spectrumequity.com

Manages more than $1 billion in capital. Invests $1 million to $100 million in seed to later-stage companies. Looks for outstanding management. Expects to maintain relationship with portfolio companies for four to seven years.

HOW TO APPLY:

Inquire to the nearest office.

Spectrum Equity Investors

333 Middlefield Road, Suite 200
Menlo Park, CA 94025
(415) 464-4600
Fax: (415) 464-4601
menlopark@spectrumequity.com

Spectrum Equity Investors

One International Place, 29th Floor
Boston, MA 02110
(617) 464-4600
Fax: (617) 464-4601
boston@spectrumequity.com

The Sprout Group

Focus: Data- and telecommunications, e-commerce, healthcare, and software
Web Address: www.sproutgroup.com/

Founded in 1969 as an affiliate of the investment bank Donaldson, Lufkin & Jenrette. Invests in early-stage, growth, mezzanine, and buyout ventures for expansion projects, recapitalizations, and management buyouts. Invests $5 million to $50 million depending on the type of project. Targets an ROI of 30 percent.

HOW TO APPLY:

Submit proposal using the E-plans form at the Web site, or send via regular mail.

Sprout Group

277 Park Ave., 21st Floor
New York, NY 10172
(212) 892-3600
Fax: (212) 892-3444

Sprout Group
3000 Sand Hill Road
Building 3, Suite 170
Menlo Park, CA 94025
(650) 234-2700
Fax: (650) 234-2779

Sprout Group
520 Lake Cook Road
Suite 450
Deerfield, IL 60015
(847) 940-1735
Fax: (847) 940-1724

SSM Ventures
Focus: E-businesses, Internet software, data- and telecommunications
Web Address: www.ssmventures.com

Focuses primarily, but not exclusively, on the Southeast and Texas. Typically provides $2 million to $10 million to companies with a unique product or service. Seeks start up, development, expansion, and buy-out ventures.

HOW TO APPLY:
Send proposals to

SSM Ventures
110 Wild Basin Road, Suite 280

Austin, TX 78746
(512) 437-7900
Fax: (512) 437-7925

or

SSM Ventures
845 Crossover Lane, Suite 140
Memphis, TN 38117
(901) 767-1131
Fax: (901) 767-1135

St. Paul Venture Capital
Focus: Consumer information technologies, communications, electronic commerce, healthcare, life sciences, enterprise systems and software, consumer products and services
Web Address: www.stpaulvc.com

Targets very early-stage and later-stage companies, as well as established businesses. Acts as lead or co-investor. Invests $1 million to $15 million over multiple rounds.

HOW TO APPLY:
Send a business plan via Web.

St. Paul Venture Capital
10400 Viking Drive, Suite 550
Eden Prairie, MN 55344
(612) 995-7474

St. Paul Venture Capital
Three Lagoon Drive, Suite 130
Redwood City, CA 94065
(650) 596-5630

Fax: (650) 596-5711

St. Paul Venture Capital
138 River Road
Andover, MA 01810
(978) 837-3198
Fax: (978) 837-3199

Summit Partners
Focus: Software, technology, healthcare, information services, and financial services industries
Web Address: www.summitpartners.com/

Founded in 1984. Invests in growing and profitable private companies with a strong management team. Offers equity and mezzanine funding. Maintain domestic and international business contacts. Takes a board seat.

Summit Partners
600 Atlantic Ave., Suite 2800
Boston, MA 02210-2227
(617) 824-1000
Fax: (617) 824-1100

Summit Partners
499 Hamilton Ave., Suite 200
Palo Alto, CA 94301
(650) 321-1166
Fax: (650) 321-1188
kdraganov@summitpartners.com
dlower@summitpartners.com

Sutter Hill Ventures
Focus: Start-ups and early-stage companies in information technology and healthcare

Web Address: www.shv.com/

Founded in 1962, currently invests from a pool of more than $400 million.

HOW TO APPLY:
Send proposals to

Sutter Hill Ventures
755 Page Mill Road, Suite A-200
Palo Alto, CA 94304-1005
(650) 493-5600
Fax: (650) 858-1854

TA Associates
Focus: Business services, consumer products and services, financial services, healthcare, the Internet, IT services, media, software, and technology
Web Address: www.ta.com/

Founded in 1968, invests $10 million to $100 for growth, acquisitions, fund share repurchases, and leveraged buyouts. Candidates must have an operating income run-rate of at least $2 million.

HOW TO APPLY:
Send proposals to

TA Associates
High Street Tower, Suite 2500
125 High St.
Boston, MA 02110
(617) 574-6700
Fax: (617) 574-6728
info@ta.com

or

TA Associates
70 Willow Road, Suite 100
Menlo Park, CA 94025
(650) 328-1210
Fax: (650) 326-4933

TA Associates
One Oxford Center, Suite 4260
Pittsburgh, PA 15219-1407
(412) 441-4949
Fax: (412) 441-5784

TAT Capital Partners
Focus: Electronics, semiconductors, and medical devices
Web Address: www.tat.ch/

Invests in early-stage and established companies (with up to $15 million in sales) in U.S. and Europe. Help companies expand into Europe and Japan. Requires a lead investor role. Early-stage companies must demonstrate the ability to become a viable global venture in two to five years.

HOW TO APPLY:
Send inquiries using electronic form at the Web site or to

TAT Capital Partners Ltd.
Attn: Mark Putney
P.O. Box 23326
San Jose, CA 95153-3326
(408) 270-9200

Fax: (408) 270-4140

Techfarm
Focus: Information technology
Web Address: www.techfarm.com/

A technology incubator, Techfarm backs seed- and early-stage companies with the potential to become a market leader in three to five years. Looks for managerial strength, technical expertise, competitive edge, and a unique product or service. Offers incubator services. Initial investments range from $750,000 to $2 million.

HOW TO APPLY:
Send business idea or complete plan to

TechFund
200 W. Evelyn Ave., Suite 100
Mountain View, CA 94041
(650) 934-0900
Fax: (650) 934-0910
gac@techfundcapital.com
kak@techfundcapital.com
jlw@techfundcapital.com

Technology Crossover Ventures
Focus: Internet infrastructure, e-business applications, Internet services, business-to-consumer and business-to-business applications
Web Address: www.tcv.com/

Founded in 1995 for Internet investments in early-stage both private through public companies. Manages $1.6 billion. Offers growth capital, staff recruiting, advice on strategic initiatives, and introductions to business resources.

HOW TO APPLY:
Send proposals to the nearest office.

TCV (Headquarters)
575 High St., Suite 400
Palo Alto, CA 94301
(650) 614-8200
Fax: (650) 614-8222
info@tcv.com

TVC
160 West 86th St., Suite 12B
New York, NY 10024
(212) 277-3900
Fax: (212) 277-3901

TCV
56 Main St., Suite 210
Millburn, NJ 07041
(973) 467-5320
Fax: (973) 467-5323

Technology Funding
Focus: Information systems, healthcare, and industrial technologies.
Web Address: www.techfunding.com/ offering.html

Backs high-growth companies throughout the country. Considers early- through later-stage businesses.

HOW TO APPLY:
Call (800) 821-5323 to gauge interest or send proposals to clients@techfunding.com.

Techxas Ventures
Focus: Computer hardware and software, communications and networking, systems integration, and information technology distribution
Web Address: www.techxas.com/

Founded in 1998. Targets technology ventures near Austin, Dallas, Houston, and San Antonio, TX. Typically invests $500,000 per round in early-stage companies that are developing products, working toward a product introductions, building new sales efforts, or launching a market-entry strategy. Usually acts as lead investor.

HOW TO APPLY:
E-mail an executive summary or business plan to general partners Bruce A. Ezell at Bruce@techxas.com or Michael P. LaVigna at Mike@techxas.com.

Techxas Ventures
8920 Business Park Drive
Austin, TX 78759
(512) 343-0118
Fax: (512) 343-1879

Telecommunications Development Fund

Focus: Small businesses in communications industry
Web Address: www.tdfund.com/

Manages $25 million for seed and early-stage businesses. Typical investments are $375,000 to $1 million per company. Seeks long-term partnerships with reltationships that usually last from four to eight years. Assists in staff development, developing business strategies, providing business contacts, and locating follow on funding.

How to Apply:

Complete electronic data sheet at the Web site. Send it and a business plan to

Telecommunications Development Fund

Attention: Business Director
2020 K Street, NW, Suite 375
Washington, DC 20006
(202)-293-8840
Fax: (202) 293-8850

TeleSoft Partners

Focus: Next-generation communications services, software, systems and Internet companies
Web Address: www.telesoftvc.com

Founded in 1997 to invest equally in early, development-phase, and later-stage companies. Typically invests $1 million to $10 million per venture.

How to Apply:

TeleSoft Partners

1450 Fashion Island Blvd., Suite 610
San Mateo, CA 94404
(650) 358-2500
Fax: (650) 358-2501
telesoft@telesoftvc.com

Telos Venture Partners

Focus: Software, the Internet, semiconductors, and communications
Web Address: www.telosvp.com/

Backs early-stage technology ventures with a roadmap for becoming public companies. Provides $500,000 to $2 million in first or second round financing. Looks for managerial experience, growth potential, and unique technologies.

How to Apply:

Send business plans or executive summaries to:

Telos Venture Partners

2350 Mission College Blvd., Suite 1070
Santa Clara, CA 95054
Fax: (408) 982-5880
asel@telosvp.com

TI Ventures

Focus: Early-stage technology companies focused on DSP software and hardware for communications, networking, audio, video, storage, display, and IC power management.

Web Address: www.ti.com/corp/docs/ventures/index.htm

Founded in 1996 by TI and H&Q Venture Associates, the fund invests with $65 million in capital for technology venture

HOW TO APPLY:

Send a business plan to:

TI Ventures L.P.
c/o H&Q Venture Associates
One Bush St.
San Francisco, CA 94104
(415) 439-3000
Fax: (415) 439-3621
Email: info@HQVA.com

TI Ventures
c/o Texas Instruments
7839 Churchill Way, M/S 3995
Dallas, TX 75251
(972) 917-5041
Fax: (972) 917-3804
tiventures@ti.com

Thoma Cressey Equity Partners

Focus: Business services, health care, distribution and information industries

Web Address: www.tc.nu/

Funds acquisitions, growth, buyouts, recapitalizations, or "going-private" projects. Takes a board seat. Often works with portfolio companies for four to six years or longer.

HOW TO APPLY:

Send inquiries to the nearest office.

Thoma Cressey Equity Partners
Sears Tower, 44th Floor
233 South Wacker Drive
Chicago, IL 60606
(312) 777-4444
Fax: (312) 777-4445
tcep@tc.nu

Thoma Cressey Equity Partners
4050 Republic Plaza
370 17th St.
Denver, CO 80202
(303) 592-4888
Fax: (303) 592-4845
tcep@tc.nu

Thoma Cressey Equity Partners
600 Montgomery St., 27th Floor
San Francisco, CA 94111
(415) 263-3660
Fax: (415) 392-6480
tcep@tc.nu

TL Ventures

Focus: Early-stage technology ventures in the Internet, software, information technology services, communications, and life sciences

Web Address: www.tlventures.com/

Founded in 1988, now has $750 million under management. Majority of investments are in California, the Northeast and Texas. Backs a variety of development stages from seed companies to established corporations.

HOW TO APPLY:

Send proposal via the Web site or to

TL Ventures
435 Devon Park Drive
700 Building
Wayne, PA 19087-1990
(610) 971-1515
Fax: (610) 975-9330
info@tlventures.com

TL Ventures Austin
221 West 6th St., Suite 1550
Austin, TX 78701
(512) 391-2850
Fax: (512) 391-2875
info@tlventures.com

TL Ventures Los Angeles
11150 Santa Monica Blvd., Suite 1500
Los Angeles, CA 90025
(310) 914-0783
Fax: (310) 477-6060
info@tlventures.com

TL Ventures Phoenix

8060 Mummy Mountain Road
Paradise Valley, AZ 85253
(310) 914-0783
Fax: (602) 922-0787
info@tlventures.com

Trans Cosmos USA

Focus: Internet new media, marketing services, e-commerce, and customer service applications

Web Address: www.trascosmos.com

Invests in North America, Europe, and Asia. Typically provides $500,000 to $20 million per venture.

HOW TO APPLY:

Send proposals to

Steve Clemons
Trans Cosmos
777 108th Avenue NE, Suite 2300
Bellevue, WA 98004
(425) 468-3900
Fax: (425) 468-3901

Trellis Partners

Focus: Early-stage Texas technology ventures in e-commerce and telecommunications

Web Address: www.trellispartners.com/

Invests $3 million and $5 million in each venture. Co-invests with other venture funds and investors.

HOW TO APPLY:

Send a business plan to businessplans@trellispartners.com

Trellis Partners
2600 Via Fortuna
The Terrace
Building One, Suite 150
Austin, TX 78746
(512) 330-9200
Fax: (512) 330-9400

Tribune Ventures
Focus: New media companies that dovetail with the parent corporation's interactive services and Internet businesses
Web Address: www.tribune.com/ventures/

Part of the Tribune Co., a conglomerate of publishing, broadcasting, and education companies. Usually invests $3 million to $10 million per venture. Acts as a lead or co-investor. Targets companies with commercial products and existing revenues. Takes a board seat when it's the lead investor.

HOW TO APPLY:

Send proposals to Shawn Luetchens, Manager, at sluetchens@tribune.com

Tribune Ventures

435 N. Michigan Ave., Suite 600
Chicago, IL 60611
(312) 222-3881
Fax: (312) 222-5993

Trident Capital
Focus: Internet, infrastructure management, outsourcing, transaction services, and information technology
Web Address: www.tridentcap.com

Seeks experienced management teams. Invests in seed-, early-, and expansion-stage ventures, "dot-com" spinoffs of established businesses, roll-ups, and buyouts.

HOW TO APPLY:

E-mail a proposal to info@tridentcap.com.

Trident Capital
2480 Sand Hill Road, Suite 100
Menlo Park, CA 94025
(650) 233-4300
Fax: (650) 233-4333

Trinity Ventures
Focus: Start-ups in e-commerce, communications, software, and application services
Web Address: www.trinityventures.com/

Founded in 1986, now invests using a $300 million fund. Prefers first- or second-round investments.Will consider later-stage expansion funding for fast-growth ventures. Usually invests $2 million to $10 million in the initial round, up to $20 million in follow-on rounds. Typically acts as the lead investor. Takes a board seat.

HOW TO APPLY:

E-mail a business plan to info@trinityventures.com or mail to

Trinity Ventures
3000 Sand Hill Road
Building 1, Suite 240
Menlo Park, CA 94025
(650) 854-9500
Fax: (650) 854-9501

TVM Techno Venture Management
Focus: Information technology and life sciences ventures in the United States and Europe, particularly Germany
Web Address: www.tvmvc.com/

Founded in 1983, maintains offices in Munich and Boston. Looks for innovative information technology and life sciences ventures with the potential for high growth. Evaluates projects according to managerial strength and market impact. Assists in recruiting and international sales efforts.

HOW TO APPLY:

Send proposals to

TVM Techno Venture Management
101 Arch St., Suite 1950

Boston, MA 02110
(617) 345-9320
Fax: (617) 345-9377
info@tvmvc.com

21st Century Internet Venture Partners
Focus: Early-stage e-commerce, enterprise systems, and electronic intermediaries.
Web Address: www.21st-century.com/

A spinoff of Hummer Winblad Partners, the fund has committed capital of $55 million. Looks for unique products or services, and revenue and market penetration potential.

HOW TO APPLY:

Send inquiries to J. Neil Weintraut, General Partner, at nweintraut@21vc.com, or Peter Ziebelman, General Partner, at peters@21vc.com.

21st Century Internet Venture Partners
Two South Park, 2nd Floor
San Francisco, CA 94107
(415) 512-1221
Fax: (415) 512-2650

U.S. Bancorp Piper Jaffray Ventures
Focus: Healthcare services, medical devices, and healthcare information systems
Web Address: www.pjc.com/

A subsidiary of U.S. Bancorp Piper Jaffray. Backs emerging-growth companies with three main funds. Seeks talented managers, ongoing competitive edge, the ability to reach sales of $100 million or more, and long-term revenues.

HOW TO APPLY:

Send a business plan using an electronic form at the Web site or to

U.S. Bancorp Piper Jaffray
222 South Ninth St.
Minneapolis, MN 55402

US Venture Partners
Focus: The Internet, communications, software, semiconductors, medical, and consumer brands
Web Address: www.usvp.com/

Specializes on early-stage ventures. Actively assists in developing business strategies, recruiting staff, honing financing plans, and cultivating partnerships. Seeks managers with successful track records. Usually acts as the lead investor. Contributes $500,000 for seed ventures up to $10 million for later-stage companies. Targets companies in Silicon Valley, but will consider proposals in other areas.

HOW TO APPLY:

Inquire to

U.S. Venture Partners
2180 Sand Hill Road, Suite 300
Menlo Park, CA 94025
(650) 854-9080

Fax: (650) 854-3018

Vanguard Venture Partners
Focus: Seed- and early-stage information technology and life sciences companies
Web Address: www.vanguardventures.com/

Founded in 1981, typically works as a lead or co-investor during a company's first funding round. Looks for ventures with the promise to return ten-times the investment through an IPO or acquisition in five to seven years. Offers incubator resources.

HOW TO APPLY:

E-mail a business plan to info@vanguardventures.

Vanguard Venture Partners
525 University Ave., Suite 600
Palo Alto, CA 94301
(650) 321-2900
Fax: (650) 321-2902

Vanguard Venture Partners
1330 Post Oak Blvd., Suite 1550
Houston, TX 77056
(713) 877-1662
Fax: (713) 877-8669

Vector Fund Management
Focus: Life sciences and healthcare
Web Address: www.vectorfund.com/

Backs later-stage private and public ventures. Acts as lead or co-lead investor in funding that typically ranges from $5 million to $15 million. Looks for ROI in one to three years.

HOW TO APPLY:

Send two copies of the business plan to

Vector Fund Management
1751 Lake Cook Road, Suite 350
Deerfield, IL 60015
(847) 374-3880
Fax: (847) 374-3899

The VenCom Group, Inc.
Focus: The convergence of telecommunications, computing, consumer electronics, and content
Web Address: www.vencom.com

Backs seed-, development-, and mezzanine-stages with investments of $1 million to $10 million. Looks for near-term growth of 30 percent or more.

HOW TO APPLY:

Complete the electronic information form at the Web site.

The VenCom Group, Inc.
2201 Waukegan Road, Suite E-200

Bannockburn, IL 60015
(847) 374-7000

VenGlobal Capital Fund
Focus: Early-stage companies in software and communications
Web Address: www.venglobal.com

Looks for an experienced management team able to carry out a well-defined business strategy. The product or service should have a foundation in a unique technology. The venture should be on track for a public offering in three to five years.

HOW TO APPLY:

Send a business plan to
info@venglobal.com

VenGlobal Capital Fund
20195 Stevens Creek Blvd., Suite 110
Cupertino, CA 95014
(408) 861-1035
Fax: (408) 861-1150

Venrock Associates
Focus: Information technology, healthcare, and life sciences
Web Address: www.venrock.com/

A venerable fund dating back to the 1930s. A majority of its investments are seed-stage or first-round fundings. Looks for managerial expertise, a breakthrough product or service, and a viable business model.

How to Apply:

Send a business plan to

Venrock Associates
30 Rockefeller Plaza, Room 5508
New York, NY 10112
(212) 649-5600
Fax: (212) 649-5788

Venrock Associates
2494 Sand Hill Road, Suite 200
Menlo Park, CA 94025
(650) 561-9580
Fax: (650) 561-9180

Venrock Associates
2494 Sand Hill Road
Suite 200
Menlo Park, CA 94025
(650) 561-9580
Fax: (650) 561-9180

Venture Investors Management LLC
Focus: Early Midwestern companies in a variety of industries
Web Address: www.ventureinvestors.com/

Looks for unique products or services, a competitive advantage, and high barriers to entry. Ventures should be able to achieve a 10 to 15 fold increase rise in value in seven years or less. Key criteria include the strengths of the management team and a

roadmap for a public offering in five to seven years.

How to Apply:

Send proposals to

Venture Investors
University Research Park
505 South Rosa Road
Madison, WI 53719
(608) 441-2700
Fax: (608) 441-2727
vi@ventureinvestors.com

Viridian Capital Partners
Focus: Early-stage technology companies
Web Address: www.@viridian-capital.com/

Typically invests $5 million to $25 million in ventures with high-growth potential. Targets first-round funding candidates, does not invest seed capital. Prefers being the sole or lead investor. Takes a board seat.

How to Apply:

Call to gauge interest or send a business plan to

Viridian Capital Partners
6100 Fairview Road
Suite 770
Charlotte, NC 28210
(704) 556-1950
Fax: (704) 556-0556
info@viridian-capital.com
frank@viridian-capital.com

smarino@viridian-capital.com
jsampson@viridian-capital.come

Voyager Capital
Focus: The Internet, software, computer communications, information technology services
Web Address: www.voyagercap.com

Targets ventures in the Pacific Northwest and technology centers on the West Coast. Invests in early- and middle-stage companies.

HOW TO APPLY:

Send a business plan to

Voyager Capital
800 Fifth Avenue, Suite 4100
Seattle, WA 98104
(206) 470-1180
Fax: (206) 470-1185
info@voyagercap.com

Vulcan Ventures
Focus: Established new-media companies
Web Address: www.paulallen.com

Established by Microsoft co-founder Paul Allen. Backs operating businesses or new ventures from existing companies; shuns start ups, film production companies, record companies, music acts, and other entertainment businesses.

HOW TO APPLY:

Submit a business plan by completing the online form at the Web site.

Vulcan Northwest Inc.
110 110th Ave. N.E., Suite 550
Bellevue, WA 98004
(425) 453-1940

Wakefield Group
Focus: Mid-Atlantic companies, particularly the Carolinas
Web Address: www.wakefieldgroup.com/

Founded in 1988, backs growth companies and management buyouts. Typically invests $1 million to $5 million per company, with a goal of receiving returns of 25 percent or more each year. Targets strong management teams and companies with the chance to dominate a particular market.

HOW TO APPLY:

Send proposals to

Thomas C. Nelson, tcnelson@wakefieldgroup.com, Anna Nelson, asnelson@wakefieldgroup.com, or Michael Elliott, mfelliott@wakefieldgroup.com.

Wakefield Group
1110 East Morehead St.
Charlotte, NC 28204
P.O. Box 36329
Charlotte, NC 28236
(704) 372-0355
Fax: (704) 372-8216

Walden Capital Partners
Focus: Manufacturing, distribution, the Internet, software, hardware, and healthcare, and medical companies
Web Address: www.waldencapital.com/

A Small Business Investment Company licensee. Looks for later stage businesses seeking expansion funds. Candidates should display a competitive advantage and managerial acumen. Invests a maximum of $4 million per company; partners with funds for additional capital.

HOW TO APPLY:

Send proposals to Martin B. Boorstein, principal, marty@waldencapital.com; John R. Costantino, principal, john@waldencapital.com; or Allen Greenberg, principal, allen@waldencapital.com.

Walden Capital Partners
150 E. 58 St.,
34th Floor
New York, NY 10155
(212) 355-0090

Warburg, Pincus Ventures
Focus: Information technology, the Internet, healthcare, life sciences, financial services, energy, media and communications, and business services
Web Address: www.warburgpincus.com/

Founded in 1971, now maintains offices worldwide. Targets start ups, early-stage, and late-stage companies, buyouts, recapi-

talizations, expansions, acquisitions. Expects to partner for five to seven years.

HOW TO APPLY:

Send proposals to

Rosanne Zimmerman
Vice President
E.M. Warburg, Pincus & Co., LLC
466 Lexington Ave.
New York, NY 10017-3147
(212) 878-0600
Fax: (212) 878-9351
rzimmerman@warburgpincus.com

Weiss, Peck & Greer Venture Partners
Focus: Early- and expansion-stage information technology and life sciences ventures
Web Address: www.wpgvp.com/

Established in 1971, now has seven venture funds worth $700 million. Backs companies in development stages from seed through mezzanine. Looks for strong managers, proprietary products or services, large markets, and viable business models. Typically invests $2 million to $7 million (seed capital may be as low as $100,000). Subsequent funding rounds can bring the total per company to $10 million. Looks for liquidity five to seven years after the first investment.

HOW TO APPLY:

Send a business plan to

Weiss, Peck & Greer Venture Partners

Suite 3130
555 California St.
San Francisco, CA 94104
(415) 622-6864
Fax: (415) 989-5108

Western States Investment Group

Focus: Medical products, telecommunications, software, transportation, and electronics
Web Address: www.wsig.com/

Established in 1976, considers investments in a wide range of industries. Helps develop growth and business strategies.

How to Apply:

Send proposals to

Scott R. Pancoast, executive vice president, at scott@wsig.com
Western States Investment Group
9191 Towne Centre Drive, Suite 310
San Diego, California 92122

Weston Presidio Capital

Focus: The Internet, telephony, specialty retailing, service businesses, manufacturing, healthcare, technology, restaurants and consumer goods
Web Address: www.westonpresidio.com/

Considers managers the primary investment criterion. Manages $900 million in capital. Focuses on growth companies, recapitalizations, and buyouts. Assists in follow on fundraising, business planning, recruiting,

and cultivating strategic relationships. Typically invests $5 million to $100 million per venture, although can help find sources for higher amounts when necessary.

How to Apply:

Send inquiries to

Michael Lazarus, managing partner (San Francisco), mlazarus@westonpresidio.com, or Michael Cronin, managing partner (Boston), mcronin@westonpresidio.com

Weston Presidio Capital

343 Sansome St.
Suite 1210
San Francisco, CA 94104-1316
(415) 398-0770
Fax: (415) 398-0990

Weston Presidio Capital

One Federal St., 21st Floor
Boston, MA 02110-2004
(617) 988-2500
Fax: (617) 988-2515

Wasserstein Perella Venture Capital Group

Focus: Early-stage companies
Web Address: www.wasserella.com/about/pro_mer_venture.htm

Targets early-stage companies with investments of $2 million to $9 million. Will act as a sole, lead or co-investor. Requires a strong management team, a viable business strategy, unique products or services, and fast growing or large, established target markets.

HOW TO APPLY:

Send a business plan to

George L. Lauro,
george_lauro@wasserella.com or Thomas Ibsen Huang,
thomas_huang@wasserella.com

Wasserstein Perella Ventures
320 Park Ave., 14th Floor
New York, NY 10022
(212) 969-2766
Fax: (212) 702-5635

Wind Point Partners
Focus: Industrial and consumer manufacturing, business-to-business services, publishing, healthcare, value-added distribution, specialty retail, telecommunications, and information technology services
Web Address: www.wppartners.com/

A Midwest-based fund that backs start-ups, acquisitions, or recapitalizations. Usually invests in Midwestern companies, but will consider opportunities in other regions.

HOW TO APPLY:

Send inquiries to the nearest office.

Wind Point Partners
One Towne Square, Suite 780
Southfield, MI 48076

(248) 945-7200
Fax: (248) 945-7220

Wind Point Partners
676 North Michigan Ave., Suite 3300
Chicago, IL 60611
(312) 255-4800
Fax: (312) 255-4820

Windamere Venture Partners
Focus: Early-stage healthcare companies
Web Address: www.windamerevp.com

Targets emerging pharmaceutical, integrated disease management, Internet-enabled, pharmacogenomics, and therapeutic devices companies. Helps in drafting a business plan, developing a business strategy, and identifying financing requirements.

HOW TO APPLY:

Send proposals to
information@windamerevp.com

or

Windamere Venture Partners, LLC
12230 El Camino Real, Suite 300
San Diego, CA 92130
(858) 350-7950
Fax: (858) 350-7951

Wolf Ventures
Focus: Business-to-business technology ventures in the Rocky Mountain area

Web Address: www.wolfventures.com/

Targets investment between $500,000 and $2.5 million. Seeks experienced management teams and companies with a business-to-business model. Also considers companies involved in the Internet, information technology, communications, software, and hardware/devices sectors.

How to Apply:
Send a business plan to businessplan@wolfventures.com

Wolf Ventures
50 South Steele St., Suite 777
Denver, CO 80209
(303) 321-4800
Fax: (303) 321-4848

Zero Stage Capital
Focus: Information technology, software, communications, and healthcare
Web Address: www.zerostage.com

Backs start up, early-stage, and established companies in the Northeastern U.S. Typically acts as the lead investor and cultivates co-investors. Initial investments are $250,000 to $3 million. Established companies may received $2 million to $3 million. Looks for companies with the potential to earn $30 million to $50 million in annual sales in three to five years.

How to Apply:
Send an executive summary as an e-mail attachment to businessplans@zerostage.com. Also, complete the form at the Web site.

VENTURE CAPITAL FUNDS
MARKET-FOCUS INDEX

Advanced Materials
Batterson Venture Partners

Aerospace
The Carlyle Group
SpaceVest

Agriculture
Alternative Agricultural Research and Commercialization Corp.
CMEA Ventures

Application Services
Trinity Ventures

Basic Industry
CeBourn Ltd.
Kestrel Venture Management
Madison Dearborn Partners

Biology
Asset Management Company

Biopharmaceuticals
Alta Partners

Biotech
Batterson Venture Partners
CMEA Ventures
Collinson Howe & Lennox
Comdisco Ventures
Community Technology Fund (CTF)
Forward Ventures
Medicus Venture Partners
Paradigm Capital Partners
Sanderling Ventures
Seaflower Ventures

Business Services
ABN AMRO Private Equity
ABS Capital Partners
BCI Partners
Berkshire Partners
Brown, McMillan & Co.
Capital Resource Partners
Capstone Ventures
Chase Capital Partners
Cornerstone Equity Investors
Crosslink Capital
EOS Partners
Frontenac Company
Mason Wells
PNC Equity Management
Patricof & Co. Ventures, Inc.
TA Associates
Thoma Cressey Equity Partners
Warburg, Pincus Ventures

Business to Business
Artemis Ventures
Chase Capital Partners
Palomar Ventures
Paradigm Capital Partners
Ridgewood Capital
Scripps Ventures
Sentinel Capital Partners
Technology Crossover Ventures
Wind Point Partners
Wolf Ventures

Cable TV
Advent International

Chemicals
Advent International
Ampersand Ventures
Roser Ventures

Communications

ABS Capital Partners
Accel Partners
Advantage Capital
Alpine Technology Ventures
Altos Ventures
Ameritech Development Corp.
Austin Ventures
Bachow & Associates
Battery Ventures
BCI Partners
Bessemer Venture Partners
Blue Chip Venture Company
Boston Capital Ventures
Burr, Egan, Deleage & Co.
Chase Capital Partners
Charles River Ventures
Columbia Capital Corp.
Comdisco Ventures
Commerce Capital
ComVentures
Community Technology Fund (CTF)
Crescendo Ventures
Doll Capital Management
Dolphin Communications
Draper Fisher Jurvetson
Dougery Ventures
DynaFund Ventures
East/West Capital Associates
El Dorado Ventures
Enterprise Partners
Euclid Partners
Exelon Capital Partners
Fidelity Ventures
Lucent Venture Partners, Inc.
M/C Venture Partners
Madison Dearborn Partners
Menlo Ventures

Mustang Ventures
Nassau Capital
Norwest Venture Partners
Oak Investment Partners
Olympic Ventures
Onset Ventures
Opus Capital
Palomar Ventures
Rader Reinfrank & Co.
Redpoint Ventures
Rein Capital
Ricoh Silicon Valley
Roser Ventures
RRE Ventures
Sevin Rosen Funds
The Shepherd Group
South Atlantic Venture Funds
Southeast InteractiveTechnology Funds
Southeastern Technology Fund
Spectrum Equity Investors
The Sprout Group
SSM Ventures
St. Paul Venture Capital
Techxas Ventures
TeleSoft Partners
Telos Venture Partners
TL Ventures
Trinity Ventures
The VenCom Group, Inc.
US Venture Partners
VenGlobal Capital Fund
Voyager Capital
Warburg, Pincus Ventures
Zero Stage Capital

Computer Hardware/Electronics

Bay Partners
Charter Ventures
CMEA Ventures

Comdisco Ventures
Community Technology Fund (CTF)
KB Partners
Matrix Partners
North Atlantic Capital Corporation
Polaris Venture Partners
Ricoh Silicon Valley
Signature Capital
Techxas Ventures
The VenCom Group, Inc.
Walden Capital Partners

Computer Sciences
Advantage Capital
Comdisco Ventures

Consumer Products and Services
Advent International
Alpha Capital Partners
Alpine Technology Ventures
Apex Investment Partners
Blue Chip Venture Company
Brand Equity Ventures
Capital Resource Partners
Enterprise Partners
EOS Partners
Foundation Capital
Frontenac Company
Keystone Venture Capital
Madison Dearborn Partners
North Hill Ventures, L.P.
Oak Investment Partners
Palomar Ventures
Patricof & Co. Ventures, Inc.
Rosewood Capital
Scripps Ventures
Sentinel Capital Partners
The Shepherd Group
South Atlantic Venture Funds

St. Paul Venture Capital
TA Associates
Technology Crossover Ventures
Telecommunications Development Fund
US Venture Partners
The VenCom Group, Inc.
Weston Presidio Capital

Customer Relationship Products
Artemis Ventures
Cambridge Technology Capital Fund
Trans Cosmos USA

Databases
Atlantic Medical Capital

Defense
The Carlyle Group

Distribution
ABN AMRO Private Equity
Agio Capital Partners
The Cambria Group
EOS Partners
Marathon Investment Partners
Roser Ventures
Thoma Cressey Equity Partners
Walden Capital Partners
Wind Point Partners

Education
Calvert Ventures
Crosslink Capital
Fidelity Ventures
PNC Equity Management
Paradigm Capital Partners
Primus Venture Partners
Ravenswood Capital

Electronic Commerce
Alta Partners
Altos Ventures
Artemis Ventures
Austin Ventures
Battery Ventures
Benchmark Capital
Bessemer Venture Partners
Brand Equity Ventures
Cambridge Technology Capital Fund
Capstone Ventures
CCG Venture Partners
CeBourn Ltd.
Chase Capital Partners
Charter Ventures
CMEA Ventures
Crosspoint Venture Partners
DigitalVentures
Draper Fisher Jurvetson
East/West Capital Associates
Encompass Ventures
FBR Technology Venture Partners
Flynn Ventures
Foundation Capital
Matrix Partners
North Atlantic Capital Corporation
Orchid Group Holdings
Palomar Ventures
Paradigm Capital Partners
Polaris Venture Partners
Primus Venture Partners
Rader Reinfrank & Co.
Ravenswood Capital
Ricoh Silicon Valley
Ridgewood Capital
Rosewood Capital
RRE Ventures
Signature Capital

Southeast Interactive Technology Funds
Spectrum Equity Investors
The Sprout Group
SSM Ventures
St. Paul Venture Capital
Technology Crossover Ventures
Trans Cosmos USA
Trinity Ventures
21st Century Internet Venture Partners

Electronic Design Automation
Dougery Ventures

Electronics
Batterson Venture Partners
Benchmark Capital
DynaFund Ventures
Ricoh Silicon Valley
Roser Ventures
Siemens Venture Capital (SVC)
TAT Capital Partners
TI Ventures
Western States Investment Group

Energy
Calvert Ventures
EnerTech Capital Partners
EOS Partners
Exelon Capital Partners
N^{th} Power Technologies, Inc.
Warburg, Pincus Ventures

Enterprise Applications
Artemis Ventures
Brentwood Venture Capital
Cambridge Technology Capital Fund
Charter Ventures
Community Technology Fund (CTF)
El Dorado Ventures

Norwest Venture Partners
Oak Investment Partners
Sand Hill Group
Southeast InteractiveTechnology Funds
St. Paul Venture Capital
21st Century Internet Venture Partners

Environmental
Calvert Ventures
The Carlyle Group
Cordova Ventures
North Atlantic Capital Corporation

Financial services
ABS Capital Partners
BG Affiliates
Capital Resource Partners
Conning & Co.
Cordova Ventures
DigitalVentures
Madison Dearborn Partners
North Atlantic Capital Corporation
North Hill Ventures, L.P.
Northwood Ventures
Patricof & Co. Ventures, Inc.
Primus Venture Partners
Shawmut Capital Partners, Inc.
Summit Partners
TA Associates
Warburg, Pincus Ventures

Healthcare
ABN AMRO Private Equity
ABS Capital Partners
Advanced Technology Ventures
Advantage Capital
Advent International
Alpha Capital Partners
Atlantic Medical Capital

BancBoston Capital and BancBoston Ventures
Beecken Petty & Company
BG Affiliates
Bessemer Venture Partners
Blue Chip Venture Company
Boston Millennia Partners
Brown, McMillan & Co.
Brentwood Venture Capital
Calvert Ventures
Canaan Partners
Capital Resource Partners
Capital Southwest Corporation
Capstone Ventures
The Carlyle Group
Chase Capital Partners
CMEA Ventures
Collinson Howe & Lennox
Commerce Capital
Commerce Capital
Community Technology Fund (CTF)
Conning & Co.
Cordova Ventures
Cornerstone Equity Investors
Crescendo Ventures
Crosslink Capital
Domain Associates
Encompass Ventures
Enterprise Partners
EOS Partners
Euclid Partners
Fidelity Ventures
Forward Ventures
Frazier & Co.
KB Partners
Kline Hawkes & Co.
Madison Dearborn Partners
Mayfield Fund

Menlo Ventures
Mitsui USA Private Equity Group
Montreux Equity Partners
Morgan Stanley Dean Witter Venture Partners
Morgenthaler
MPM Capital Advisors
Nassau Capital
New Enterprise Associates
Noro-Moseley Partners
North Atlantic Capital Corporation
North Bridge Venture Partners
Northwood Ventures
Olympic Ventures
PNC Equity Management
Pacific Horizon Ventures
Pacific Venture Group's
Paradigm Capital Partners
Patricof & Co. Ventures, Inc.
Polaris Venture Partners
Prism Venture Partners
Salix Ventures
Sequel Venture Partners
SGI Capital
Sequoia Capital
Sierra Ventures
Signature Capital
Skywood Ventures
South Atlantic Venture Funds
St. Paul Venture Capital
Summit Partners
Sutter Hill Ventures
TA Associates
Technology Funding
Thoma Cressey Equity Partners
U.S. Bancorp Piper Jaffray Ventures
Vector Fund Management
Venrock Associates

Walden Capital Partners
Warburg, Pincus Ventures
Weston Presidio Capital
Wind Point Partners
Windamere Venture Partners
Zero Stage Capital

Information Technology
ABN
ABS Capital Partners
AMRO Private Equity
Avalon Investments
Advantage Capital
Advanced Technology Ventures
Advent International
Aegis Capital
Alliance Technology Ventures
Alloy Ventures Inc.
Alpha Capital Partners
Alpine Technology Ventures
Apex Investment Partners
Arch Ventures
Aspen Ventures
Asset Management Company
Associated Venture Investors
Atlantic Medical Capital
Atlas Venture
Aurora Ventures Inc.
Bachow & Associates
BancBoston Capital and BancBoston Ventures
Berkeley International Capital Corp.
Blue Chip Venture Company
Boston Millennia Partners
Burr, Egan, Deleage & Co.
Canaan Partners
Capital Southwest Corporation
The Carlyle Group
Chase Capital Partners

Charles River Ventures
Columbia Capital Corp.
Cordova Ventures
Crescendo Ventures
Draper Fisher Jurvetson
East/West Capital Associates
Edelson Technology Partners
Enterprise Partners
EOS Partners
Euclid Partners
First Analysis Venture Capital
Frontenac Company
JK&B Capital
JMI Equity Fund
KB Partners
Keystone Venture Capital
Kleiner, Perkins, Caufield, & Byers
Kline Hawkes & Co.
The Long Island Venture Fund
M/C Venture Partners
Mayfield Fund
Mitsui USA Private Equity Group
Montreux Equity Partners
Morgan Stanley Dean Witter Venture Partners
Morgenthaler
NCIC Capital Fund
New Enterprise Associates
New Vista Capital
Nokia Ventures
Noro-Moseley Partners
North Hill Ventures, L.P.
Novak Biddle Venture Partners
One Liberty Ventures
Pacific Venture Group's
Prism Venture Partners
Red Rock Ventures
Rein Capital

Ricoh Silicon Valley
Selby Venture Partners
Sequel Venture Partners
Sevin Rosen Funds
SGI Capital
Sequoia Capital
Siemens Venture Capital (SVC)
Sierra Ventures
Sigma Partners
Silver Lake Partners
Skywood Ventures
Sloan Ventures
South Atlantic Venture Funds
Southeastern Technology Fund
Summit Partners
Sutter Hill Ventures
TA Associates
Techfarm
Technology Funding
Techxas Ventures
Thoma Cressey Equity Partners
TL Ventures
Trident Capital
TVM Techno Venture Management
Vanguard Venture Partners
Venrock Associates
Viridian Capital Partners
Voyager Capital
Warburg, Pincus Ventures
Weiss, Peck & Greer Venture Partners
Weston Presidio Capital
Wind Point Partners
Wolf Ventures
Zero Stage Capital

Insurance
Conning & Co.

Internet

ABS Capital Partners
Accel Partners
Alpine Technology Ventures
Alta Partners
Altos Ventures
Artemis Ventures
The Barksdale Group
Battery Ventures
Bay Partners
BCI Partners
Brentwood Venture Capital
The Carlyle Group
Castile Ventures
CCG Venture Partners
CeBourn Ltd.
Chase Capital Partners
Charter Ventures
CMEA Ventures
Community Technology Fund (CTF)
Crosslink Capital
Dawntreader LP
Doll Capital Management
Dougery Ventures
DynaFund Ventures
El Dorado Ventures
Encompass Ventures
EnerTech Capital Partners
FBR Technology Venture Partners
Flynn Ventures
Foundation Capital
Fusient Media Ventures
KB Partners
Matrix Partners
North Atlantic Capital Corporation
Northwood Ventures
Novell Ventures
Oak Investment Partners
Ohana Ventures

Olympic Ventures
Onset Ventures
Orchid Group Holdings
Patricof & Co. Ventures, Inc.
Polaris Venture Partners
Primedia Ventures
Primus Venture Partners
Ravenswood Capital
Redleaf Venture Management
Redpoint Ventures
Rosewood Capital
Scripps Ventures
Selby Venture Partners
The Shepherd Group
SOFTBANK Venture Capital
Southeast InteractiveTechnology Funds
Southeastern Technology Fund
SpaceVest
Sparkventures
SSM Ventures
Technology Crossover Ventures
TeleSoft Partners
Telos Venture Partners
TL Ventures
Trans Cosmos USA
Tribune Ventures
Trident Capital
US Venture Partners
Voyager Capital
Walden Capital Partners
Warburg, Pincus Ventures
Weston Presidio Capital

Intranets
Accel Partners
FBR Technology Venture Partners
Redleaf Venture Management

Life Sciences

Advantage Capital
Alliance Technology Ventures
Alloy Ventures Inc.
Arch Ventures
Atlas Venture
Aurora Ventures Inc.
Boston Millennia Partners
Burr, Egan, Deleage & Co.
Charter Ventures
Kleiner, Perkins, Caufield, & Byers
The Long Island Venture Fund
MPM Capital Advisors
New Enterprise Associates
Olympic Ventures
Pacific Horizon Ventures
St. Paul Venture Capital
TL Ventures
TVM Techno Venture Management
Vanguard Venture Partners
Vector Fund Management
Venrock Associates
Warburg, Pincus Ventures
Weiss, Peck & Greer Venture Partners

Manufacturing
Agio Capital Partners
Alpha Capital Partners
Bachow & Associates
BG Affiliates
Berkshire Partners
The Cambria Group
Capital Resource Partners
Capital Southwest Corporation
Commerce Capital
Frontenac Company
Marathon Investment Partners
Northwood Ventures
PNC Equity Management
Roser Ventures

Sentinel Capital Partners
SGI Capital
The Shepherd Group
South Atlantic Venture Funds
Walden Capital Partners
Weston Presidio Capital
Wind Point Partners

Media
ABS Capital Partners
Advent International
Ameritech Development Corp.
Associated Venture Investors
BCI Partners
Brown, McMillan & Co.
Cambridge Technology Capital Fund
Comdisco Ventures
Crosslink Capital
East/West Capital Associates
Northwood Ventures
Rader Reinfrank & Co.
Redpoint Ventures
Ricoh Silicon Valley
The Shepherd Group
Spectrum Equity Investors
TA Associates
Trans Cosmos USA
Tribune Ventures
Vulcan Ventures
Warburg, Pincus Ventures
Wind Point Partners

Medical
Alpha Capital Partners
Alta Partners
Batterson Venture Partners
Berkeley International Capital Corp.
Canaan Partners
Collinson Howe & Lennox

Comdisco Ventures
Community Technology Fund (CTF)
Cordova Ventures
KB Partners
Medicus Venture Partners
New Enterprise Associates
One Liberty Ventures
Opus Capital
Polaris Venture Partners
Primus Venture Partners
Roser Ventures
Sanderling Ventures
Seaflower Ventures
Siemens Venture Capital (SVC)
Signature Capital
TAT Capital Partners
U.S. Bancorp Piper Jaffray Ventures
US Venture Partners
Walden Capital Partners
Western States Investment Group

Multimedia
Alpine Technology Ventures
Associated Venture Investors
Encompass Ventures
Onset Ventures

Networking
Alta Partners
Altos Ventures
Battery Ventures
Bay Partners
Benchmark Capital
Brentwood Venture Capital
Castile Ventures
CeBourn Ltd.
The Centennial Funds
Charter Ventures
Comdisco Ventures

ComVentures
Community Technology Fund (CTF)
Cornerstone Equity Investors
Doll Capital Management
Dougery Ventures
EnerTech Capital Partners
Foundation Capital
Lucent Venture Partners, Inc.
Matrix Partners
Mustang Ventures
North Bridge Venture Partners
Novell Ventures
Onset Ventures
Palomar Ventures
Polaris Venture Partners
Redpoint Ventures
Rein Capital
Sevin Rosen Funds
Spectrum Equity Investors
The Sprout Group
SSM Ventures
Techxas Ventures
Warburg, Pincus Ventures

Oil, Gas, Natural Resources
Altira Group
Madison Dearborn Partners

Outsourcing
ABN AMRO Private Equity Communications
ABN AMRO Private Equity
Artemis Ventures
First Analysis Venture Capital
Keystone Venture Capital
Primus Venture Partners
Sentinel Capital Partners
Trident Capital

Pharmaceuticals
Charter Ventures
Collinson Howe & Lennox
Community Technology Fund (CTF)
Polaris Venture Partners

Physical Sciences
Arch Ventures

Production
Agio Capital Partners

Real Estate
BG Affiliates
The Carlyle Group
Nassau Capital

Recreation and Leisure
Paradigm Capital Partners
Weston Presidio Capital

Regional
Abell Venture Fund (Baltimore-area)
Alpha Capital Partners (Midwest)
Angels' Forum Management Co. (San Francisco area)
Arbor Partners (Michigan)
C3 Holdings (Midwest)
Capital Insights (the Carolinas)
Chinavest (China, Taiwan, and Hong Kong)
CID Equity Partners (Midwest)
Coastal Enterprises Inc. (Maine)
CenterPoint Ventures (Texas)
Chisholm Private Capital Partners (Oklahoma/Texas area)
Commonwealth Capital Ventures (New England)
The Community Development Ventures, Inc. (Baltimore)

Draper International (India)
Early Stage Enterprises (Mid-Atlantic region)
Edison Venture Fund (Mid-Atlantic region)
Egan-Managed Capital (New England)
Eno River Capital (North Carolina)
Evanston Business Investment Corp. (Chicago area)
First Capital Group (the Southwest)
Flatiron Partners (New York City area)
Fluke Venture partners (Pacific Northwest)
Kansas City Equity Partners (Midwest)
Kestrel Venture Management (New England)
Massachusetts Technology Development Corp. (Massachusetts)
Mentor Capital Partners, Ltd. (Pennsylvania, New Jersey, Mid-Atlantic)
Millennium Three Venture Group (Phoenix, Reno, Las Vegas, Sacramento, Stockton/Modesto)
MMG Ventures, L.P (Delaware, Maryland, New Jersey, Pennsylvania, Virginia, Washington, D.C.)
Nippon Investment & Finance Co. Ltd (Asia)
North Coast Technology Investors, LP (Indiana, Michigan, Ohio)
North Carolina Enterprise Fund, L.P (North Carolina)
North Dakota Development Fund (North Dakota)
Quantum Capital Partners (Southeast)
River Cities Capital (Midwest and Southeast)
Sequel Venture Partners (Rocky Mountains)
Sparkventures (New England)
Trellis Partners (Texas)

Venture Investors Management LLC (Mid-west)
Wakefield Group (Mid-Atlantic)
Wolf Ventures (Rocky Mountains)

Retailing
ABN AMRO Private Equity
Advent International
Altos Ventures
Apex Investment Partners
Berkshire Partners
Blue Chip Venture Company
Brand Equity Ventures
Capital Resource Partners
Capital Southwest Corporation
Flynn Ventures
Marathon Investment Partners
Northwood Ventures
Patricof & Co. Ventures, Inc.
South Atlantic Venture Funds
Weston Presidio Capital
Wind Point Partners

Semiconductors
Alpine Technology Ventures
Austin Ventures
Benchmark Capital
Bessemer Venture Partners
Comdisco Ventures
Crosslink Capital
El Dorado Ventures
Lucent Venture Partners, Inc.
Matrix Partners
Mayfield Fund
Patricof & Co. Ventures, Inc.
Sevin Rosen Funds
Signature Capital
TAT Capital Partners
Telos Venture Partners

US Venture Partners

Software
ABN AMRO Private Equity
Alpine Technology Ventures
Altos Ventures
Apex Investment Partners
Bachow & Associates
Batterson Venture Partners
Battery Ventures
Bay Partners
BCI Partners
Boston Capital Ventures
Charles River Ventures
CMEA Ventures
Comdisco Ventures
Crosspoint Venture Partners
Draper Fisher Jurvetson
Fidelity Ventures
JK&B Capital
JMI Equity Fund
KB Partners
Levy Trajman Management Investment Inc.
Mason Wells
Matrix Partners
Mayfield Fund
Menlo Ventures
North Atlantic Capital Corporation
North Bridge Venture Partners
Norwest Venture Partners
Olympic Ventures
Onset Ventures
Opus Capital
Patricof & Co. Ventures, Inc.
Primedia Ventures
Rein Capital
Ricoh Silicon Valley
Roser Ventures
RRE Ventures

Sevin Rosen Funds
The Shepherd Group
Signature Capital
SpaceVest
Sparkventures
The Sprout Group
St. Paul Venture Capital
Summit Partners
TA Associates
Techxas Ventures
TeleSoft Partners
Telos Venture Partners
TL Ventures
Trinity Ventures
US Venture Partners
VenGlobal Capital Fund
Voyager Capital
Western States Investment Group
Zero Stage Capital

Specialty Materials
Ampersand Ventures
Sparkventures

Telecommunications
Alpine Technology Ventures
Alta Partners
Apex Investment Partners
Batterson Venture Partners
Bay Partners
Benchmark Capital
Berkshire Partners
Boston Millennia Partners
The Carlyle Group
Castile Ventures
CeBourn Ltd.
The Centennial Funds

Charter Ventures
Cordova Ventures
Cornerstone Equity Investors
Crosspoint Venture Partners
EnerTech Capital Partners
FBR Technology Venture Partners
Flynn Ventures
Foundation Capital
Frontenac Company
JK&B Capital
KB Partners
North Atlantic Capital Corporation
North Hill Ventures, L.P.
Northwood Ventures
Ohana Ventures
OneLiberty Ventures
PNC Equity Management
Palomar Ventures
Patricof & Co. Ventures, Inc.
Primus Venture Partners
Prism Venture Partners
Rader Reinfrank & Co.
Rein Capital
Sequel Venture Partners
Sevin Rosen Funds
Siemens Venture Capital (SVC)
Signature Capital
Southeast InteractiveTechnology Funds
SpaceVest
Telecommunications Development Fund
The VenCom Group, Inc.
Weston Presidio Capital
Wind Point Partners

Transportation
Berkshire Partners
Western States Investment Group

MATCHES MADE IN HEAVEN: SEED FUNDS, ANGEL INVESTORS, AND INTRODUCTION SERVICES

No doubt the venture capital industry is hot: Business monthlies cover fund managers like *People* covers entertainment celebrities. Unfortunately for many small companies, especially those that don't offer a technology-oriented product or service, venture capital backs less than 10 percent of the new ventures that emerge each year. The reason is partly ROI: high tech is risky, but the rewards are also potentially weighty: venture capitalists routinely seek returns of 25 to 50 percent or more on their investments.

Investment size is another factor that puts venture funds in only select entrepreneurial pockets. Managers on and off Sand Hill Road sweat out the background checks and business-model vetting that they must do to find investment candidates that are worth risking millions of dollars on. Due diligence isn't significantly less for smaller, under $1 million investments. So if you're going to spin the wheel, why not bet high, say $2 million to $10 million, on something like the Internet or a breakthrough software application that has the possibility of creating a new generation of blue ribbon companies?

What makes sense from an investor's perspective doesn't necessarily help the start up retailer or manufacturing outfit that's come up with a killer marketing plan and has the managerial experience to make it succeed. So where does an entrepreneur turn if he or she needs $100,000 to $1 million and doesn't want to incur debt? Two important investment sources focus specifically on investments of this size range. One is a special class of venture funds called seed funds, the other is well-heeled individual investors known as angels.

Both groups specialize in making investments of $1 million or less—sometimes far less—in very early stage companies that may not have a commercial product or service, or even a business plan. Like higher-profile venture capitalists, seed funds and angels take a share of the new company in return for their capital, and depending on the individual investors, may expect to have an influential voice in business decisions.

Because you're giving up a piece of your company to seed-fund managers or angels, you need to look beyond a potential investor's checkbook to find the right fit. The ability of the investor and your management team to work together is essential. That means not only being in sync with the business idea and the exit or liquidity strategy, but if possible, finding complementary backgrounds. An investor who rounds out your company's gaps in start up experience, technology, or marketing means you're more likely to have a business partner rather than a bean counter. You can help make sure that happens by doing your own due-diligence: check the backgrounds of potential investors by interviewing the executives of existing investments, as well as accountants and attorneys with entrepreneurial expertise.

Traditionally, the trouble with angel investors has been the fact that they were often as ephemeral as their namesakes. The Web has changed that. A number of Web sites now exist to match angels and entrepreneurs, so start ups don't have to rely solely on their local networks of accountants, lawyers, and business executives to introduce them to wealthy investors. Now, the Internet opens the investor pool to the entire country and even the world.

Most matchmaking sites manage a database that allows registered investors to browse business proposals submitted by entrepreneurs. One of the most famous angel/entrepreneur matchmakers is ACE-Net, an online database managed in part by the Small Business Administration. One of ACE-Net's biggest benefits to cash-starved start ups is its requirement that investors be accredited before they are allowed to browse prospective candidates. Accreditation is a formal definition developed by the U.S. Securities and Exchange Commission. In essence, this requires investors to have a net worth of $1 million or more or an annual income of over $200,000 ($300,000 for a married couple). Being accredited doesn't guarantee the investor is right for your company, only that he or she has the resources to back your company, rather than waste your time, if everything else checks out.

In addition to offering databases, a small number of sites are now duplicating the elevator-pitch presentations that are a staple of capital-investment forums and luncheons across the country. In the real world, entrepreneurs at these forums have a short time—often 10 or 15 minutes—to pitch their business plans to an audience of deep-pocket investors. In the virtual world, the same opportunity exists in the form of pithy 150-word summaries and in some cases short video and audio messages designed to bowl over online investors. Both the real and virtual presentations put almost unbearable pressure on entrepreneurs to sum up their dreams in a short sound, or video, bite. But the payoff of communicating directly with business people who have money to risk can mean the difference between a dream that fades or one that thrives.

The following directory lists seed funds, angel investment groups, and angel/entrepreneur matchmakers. Seed funds (identified with a ⛁ symbol) have only abbreviated listings here. See the full venture capital directory beginning on page 36 for additional information about the individual funds.

DIRECTORY OF SEED FUNDS, ANGEL INVESTORS, AND MATCHMAKERS

In the following directory, venture funds identified with a icon are those that use the Web to make it easy for entrepreneurs to electronically submit business ideas, executive summaries, or business plans. A icon denotes funds that target young companies seeking investments of less than $1 million.

Full write ups of listings noted with can be found in the Venture Capital directory beginning on page 190.

Abell Venture Fund
Focus: Baltimore-area companies in a variety of industries
*Web Address:*www.abell.org/venturef.htm

Ace-Net
Focus: Start ups seeking $250,000 to $5 million
Web Adress: www.ace-net.org

A fee-based service, sponsored by the Small Business Administration, that matches entrepreneurs needing $5 million or less with registered angels—private investors that meet the Security and Exchange Administration's definition of accredited individual investors. Companies list their business data and financial needs on a secure site that is accessible to accredited investors nationwide. Investors contact entrepreneurs directly. Annual fees to entrepreneurs vary depending on the state, but the maximum is $450. See Web site for the 40 regional Network Operators—universities, non-profits, and development centers—that manage the program throughout the country. Operators also provide mentoring and managerial support.

Ace-Net also publishes a model contract of terms and conditions common to angel investments. Ace-Net short form registration helps entrepreneurs bypass multi-state securities registrations for investments below $1 million. Ace-Net is not available for companies seeking more than $5 million, or sole proprietorships, partnerships, limited liability partnerships, and some other business types (see Web site for complete list).

HOW TO APPLY:

Submit a completed Entrepreneur Application form (at the Web site) to the nearest Network Operator.

Advantage Capital
Focus: Communications, information processing, computer sciences, health care, life sciences
Web Address: www.advantagecap.com

Ad-Ventures
Focus: Internet and real-estate
www.ad-ventures.com

Picks investment candidates in the target markets for the venture capital division of Softbank. Provides management advice for portfolio companies.

How to Apply:

Attach business plan to e-mail message, and send to brn@ad-ventures.com.

Ad-Ventures

ATTN: Submissions
10926 Alta View Drive
Studio City, CA 91604
(323) 417-4797
Fax: (323) 417-4995

Aegis Capital

Focus: Computers and information systems
Web Address: www.aegis-capital.com

Alliance Technology Ventures

Focus: Early-stage information technology and life sciences
Web Address: www.atv.com/

Alloy Ventures Inc.

Focus: Seed and early-stage technology companies in information and life sciences
Web Address: www.alloyventures.com/

Alpha Capital Partners

Focus: Information technology, medical and healthcare, consumer businesses and manufacturing companies, mainly in the Midwest
Web Address: www.alphacapital.com

Altira Group

Focus: Technologies for the oil and gas industry
Web Address: www.altiragroup.com/

Alternative Agricultural Research and Commercialization Corp.

Focus: Industrial uses of agricultural materials
Web Address: www.usda.gov/aarc/

Altos Ventures

Focus: Early-stage investments in business-to-business e-commerce, software, e-retailing, the Internet, networking, and communications
Web Address: www.altosvc.com

Ameritech Development Corp.

Focus: Communications and media companies
Web Address: www.ameritech.com/products/venture_rm/adc.html

Ampersand Ventures

Focus: Specialty Materials and Chemicals (SMC) industry
Web Address: www.ampersandventures.com/

Angels' Forum Management Co.

Focus: New technologies from the greater San Francisco Bay area of California
Web Address: www.angelsforum.com

Angel Money

Focus: Internet hardware and software
Web Address: Angelmoney.com

Typically invests $50,000 to $500,000, but accumulate as much as $5 million with other sources. Shuns real-estate, restaurants, retail or entertainment companies. Requires a complete business-plan, a market analysis, and a business-model showing profit potential over multiple years.

How to Apply:

Send a business plan, with an executive summary, managers' resumes, and contact information to: jimpinto@angelmoney.com

Angels 2000

Focus: High-tech and general business start ups

Web Address: www.angels2000.com/

A network of accredited investors with access to a secure database of entrepreneurs seeking capital. Investors also offer management, marketing, engineering, and other expertise. Note: at press time, the network was waiving fees for new members. Check the site for current fees.

How to Apply:

Complete the online application and e-mail an executive summary to www.angels2000.com/EXECsum.html.

Angels 2000

4165 Thousand Oaks Blvd., Suite 211
Westlake Village CA 91362
(805) 371-8419
Fax: (805) 371-8424

Apex Investment Partners

Focus: Telecommunications, software, information technology, specialty retail and consumer products
Web Address: www.apexvc.com/

Artemis Ventures

Focus: Seed-stage business-to-business software, Internet software and services, e-commerce, outsourced services, customer relationship management, enterprise applications, and enabling technologies
Web Address: www.artemisventures.com/

Arch Ventures
Focus: Seed and early-state investments in information technology, life sciences, and physical sciences
Web Address: www.archventure.com/

Asset Management Company
Focus: Seed and early-stage companies in information and biological sciences
Web Address: www.assetman.com

Associated Venture Investors
Focus: Convergence of information, communications, and entertainment technologies and services
Web Address: www.avicapital.com/

Atlas Venture
Focus: Transatlantic information technology and life sciences
Web Address: www.atlasventure.com

Aurora Ventures Inc.
Web Address: www.aurorafunds.com/
Focus: Life science and information science

Austin Ventures
Focus: E-commerce (business-to-business and business-to-consumer), communications, semiconductors

Web Address: www.austinventures.com

Batterson Venture Partners
Focus: Electronics, software, telecommunications, advanced materials, biotech and other medical applications
Web Address: www.vcapital.com

Bay Angels
Focus: Early-stage technology companies in the San Francisco area
Web Address: www.bayangels.com

Organizes monthly and special meetings where entrepreneurs introduce their companies to angel investors. Alternately, entrepreneurs can post video or text presentations on a password-protected area of the Web site.

HOW TO APPLY:

Complete a preliminary registration form at the Web site and send an executive summary or business plan to Star@bayangels.com. For information contact Mike Pogue at (415) 289-4618 or Mike@bayangels.com

Bay Partners
Focus: Early-stage companies in data networking, telecommunications infrastructure, hardware and software, and Internet markets
Web Site: www.baypartners.com/

Ben Franklin Technology Partners
Focus: Pennsylvania start ups
Web Address: www.benfranklin.org/

A business development network created by the state's Department of Community and Economic Development for connecting angel investors with entrepreneurs. Also supported by educators and area business executives. Helps young companies that might not receive capital from traditional sources. Also helps locate follow-on funding sources.

HOW TO APPLY:

Inquire to info@benfranklin.org or the nearest office:

Northeastern PA:
125 Goodman Drive
Bethlehem, PA 18015
(610) 758-5200
Fax: (610) 861-5918
http://www.nep.benfranklin.org

Central and Northern PA:
115 Technology Center
University Park, PA 16802
(814) 863-4558
Fax: (814) 865-0960
http://www.cnp.benfranklin.org

Southeastern PA:
Eleven Penn Center
1835 Market St., Suite 1100
Philadelphia, PA 19103
(215) 972-6700
Fax: (215) 972-5588

http://www.sep.benfranklin.org

Western PA:
Innovation Works, Inc.
2000 Technology Drive, Suite 250
Pittsburgh, PA 15219
(412) 681-1520
Fax: (412) 681-2625
http://www.iw.benfranklin.org

State Coordinator:
Susan Rhoades
200 N. Third St., Suite 400
Harrisburg, PA 17101
(717) 234-1748
Fax: (717) 234-1824

The Bizboard
Focus: Matchmaker for international investors and start-up managers
Web Address: www.thebizboard.com/

A free site for connecting investors around the world to entrepreneurs. Investors can browse company listings by geographic area, industry, investment size, and other criteria.

HOW TO APPLY:

Submit a listing via an electronic form at the Web site. Each listing costs $13.95 for an indefinite-length posting.

The Bizboard
c/o C.R.F Inc.
P.O. Box 6252
Tallahassee, Florida 32314

Calvert Ventures

Focus: Healthcare, education, the environment, and energy

Web Address: http://www.calvertventures.com/

The Cambria Group

Focus: Manufacturing, processing, distribution, transportation, resource or service businesses

Web Address: www.cambriagroup.com/

Cambridge Technology Capital Fund

Focus: Enterprise software, e-commerce, customer management systems, knowledge management systems, interactive media, supply chain management, strategic consulting, services, and money management and trading

Web Address: www.ctc.ctp.com/html/ctc-mission.html

Canaan Partners

Focus: Information technology, healthcare, medical

Web Address: www.canaan.com/

Capital Matchmaker

Focus: Communications/publishing, computers, software, consumer products, education and training, entertainment, manufacturing

Web Address: http://www.matchmaker.org/capital/

Matches investors throughout the world with entrepreneurs needing $25,000 or more in capital. Start ups post a business summary arranged by industry on the site. Investors contact entrepreneurs directly.

How to Apply:

List new companies at www.matchmaker.org/capital/register.htm or send questions to capital@matchmaker.org.

The Capital Network

Focus: Angel/entrepreneur introductions

Web Address: www.thecapitalnetwork.com

A non-profit, economic development group that introduces entrepreneurs and investors. Also hosts venture capital forums that feature presentations by start ups.

How to Apply:

Inquire at

The Capital Network
3925 West Braker Lane, Suite 406
Austin, TX 78759-5321
tcn@ati.utexas.edu

Castile Ventures

Focus: Data networking, telecommunications, and the Internet

Web Address: http://www.castileventures.com

CCG Venture Partners
Focus: Internet and e-business businesses
Web Address: www.ccgvp.com/

Coastal Enterprises Inc.
Focus: Maine people and communities, particularly those with low incomes
Web Address: http://www.ceimaine.org/

The Centennial Funds
Focus: Computer networking, electronic media, telecommications
Web Address: www.centennial.com/

Charter Ventures
Focus: Data networking, telecommunications, enterprise software, systems and peripherals, Internet software, and electronic commerce; life sciences, including biotechnology, medical devices, diagnostics, pharmaceuticals, and health care services.
Web Address: www.charterventures.com

Chisholm Private Capital Partners
Focus: Oklahoma, Texas and adjacent-state manufacturing companies, or those selling information technologies, life sciences products and services
Web Address: www.chisholmvc.com/

CMEA Ventures
Focus: Computer software and hardware, communications, E-commerce, the Internet, agriculture, electronic-bioindustry applications, healthcare, genomics, bioinformatics, and proteomics
Web Address: www.cmeaventures.com/

Collinson Howe & Lennox
Focus: Biotechnology, pharmaceuticals, genomics, drug delivery technology, medical and diagnostic devices, and health care services
Web Address: www.chlmedical.com/

The Colorado Capital Alliance, Inc.
Focus: Colorado Start ups needing $1 million or less
Web Address: www.angelcapital.org

A not-for-profit service that introduces angel investors and managers of start ups. Entrepreneurs should have a complete business plan and demonstrate high growth and profit potentials as well as managerial strength. Annual fee for entrepreneurs is $395.

HOW TO APPLY:

Colorado Capital Alliance, Inc.
P.O. Box 19169

Boulder, CO 80308-2169
Tel: (303) 499-9646
Fax: (303) 494-4146
email: info@angelcapital.org

The Connecticut Venture Group
Focus: Start ups in the Northeast
Web Address: www.ct-venture.org/

A not-for-profit development group that organizes entrepreneur's demonstrations and expositions to introduce new companies to angel investors. Members also include public investors, commercial and investment bankers, and professional service providers.

HOW TO APPLY:
Complete the registration form at the Web site. Fees for individual memberships are $375.

Connecticut Venture Group
1895-B Post Road
Fairfield, CT 06430

Comdisco Ventures
Focus: The Internet, software, computer services, communications, networking, hardware, semiconductors/EDA, biotech, medical devices and services, mass media
Web Address: www.comdisco.com/products/ventures/

Commonwealth Capital Ventures
Focus: Technology, healthcare, and other high-growth opportunities in New England
Web Address: www.ccvlp.com/

The Community Development Ventures, Inc. (CDVI)
Focus: Companies near Baltimore's Empowerment and Enterprise Zones
Web Address: www.mmggroup.com/

Community Technology Fund (CTF)
Focus: Communications and networking, Internet and enterprise software, computer systems and components, healthcare information systems, medical devices, clinical diagnostics, biotechnology, pharmaceuticals, and drug delivery systems
Web Address: http://www.bu.edu/ctf/

ComVentures
Focus: Early-stage communications and networking companies
Web Address: http://www.comven.com/

Cordova Ventures
Focus: Telecommunications, financial services, healthcare, medical devices and services, environmental, and information technology

Web Address: www.cordovaventures.com

Davis, Tuttle Venture Partners
Focus: Diversified by industry, growth stage, and geography
Web Address: www.davistuttle.com/

Dawntreader LP
Focus: Seed and early-stage Internet businesses
Web Address: www.dawntreaderlp.com

DigitalVentures
Focus: E-commerce and financial services
Web Address: www.dtpnet.com

Doll Capital Management
Focus: Communications, networking, and Internet services
Web Address: www.dollcap.com

The Early Stage Investment Forum
Focus: Start ups in the Pacific Northwest
Web Address: www.investmentforum.org/

Hosts the Northwest Connection for Investors and Entrepreneurs, a series of meetings between entrepreneurs seeking seed capital and a syndicate of angel investors. Entrepreneurs present a 15-minute introduction of their business to angels, venture capitalists, and investment firms. Select companies also man an exhibit booth to promote their product or service.

How to Apply:
To be considered as a presenter, send a business plan to
Screening@InvestmentForum.org.

Early Stage Enterprises
Focus: Early-stage, mid-Atlantic companies in information technology, computer software, Internet software and services, medical devices and diagnostics, life sciences, and healthcare services
Web Address: www.esevc.com

Edelson Technology Partners
Focus: International technology companies
Web Address: www.edelsontech.com

The Elevator
Focus: Start ups
Web Address: www.thelevator.com/

An on-line introduction service for entrepreneurs and investors. Start ups post a 150-word pitch and business plan on the secure site. Postings are free, unless site organizers require more information in the pitch. Start ups pay $79.95 to resubmit pitches. Registered investors pay a $150 fee to receive a password to access the postings. Interested parties discuss the potential partnership in a private chat room.

How to Apply:

Register at the Web site or inquire to info@thelevator.com.

Encompass Ventures

Focus: Western U.S. and Canadian companies in electronic commerce, Internet/intranet, digital audio and video, embedded systems, home computing, and healthcare

Web Address: www.encompassventures.com

Eno River Capital

Focus: Bioscience companies in North Carolina

Web Address: www.enorivercapital.com/

Enterprise Partners

Focus: Information technology, communications, healthcare, and select consumer products and services

Web Address: www.ent.com

Evanston Business Investment Corporation

Focus: Early-stage ventures in the Chicago area, particularly those in Evanston, IL, or affiliates of Northwestern University

Web Address: www.ebic.com/

Fidelity Ventures

Focus: Healthcare, software, communications, employer services, and education

Web Address: www.fidelityventures.com

First Analysis Venture Capital

Focus: Information technology, outsourced services, and infrastructure industries

Web Address: www.facvc.com/

Florida Venture Forum

Focus: South Florida entrepreneurs

Web Address: www.flvencap.org/

Organizes meetings throughout the year for area entrepreneurs, angels, and other investors. Start ups that pass a business-plan screening are invited to showcase their products or services. A panel of experts in the start up's target industry critiques the plans and offers management advice.

How to Apply:

Inquire at

The Florida Venture Forum

255 Alhambra Circle, Suite 500
Coral Gables, Florida 33134

Fluke Venture Partners

Focus: Unique products, technologies, services, or market ventures

Web Address: www.flukecapital.com/

Flynn Ventures

Focus: Retail, lifestyle, e-commerce, the Web, information technology, telecommunications and restaurant chains
Web Address: www.flynnventures.com/

Forward Ventures

Focus: Early-stage biotechnology and healthcare companies
Web Address: www.forwardventures.com/

Foundation Capital

Focus: Consumer e-commerce, e-business, Internet infrastructure, telecommunications, and networking
Web Address: www.foundationcapital.com/

Garage.com

Focus: Seed-stage companies in networking, software, computer hardware and peripherals, semiconductors, the Internet, telecommunications, biotechnology, or medical devices
Web Address: www.garage.com

Maintains a network of angels and other investors seeking seed-stage start ups. Entrepreneurs and investors must go through a screening process, the latter for growth potential, the former for experience with young companies. Companies and investors deal directly once the relationship is established.

How to Apply:

Begin the screening process by completing an electronic form at the Web site. Final acceptance will take additional information and a personal meeting with Garage.com. Start ups that receive funding through the site pay a percentage of the funded amount to Garage.com.

Garage.com
420 Florence Ave.
Palo Alto, CA 94301
(650) 470-0950
Fax: (650) 470-0940

Note: see Web site for locations of offices in Boston, MA, Austin, TX, and Seattle, WA.

The Gathering of Angels

Focus: Seed-level companies in Southwest
Web Address: www.gatheringofangels.com

Holds monthly meetings in Santa Fe, NM, with angels, venture capital managers, and bankers to evaluate early-stage investment opportunities and establish mentoring relationships with young companies. This year began organizing similar meetings in Scottsdale, AZ, Atlanta, GA, and Hilton Head, SC.

How to Apply:

Submit an electronic request form at the Web site for schedules of upcoming meetings. Entrepreneurs also must complete a registration form to be considered as a presenter at one of the meetings.

The Gathering of Angels

1360 Vista Colorado
Santa Fe, NM 87501
tbryant@nm.net

i-Hatch Ventures

Focus: Northeast, early-stage Internet companies
Web Address: http://www.i-hatch.com/

Established in 1999, offers capital and consulting for early-stage Internet ventures. Targets companies selling e-commerce applications, new media content, Web-enabling technology, network infrastructure products, and Internet services. Also looks for ventures with a connection to Europe for spin-offs and other projects.

How to Apply:

Send an executive summary and managers' resumes to plans@i-hatch.com.

i-Hatch Ventures

200 Park Avenue, 17th floor
New York, NY 10166
Voice and Fax: (212) 208-4590

International Capital Resources

Focus: Early-stage companies throughout the country
Web Address: www.icrnet.com

A commercial service for matching entrepreneurs and angels wanting to invest $25,000 to more than $1 million. Publishes a bi-monthly publication (subscription: $450 for five issues) for investors with profiles of new companies referred to the service by attorneys and business services executives. Entrepreneurs receive contact information for investors who are interested in the start up.

How to Apply:

Send a business plan, a private placement memorandum, and financial needs to

Gerald Benjamin

Senior Managing Partner
388 Market St., Suite 500
San Francisco, CA 94111
(415) 296-2519
Fax: (415) 296-2529
jab@icrnet.com

I-nterpriseZone

Focus: Kentucky-based e-commerce, e-business, telecommunications ventures, or those that capitalize on the overnight package-delivery hub at Louisville's airport
Web Address: www.i-nterprisezone.com

A combination angel investment vehicle and for-profit incubator. Solicits capital from angels to invest in entrepreneurs who use the I-nterpriseZone incubator infrastructure. Typically seeks a five- to ten-year payoff on investments. The incubator includes computer, networking, and security hardware, Internet connections, software development programs and financial applications, office space, and business equipment. Start ups outside the incubator's Louisville location may use only the technology services if they don't require the physical resources. "Zone" staff advises entrepreneurs in business strategy, finance, accounting, and technology.

HOW TO APPLY:

Send inquiries to

Stephen Zarick, CEO
The i-nterpriseZONE
PO Box 6386
Louisville, KY 40206
(502) 899-3227
szarick@i-nterprisezone.com

NVST.com
Focus: Matching investors and entrepreneurs
Web Address: www.nvca.org/

Online matchmaking service publishes proposals by businesses seeking funding, as well as a directory of investors.

HOW TO APPLY:

Complete the online membership registration form. For inquiries about the match-

ing service, send e-mail to Chris Brown at chrisb@nvst.com.

NVST.com, Inc.
777 108th Ave. NE, Suite 1750
Bellevue, WA 98004
(425) 454-3639
Fax: (425) 688-8098
info@nvst.com

Kansas City Equity Partners
Focus: Information technology, telecommunications, retail, consumer products, and industrial manufacturing in the Midwest
Web Address: www.kcep.com/

KB Partners
Focus: Start up and early-stage Internet products and services, information technology, computer hardware and software, telecommunications, medical devices and healthcare products, industrial and engineering technology, and analytical instrumentation
Web Address: www.kbpartners.com/

Kestrel Venture Management
Focus: New England-based Basic manufacturing, healthcare, software, computer devices, service companies, media communications, and food products
Web Address: www.kestrelvm.com

The Long Island Venture Fund
Focus: Information technology and life sciences
Web Address: www.livf.com/

Lucent Venture Partners, Inc.,
Focus: Early-stage ventures in high-growth communications technologies, including wireless communications, data networking, semiconductors, communications software, and professional services
Web Address: www.lucentventurepartners.com

Massachusetts Technology Development Corporation
Focus: Start up and expansion stage technology companies operating in Massachusetts
Web Address: www.mtdc.com/

Matrix Partners
Focus: Software, networking equipment, semiconductors, computers, storage, the Internet, and e-business applications
Web Address: www.matrixpartners.com/

Mayfield Fund
Focus: Healthcare and information technologies, software, and semiconductors
Web Address: www.mayfield.com

Medicus Venture Partners
Focus: Early stage medical and biotechnology companies based in the Western U.S.
Web Address: www.medicusvc.com/

MIT Enterprise Forum
Focus: Technology start ups
Web Address: web.mit.edu/entforum/

Organizes meetings and programs through 18 chapters across the country to provide business advice and introductions to investors and business experts. MIT alumni run the chapters, but membership is open to all entrepreneurs. Programs include a case study forum where industry experts critique and suggest improvements on individual business strategies.

How to Apply:
Contact the national chapter or local chapters:

MIT Enterprise Forum, Inc.
28 Carlton St., Building E32-330
Cambridge, MA 02139
(617) 253-0015
Fax: (617) 258-0532
Email: mitef@mit.edu

Pasadena, CA: broccoli.caltech.edu/entforum/

San Diego: www.sddt.com/mitforum/

San Francisco Bay Area: www.vlab.org/

Santa Barbara: cenforum@mit.edu

Connecticut: www.mitforumct.org/

Chicago: chiforum@mit.edu

Boston: www.mitforum-cambridge.org/

New Hampshire: www.nhhtc.org/

New York City: www.mitef-nyc.org/

Portland, OR: www.oef.org/

Dallas: www.mitforum.com/

Houston: www.miteftx.org/

Seattle: www.mitwa.org/shop/

Washington, D.C.: www.mitef.org/

Mitsui USA Private Equity Group
Focus: Information technology and healthcare
Web Address: www.mitsuipe.com/

MMG Ventures, L.P
Focus: Communications and computer, information, and healthcare services companies in Delaware, Maryland, New Jersey, Pennsylvania, Virginia, and Washington, D.C.
Web Address: www.mmggroup.com/

Montreux Equity Partners
Focus: Early-stage technology and healthcare ventures
Web Address: www.montreuxequity.com/

Mustang Ventures
Focus: Early-stage companies in data and communications networking, applications, and services
Web Address: www.mustangventures.com

NCIC Capital Fund
Focus: Early-stage technology ventures
Web Address: www.ncicfund.org

New Enterprise Associates
Focus: Early stage companies in information technology, medical and life sciences, healthcare services, medical devices, instrumentation and information management
Web Address: www.nea.com/

New Vista Capital
Focus: Early-stage information technology ventures
Web Address: www.nvcap.com/

North Bridge Venture Partners
Focus: Healthcare, software, and data communications

Web Address: www.nbvp.com/

North Coast Technology Investors, LP

Focus: Early-stage enterprise software, manufacturing, distribution, and materials science companies in Indiana, Michigan, and Ohio
Web Address: www.northcoastvc.com/

North Carolina Enterprise Fund, L.P

Focus: Small to medium-sized North Carolina-based companies
Web Address: www.ncef.com/

North Dakota Development Fund

Focus: Businesses expanding or relocating to the state
Web Address: www.growingnd.com/

Northwest Capital Network

Focus: Early-stage, high-growth ventures in the Northwest
Web Address: www.investmentforum.org

Non-profit network for matching entrepreneurs needing $50,000 to $2 million in capital with more than over 850 accredited investors throughout Washington state and Oregon. An ACE-Net Network Operator. Investors receive business summaries of potential ventures screened by the net-

work's board. Investors are then responsible for contacting entrepreneurs. The two parties work out equity terms for any subsequent investment agreements.

HOW TO APPLY:

Send a completed Northwest Capital application and business plan, along with an initial entry-fee deposit of $100. A total of $650 is required to participate in the network for six months. An additional fee of $450 is required to join the national ACE-Net network (At press time, Northwest Capital offered an $850 package price to entrepreneurs wanting to join both networks. Check the Web sites for prevailing discounts.)

Northwest Capital Network

(206) 441-3123
Fax: (206) 328-4708
nwcapital@seanet.com

Northwest Venture Group

Focus: Seattle-area start ups
Web Address: www.nwvg.org/

Founded in 1985, the non-profit organization hosts monthly breakfast meetings, presentation forums, and other programs to help entrepreneurs network with angels and other investors. Recently launched a Web portal designed to link angels and entrepreneurs.

HOW TO APPLY:

To register for upcoming programs contact

Northwest Venture Group
P.O. Box 21693
Seattle, WA 98111-3693
Reservations: (425) 746-1973
Email: nwvg@businesscity.com

Norwest Venture Partners
Focus: Enterprise software, communications systems, and communications services
Web Address: www.norwestvp.com/

Novak Biddle Venture Partners
Focus: Information technology
Web Address: www.novakbiddle.com/

Nth Power Technologies, Inc.
Focus: Energy companies
Web Address: www.nthfund.com

Ohana Ventures
Focus: Internet and telecommunications
Web Address: www.ohanaventures.com/

OneLiberty Ventures
Focus: Information and medical technologies and telecommunications
Web Address: www.oneliberty.com/

Onset Ventures
Focus: Software and Internet products and services, communications, networking, and medical technology
Web Address: www.onset.com/

Palomar Ventures
Focus: Data- and telecommunications, broadband, e-business software, business-to-business and business-to-consumer applications
Web Address: www.palomarventures.com/

Paradigm Capital Partners
Focus: Biotechnology, business-to-business e-commerce, education, healthcare, recreation and leisure, and service businesses
Web Address: www.paradigmcp.com

Polaris Venture Partners
Focus: Internet software, e-commerce, networking, computer systems, medical devices, pharmaceuticals, genomics, and healthcare
Web Address: www.polarisventures.com/

Ravenswood Capital
Focus: The Internet, e-commerce, direct marketing, and educational services
Web Address: www.ravenswoodcapital.com/

Red Rock Ventures

Focus: Early-stage information technology
Web Address: www.redrockventures.com/

Rein Capital

Focus: Data- and telecommunications, software, and information services
Web Address: www.reincapital.com/

Ricoh Silicon Valley

Focus: Communications, computer hardware, office services, electronics, electronic commerce, information technologies, media, and software
Web Address: www.rsv.ricoh.com

The Rockies Venture Club

Focus: Colorado Entrepreneurs
Web Site: www.rockiesventureclub.org/

A non-profit, group founded in 1983 to network entrepreneurs, angel investors, and others.

How to Apply:

Complete the online membership form.

Rockies Venture Club

190 East 9th Ave., Suite 440
Denver, CO 80203
(303) 831-4174
Fax: (303) 832-4920

Maita@rockiesventureclub.org or
Josh@rockiesventureclub.org

Roser Ventures

Focus: Capital equipment and services, communications, distribution, electronics, medical medical products, software, specialty chemicals and manufacturing
Web Address: www.roserventures.com/

Sanderling Ventures

Focus: Biomedical companies
Web Address: www.sanderling.com/

Seaflower Ventures

Focus: Early-stage biomedical firms
Web Address: www.seaflower.com/

Selby Venture Partners,

Focus: Seed and early-stage technology and Internet ventures in Silicon Valley
Web Address: www.selbyventures.com/

Sequel Venture Partners

Focus: Early-stage healthcare, information technology, and telecommunications companies in the Rocky Mountain states
Web Address: www.sequelvc.com/

Seraph Capital Forum
Focus: Pacific Northwest start ups
Web Address: www.seraphcapital.com/

An organization of businesswomen accredited as angel investors. Regular meetings are scheduled for six times a year, during which two entrepreneurs from emerging companies present their business plans for consideration.

HOW TO APPLY:

Entrepreneurs submit plans and an application via the Web site to be considered as presenters. Companies picked by the selection committee pay $150 to make the presentation. For information contact Anna Kearns at annak@woodscreek.com

Sevin Rosen Funds
Focus: Data communications, telecommunications, semiconductors, software and information services
Web Address: www.srfunds.com/

Sequoia Capital
Focus: Start ups in information technology and healthcare
Web Address: www.sequoiacap.com/

Siemens VentureCapital (SVC)
Focus: Information technology, telecommunications, medical engineering, and microelectronics
Web Address: www.siemens.com/svc/

The Shepherd Group
Focus: Communications, consumer products, Internet commerce and media, traditional media, niche manufacturing, software and technology
Web Address: www.tsgequity.com/

The Silicon Alley Breakfast Club
Focus: Internet start ups
Web Address: www.ibreakfast.com/faq.cfm

Holds free breakfast meetings for entrepreneurs and investors in New York, Washington, D.C., Boston, San Francisco, Santa Clara, and Los Angeles.

HOW TO APPLY:

To be considered as a business-proposal presenter at an upcoming breakfast, e-mail a 150-word pitch to pitch@ibreakfast.com. Six proposals are accepted, based on audience appeal. Businesses not chosen for presentations may still attend meetings and circulated business proposals.

TECHmarketing
91 Highland Rd.
Scarsdale, NY 10583

(914) 723-4464
Fax: (914) 472-5489

Sloan Ventures
Focus: Early-stage technology companies
Web Address: www.sloanenterprises.com

SOFTBANK Venture Capital
Focus: Internet companies
Web Address: www.sbvc.com/

SourceCapital InterNetwork
Focus: Fast-growth start ups nationwide
Web Address: www.sourcecapitalnet.com

Provides a private Web site where entrepreneurs can make electronic, multimedia presentations of their business plans to accredited angel investors. The network charges fees to presenters (see below) but doesn't take finder's fees or shares in the emerging company. Entrepreneurs can pay to have presentations stay online for six or 12 months, with updates as needed. Angels, verified to have made at least one significant investment in the last two years, scan the presentations and contact any companies they're interested in pursuing. The network provides advice on creating, scripting, and rehearsing presentations.

How to Apply:
E-mail an application (available at the site) and a text-version of the business plan.

Plans aren't screened by the network before they're posted. Text-only presentations are $1,200 and $1,400 for six-month and one-year postings, respectively. Presentations combining text, audio, and still photos are $1,445 and $1,645 per time period. Text and video presentations cost $1,945 or $2,145.

Southeastern Technology Fund
Focus: Early-stage companies in the Internet, information technology, and communications
Web Address: www.setfund.com/

Spectrum Equity Investors
Focus: Communications services, networking infrastructure, electronic commerce, and media industries
Web Address: www.spectrumequity.com

Techfarm
Focus: Information technology
Web Address: www.techfarm.com/

Start-Up University
Focus: Start-up companies nationwide
Web Address: www.startupuniversity.com/

A forum to introduce entrepreneurs to angel investors. Doesn't screen proposals or investors or charge fees. Entrepreneurs post company descriptions and capital needs on the Web site. Investors contact companies depending on interest.

HOW TO APPLY:

Submit electronic Investment Opportunity Profile.

wayne@StartUpUniversity.com
1390 Market St.
25th Floor, Suite 26
San Francisco, CA 94102
(800) 361-4109

Tech Coast Angels
Focus: Early-stage Southern California ventures
http://www.techcoastangels.org/

Looks for technology start-ups with business plan for national or international success. Introduces accredited investors to entrepreneurs. Investors offer capital and management expertise.

HOW TO APPLY:

Send a proposal and an executive summary or business plan as an e-mail attachment to proposal@Slocumb.com. Include the company name in the subject line.

Techxas Ventures
Focus: Computer hardware and software, communications and networking, systems integration, and information technology distribution
Web Address: www.techxas.com/

Telecommunications Development Fund
Focus: Small businesses in communications industry
Web Address: www.tdfund.com/

Telos Venture Partners
Focus: Software, the Internet, semiconductors, and communications
Web Address: www.telosvp.com/

TL Ventures
Focus: Early-stage technology ventures in the Internet, software, information technology services, communications, and life sciences
Web Address: www.tlventures.com/

Trans Cosmos USA
Focus: Internet new media, marketing services, e-commerce, and customer service applications
Web Address: www.trascosmos.com

Trident Capital
Focus: Internet, infrastructure management, outsourcing, transaction services, and information technology

Web Address: www.tridentcap.com

21st Century Internet Venture Partners
Focus: Early-stage e-commerce, enterprise systems, and electronic intermediaries
Web Address: www.21st-century.com/

US Venture Partners
Focus: The Internet, communications, software, semiconductors, medical, and consumer brands
Web Address: www.usvp.com/

Vanguard Venture Partners
Focus: Seed- and early-stage information technology and life sciences companies
Web Address: www.vanguardventures.com/

The VenCom Group, Inc.
Focus: The convergence of telecommunications, computing, consumer electronics, and content
Web Address: www.vencom.com

Venrock Associates
Focus: Information technology, healthcare, and life sciences
Web Address: www.venrock.com/

Venture Capital Access Online
Focus: International investor matching service
Web Address: www.vcaonline.com

Matching service for entrepreneurs and international investors. Start up managers post executive summaries for $30 per year.

HOW TO APPLY:

Send inquiries via the electronic form at the Web site.

The Venture Club of Louisville
Focus: Louisville, KY, ventures
Web Address: www.ventureclub-louisville. org/clubinfo.html

Founded in 1995, the not-for-profit club holds monthly meetings where entrepreneurs and angels can meet socially. Also, selected companies make a seven-minute presentation to introduce their business plans to investors.

HOW TO APPLY:

Contact the club for application to be considered for presenting at a future meeting. Club members pay annual dues of $250. Contact: Rebecca Craig at (502) 589-6868 for information.

The Venture Club of Louisville
310 West Liberty St., Ste. 505,
Louisville, KY 40202

The Venture Forum

Focus: Entrepreneurs in central Virginia
Web Address: www.ventureclub.com

Organizes the "Five Minute Forum," where young businesses present their plans at bimonthly luncheons. Each month, three people are given five minutes to tell us their plans. Open to any interest parties in the area. Annual dues for individuals is $100.

HOW TO APPLY:

To be considered as a presenter, send e-mail to forum@ventureclub.com, or call Bob Louthan at (804) 267-3216; fax (804) 272-0347.

Venture Investors Management LLC

Focus: Early Midwestern companies in a variety of industries
Web Address: www.ventureinvestors.com/

VentureList.com

Focus: Start ups needing $50,000 to $1.5 million
Web Address: www.venturelist.com

Manages an entrepreneurs' database of seed-level companies. Database is available accredited investors around the world. Investors contact entrepreneurs.

HOW TO APPLY:

E-mail a funding proposal (available at the site) and an executive summary to info@venturelist.com. Fees at press time for entrepreneurs were $100 to have proposals posted for three months.

Viridian Capital

Focus: Women-owned businesses or those who market to women
Web Address: www.viridiancapital.com

Targets emerging ventures with products or services for the Internet, software, telecommunications, life sciences, medical devices, healthcare services and bio-informatics.

HOW TO APPLY:

Send an executive summary or business plan to Christine Cordaro, for life sciences, healthcare, and medical-devices proposals; Willa Seldon, for Internet, telecommunications, and information technology ventures (willa@viridiancapital.com).

Viridian Capital

220 Montgomery St., Suite 946
San Francisco, CA 94104
(415) 391-8950
Fax: (415) 391-8937

Weiss, Peck & Greer Venture Partners

Focus: Early- and expansion-stage information technology and life sciences ventures

Web Address: www.wpgvp.com/

Wellspring Angel Fund
Focus: North American start ups in software, the Internet, e-business, and electronics
Web Address: www.wellspringfund.com

An organization of angel investors with business experience in high tech. Manages an angel-investment fund and provides business mentoring services. Affiliated with the Hexa Incubator LLC, an independent subsidiary. Helps recruit staff and cultivate follow-on funding sources.

HOW TO APPLY:
Send a business plan, including managers' resumes, to Julian Chan at jchan@ wellspringfund.com

Wolf Ventures
Focus: Business-to-business technology ventures in the Rocky Mountain area

Web Address: www.wolfventures.com/

Wye River Capital
Focus: Start ups in information technology and healthcare in Maryland, Washington, D.C., and Virginia.
Web Address: www.wyeriver.net

Invests private funds and co-invests with other angels, depending on the need.

HOW TO APPLY:
Send inquiries to

Kevin Quinn
7 King Charles Place
Annapolis, MD 21401
(410) 267-8811
Fax: (410) 267-8235
Email: kquinn@wyeriver.net

Zero Stage Capital
Focus: Information technology, software, communications, and healthcare
Web Address: www.zerostage.com

BUSINESS INCUBATORS: SAFE HAVENS FOR YOUNG COMPANIES

Like their down-on-the-farm namesakes, business incubators are hot. At no other time have incubators spawned more offspring than in 1999 and 2000, according to the National Business Incubation Association, a trade group that serves the industry. In fact, incubators are becoming the driving force for today's start ups that are looking to accomplish that all-important breakthrough step from cocktail-napkin idea to commercial business.

There are a handful of reasons why incubators are suddenly the rage for resource strained entrepreneurs. First, incubators have changed with the times to offer a new version of entrepreneur helper. Once almost exclusively non-profit endeavors, often run by the business department of a university, many of today's incubators are now commercial enterprises that exist to make money for their operators in addition to giving a boost to new companies. In ideal situations, both investors and entrepreneurs enjoy a profitable trade off with for-profit incubators. Growing companies get business expertise from the incubator's directors, not to mention the investment and professional contacts these people maintain. Many young also companies receive office space and essential but otherwise costly infrastructure items like PCs, copiers, fax machines, and furniture.

In return, incubators increasingly are taking an equity stake in a start up, so a significant holding in an early-stage company that goes on to strike gold can mean runaway profits for the incubator. The fledgling company gets goods and services without spending scarce dollars, while the host organization gets a piece of the company at the ground floor before other investors overly dilute the ownership. If the start up becomes an acquisition target or a successful public launch, the incubator reaps the profits of an early investor. Unfortunately, some for-profit incubators have gotten a bad rap in the last year from unscrupulous managers who sought large equity stakes but didn't deliver on business resource promises. When the relationship works, whether non-profit or for-profit, modern incubators are reaching out to entrepreneurs using the Internet to promote themselves and connect with business people.

Making it in New York

One of the oldest incubators, and the first tied to a university, is the Incubator Program at the Rensselaer Polytechnic Institute, in Troy, NY. Opened in 1980, the not-for-profit program focuses on helping technology companies gain a commercial foot hold, however, the organization's broad interpretation of technology means it considers far more than just computer and Web companies, according to Bela Musits, the program's director. "If you want to open a pizza company, we'll take a look at what you have to offer," he says. Companies don't have to be affiliated with the Institute, nor do they have to be run by students, alumni, or faculty. However, because of the close ties between the program and the Rensselaer community, incubator-backed companies have been split in even thirds among current or former students, faculty, and the general public. The companies include MapInfo, a creator of computer-based mapping software.

Start ups make a three- to four-year commitment to the incubation program. In return, they get tangible and intangible help. The program provides offices, conference rooms, telephone systems, Internet connections, and "all the other things they need but don't add value to the business," Musits says. He admits that this is standard incubator fare that in itself doesn't distinguish Rensselaer's program.

The unique piece is its intellectual resources, including the management advice of business people with multiple start ups on their resumes. Musits himself, as well as participating faculty and alumni, share their real-world experiences from creating one or more start ups. Entrepreneurs who have graduated from incubator also contribute advice. "There's a real sense of community here. Entrepreneurs get a lot of insight, knowledge, and wisdom. We also provide links to the campus and to the general community, including attorneys, accountants, and investors," Musits says.

At the beginning of 2000, 24 companies were part of the program, which offers a total of 10,000 square feet of business space. Relationships between the incubator and start-up managers usually begins with a business plan. Musits or another member of the Rensselaer program helps business people write or hone plans to create a focused business strategy and answer the financial questions that potential investors will eventually want answered. Among these big money questions are the two basic considerations essential to every business: How much money does the enterprise need and when does it need it? "We'll think through the financial aspects unique to each business," Musits explains. "If the company wants to go into injection-molded widgets, it will require a lot of initial capital—hundreds of thousands of dollars just to get started. Contrast that with an Internet business, where the capital requirements may initially be just a couple of computers and a couple of folks."

In a similar way, the specific funding sources Rensselaer helps cultivate for members of its incubator program depend on the unique requirements of each start up. "Sometimes, it depends on potential. Venture capitalists are interested in only certain types businesses, the ones with the potential to go public or be acquired," Musits explains. "Out of a hundred business plans I might see, only a small percent have the potential of going public. Entrepreneurs need to realize this. Venture capital funds get a lot of press, but if your business is regional or has the potential of making only $30 million in sales, it's probably not a business venture capitalists would be interested in."

In addition to not keeping an open mind about funding sources, first-time start-up managers often make the mistake of falling in love with the business idea or technology they're bringing to market, and forget to look at the company from an outside investor's point of view. "With the first company I started, I fell in love with the technology," Musits admits. "We had the best widget, but customers didn't care," he says, explaining that pricing, availability, and marketing prowess can also determine success and failure of a new product or service.

All the work of the incubator isn't confined to preparing the start-up for it's financial coming out party. Mustis and his staff also coach entrepreneurs on how to evaluate and negotiate funding deals. "We want investors who bring more than money to the table," he says. "If we just wanted money, we could go to a bank. On the other hand, if we're going after a venture capitalist or an angel, we find out what expertise can they bring to the start up? What business connections, including connections to distribution channels, do they have? What potential [acquisition] suitors do they know? We have to look investors in the eye and be very comfortable with them."

Musits also helps jazzed up entrepreneurs learn what can be the hardest business lesson of all: Just because he or she creates a business, the entrepreneur may not be the best person to run it. "Most people who put a significant amount of capital in a business will want to have a significant influence on the business. If you're a person who wants to start a business and you want a significant amount of outside money, you're probably not going to be the one driving the bus. Investors will insist on bringing in someone to broaden out the team," Musits says.

GATEWAY TO THE INTERNET

Gateway Alliance II, a St. Paul, MN, incubator founded in 1996, began as a business nurturer for medical industry start ups. Reacting to the omnipresent Internet, Gateway recently adopted more of a technology focus and is now backing two Web-based businesses. The business backing Gateway provides young companies is clear: it ranges from helping to evaluate an entrepreneur's budding commercial idea, to working with founders to develop a corporate structure that can help promising ideas grow, pumping up the young business with financial and talent resources to fuel growth, and finally to lay the groundwork for an IPO. Most of the companies Gateway considers to bring into its fold emerge from word-of-mouth recommendations from business people in and around St. Paul. "We get two to three ideas a month," says Arnold Angeloni, Gateway president. "We're not looking for successful private companies; we seek companies that have a high probability going public or being acquired within two to five years."

In most cases, entrepreneurs need to find a business-community partner to spread the word about the start up to local business people, Angeloni says. Partners might include incubators, like Gateway, or accountants, lawyers, or angels. Besides opening the right investment doors, a seasoned partner can help entrepreneurs avoid scam artists who exist to prey on the inexperience and exuberance of company founders. One example is a breed of "investment advisors" who ask for retainers, sometimes amounting to $5,000 or more, before pitching a start up to the advisor's so-called connections. In one example, an advisor who had only phantom connections, asked an entrepreneur associated with Gateway for upfront money. "This 'advisor' made a living at getting $5000 retainers," Angeloni says. "If we hadn't been sitting in on the call, one of the founders would have signed the check. Entrepreneurs are desperate for money, but they have to make sure to check references."

When a company first visits Gateway, the start up's managers usually come armed with a business plan—often created with the help of a commercial, fill-in-the-blanks software program. Angeloni says the quality of these plans usually rate a "three" on a scale of ten. The biggest misconception he sees in inexperienced entrepreneurs is the belief that a good idea is incentive enough for investors to "throw money at the company." In reality, wily investors are much more demanding, and often insist on seeing a prototype of a new product before they sign any checks.

The specific steps of the incubation process can include seed capital, hands-on help in writing business plans, recruiting members of an experienced management team, and tracking down deep-pocket investors. "We get entrepreneurs in front of venture capitalists and angels," says Angeloni. "We typically serve on [the start up's] board until it's sold or there's an IPO." Cash-strapped start ups don't pay for these services, they reimburse Gateway with equity: typically 15 to 30 percent of the founders stock.

Beneficiaries of Gateway's business expertise include the 1997 start up Vascular Solutions, which is due to receive Federal Drug Administration (FDA) approval for a new device that seals the femoral artery of angioplasty patients. The FDA go-ahead is the last hurdle Vascular Solutions faces before being able to go public. "In the U.S., not one medical device company has gone public [in 1999]. When Vascular goes public, it will be the first medical device company formed after 1994 to do so," Angeloni says. "A lot of money just got pulled away because medical device companies have risk. The thing that hurts them is they have to wait three or four years for the FDA approval process. Instead, investors looked at Internet start ups and realized they could get their money back in a year."

A second company, InnerPulse Inc., is another medical device company that's also begun the IPO process. Outside the medical industry, Gateway is backing Rave Sports, creator of a trampoline designed for use in water. Rave is in an encouraging growth stage, with sales approaching $10 million. Gateway helped Vascular Solutions raise a total of $2.25 million in early funding through retail brokers, angel investors, and individuals.

The new millennium could mean a time of new investment money flowing in for companies, like medical device designers, that aren't pure Internet plays. "Reality is coming back to the Internet technology marketplace. The path to profitability is becoming the flag that everyone is waving. For the Internet companies, the days of running ads on the Super Bowl are gone. That era wasn't healthy for anyone. There are billions of dollars available from the venture market. The money is going to find places to go. Now that market become more rational, it has opened up attention to medical devices," according to Angeloni.

BUSINESS INCUBATOR DIRECTORY

The following is a list of many of the for-profit and non-profit incubators operating today in the United States. Incubators marked with a icon are those that use the Web to make it easy for entrepreneurs to electronically submit business ideas, executive summaries, or business plans.

Acacia Research Corp.

Focus: Internet, life sciences, communications, media, entertainment, network infrastructure and software
Web Address: www.acaciaresearch.com

Offers seed capital and mentoring, office space, and business contacts. Technology staff can help start ups develop and test commercial Web sites. Acacia staff sit on boards of start ups to provide Internet and high-tech industry expertise. Acacia helps incubated companies find growth financing and executive staff. May remain in mentoring role after a start up leaves the incubator or completes an IPO.

HOW TO APPLY:

E-mail an executive summary to great-ideas@acaciaresearch.com. Include an "elevator pitch," concise market analysis, description of the business opportunity, and revenue projections.

The Advanced Technology Development Center

Focus: Georgia technology companies in telecommunications, digital media, software, Internet applications, biotechnology, robotics, electronics, environmental applications, manufacturing, and materials processing.
Web Address: http://www.atdc.org/

Opened in 1980 at the Georgia Institute of Technology, the incubator currently backs 40 start ups. Offers office space, light manufacturing facilities, and laboratories. Helps entrepreneurs focus business strategies, develop financing and business networks, and scope out partnering opportunities. Maintains close connections with state research universities.

HOW TO APPLY:

Demonstrate that the business idea involves an advanced technology with a long-term market advantage, high growth potential, backing by a strong managerial team, and the potential to attract outside financing. Send proposals to:

The Advanced Technology Development Center
430 10th St., NW
Suite N-116
Atlanta, GA 30318
(404) 894-3575
Fax: (404) 894-4545
info@atdc.org

or

The Advanced Technology Development Center
250 14th St., NW
4th Floor

Atlanta, GA 30318
(404) 894-5708
Fax: (404) 894-5712

or

The Advanced Technology Development Center
151 Osigian Blvd.
Warner Robins, GA 31088
(912) 953-3155
Fax: (912) 953-3169

Aquarium Ventures
Focus: High-tech start ups new Yale University
Web Address: www.aquariumventures.com/

Targets entrepreneurs at Yale University and in outlying New Haven, CT. Provides funding, offices, computers and office equipment, professional services such as legal and accounting expertise, and technical and business mentoring. Also helps attract growth funding and management candidates. Takes an equity stake in the start up. Does not have to see a full business plan. It can be a two- or three-page plan, a one-page executive summary, or just an informal letter describing your idea.

HOW TO APPLY:

Send a description of the business idea (may be in the form of a short letter, an executive summary, or a complete business plan) to plans@aquariumventures.com.

Written ideas may also be delivered in person at:

Aquarium Ventures, L.L.C.
1221 Chapel St.
New Haven, CT 06511
(203) 782-0065
Fax: (203) 782-5987

or mailed to:

Aquarium Ventures, L.L.C.
P.O. Box 209025
New Haven, CT 06520

Arizona Technology Incubator
Focus: Arizona technology start ups
Web Address: www.accessarizona.com

A non-profit organization affiliate with Arizona State University that promotes high-tech start ups in the state. Operates 23,000 sq. ft. of office space in Scottsdale, AZ. Offers economical office space, support services, as well as promotional, financial, and managerial expertise. Start ups typically use the incubator for two to three years.

HOW TO APPLY:

Looks for technology-based, Arizona companies with a unique product or manufacturing process. Shuns wholesalers and consulting businesses. Send a proposal that addresses the following: the significance and competitive advantage of the technology, market growth potential including the projected size of the market in the company's fifth year, potential to create jobs in the state, research and development needs, and the management team's expertise. Note: incubator companies are required to attend regular management and finance meetings and to provide monthly or quarterly financial reports.

Arizona Technology Incubator

1435 N. Hayden Road
Scottsdale, AZ 85257
(480) 990-0400
Fax: (480) 970-6355
E-mail: ati@getnet.com

Astra Ventures

Focus: Start-up and early-stage Internet and high technology companies.
Web Address: www.astraventures.com/

Founded in 1998, provides business planning, marketing, and product development. Attracts growth funds through a network of investors. Helps start ups hone business strategies, write business plans, and evaluate opportunities for mergers, acquisitions, and alliances. Recruits executives for young companies.

How to Apply:

Send proposals to:

Astra Ventures LLC

140 West 57th St.
Suite 8D
New York, NY 10019
(212) 245-4447
Fax: (212) 245-4448
info@astraventures.com

The Austin Technology Incubator

Focus: Technology-based start ups with high growth potential
Web Address: www.ic2-ati.org/

This non-profit incubator provides business strategy consulting, financial contacts, promotional services, business mentoring, and office facilities. Although affiliated with the University of Texas, the organization doesn't limit its involvement only to local companies. Will consider proposals from U.S. and international businesses.

ATI has helped launch 56 companies. Accepts companies for on-site or off-site incubation. Maintains contacts with a host of venture capital and angel investors, including the IC2 Seed Fund, part of the IC2 Institute of The University of Texas at Austin.

How to Apply:

Send a business plan that details the underlying technological uniqueness of the business's product or service. Targets software, computer or peripheral hardware, telecommunications equipment, Internet or Web-based applications, multimedia, biotechnology, and energy-related ventures. Also looks for managerial expertise, existing financial resources to fund the company for six months, the ability to market the product or service within 18 months, and a revenue potential of $100 million within seven years.

Mail or e-mail full business plan or executive summary to prospects@ati.utexas.

edu. Looks for proof that the management team has fully considered the financial and competitive challenges of the business. Final selection rests on the success of presentations to ATI committees

Austin Technology Incubator
3925 West Braker Lane
Austin, TX 78759
(512) 305-0026
(512) 305-0019
Fax: (512) 305-0009

Bainlab
Focus: Seed and first stage investments in business-to-business, business-to-consumer, network infrastructure, and e-services companies
Web Address: www.bainlab.com/

Cultivates early-stage companies to bring them to their first venture capital financing round. Offers seed-round financing, office space and equipment, business mentoring, business-plan and technology development, staff recruiting, and support in raising growth capital. Looks for business ideas with the potential to tap a large market and to fundamentally improve the efficiency of industry supply chains.

HOW TO APPLY:

E-mail proposals to info@bainlab.com. Company will confirm receipt within a working day and respond to proposal within two weeks. Send a full business plan

or an executive summary with backgrounders on the management team, a competitive analysis, market potential, and financial projections.

Contact Alan Colberg or Jim McCurry

Bain & Company Inc.
The Monarch Plaza
Suite 1200
3424 Peachtree Rd., NE
Atlanta, GA 30326
(404) 869-2727
Fax: (404) 869-2222

Contact: Robert Bechek, John Blasberg

Bain & Company, Inc.
Two Copley Place
Boston, MA 02116
(617) 572-2000
Fax: (617) 572-2427

The Barksdale Group
Focus: Early-stage e-commerce, Internet infrastructure, application services, networking equipment, wireless telecommunications, and software ventures
Web Address: www.barksdalegroup.com

Early round investments range from less than $2 million to several million dollars, with multiple round contributions up to $20 million. Looks for successful entrepreneurial management and unique business ideas.

HOW TO APPLY:

E-mail proposals to ideas@barksdalegroup.com. Does not read hard copies or faxes or accept pitches via the phone. Proposals may be capsule summaries of the business, an executive summary, or a financial projection for the business.

The Barksdale Group
2730 Sand Hill Road
Menlo Park, CA 94025
(650) 234-5200
Fax: (650) 234-5201

Batavia Industrial Center
Focus: Western New York state start ups
Web Address: www.iinc.com/mancusogroup/

A pioneering incubator run by Mancuso Real Estate & Management Group, the Batavia Industrial Center helps develop small industry and other businesses in the upstate New York region. Provides 850,000 sq. ft. of business facilities and support, including secretarial services, business equipment, warehouse space and equipment, and shipping and receiving support.

HOW TO APPLY:

Send proposals to:

Batavia Industrial Center
56 Harvester Ave.
Batavia, NY 14020
(716) 343-2800
Fax: (716) 343-7096
E-mail: mancuso@iinc.com

BizVestors
Focus: Internet start ups
Web Address: www.bizvestors.com/

Offers small capital investments, business advice, and physical resources for young Web-based businesses.

HOW TO APPLY:

Send proposals to:

BizVestors Investment Partners, Inc.
915 Woodhill Court
Hopkins, MN 55343
(612) 935-3615
Fax: (612) 933-6944
E-mail: info@bizvestors.com

BLG Ventures
Focus: Incubator for minority-owned technology businesses in the United States
Web Address: www.blgventures.com/

Targets minority-owned technology companies for financial, management, and operations development. Looks for start ups that can rapidly become ready for an IPO, with the potential to become market leaders. Provides business consulting and investment capital. Consulting help includes developing the start up's financial and business models by honing competitive analyses and product positioning. BLG can also help entrepreneurs in the valuation of their companies, as well as introduce business managers to a network of possible business associates and customers. Other services include executive recruitment and IT consulting.

HOW TO APPLY:

Demonstrate that the business is capable of securing large market share in a growing market. Show how the talent and experience of the managers dovetail with the business strategy. The business plan should outline aggressive an aggressive growth strategy, with milestones for reaching market dominance and profitability within three years.

Send a proposal of four pages or less, with details about the business, the market, funding, and an analysis of competitors to submissions@blgventures.com.

BLG Ventures, Inc.
104 West 27th St.
6th Floor
New York, NY 10001
(212) 462-4770
Fax: (212) 462-4771
info@blgventures.com

Bold New World
Focus: Internet start ups
Web Address: www.boldnewworld.com/2000/

A spin-off of GeoCities, the Hollywood, CA, incubator targets large undeveloped markets and companies with a unique market position. Manages $30 million for new-company investments. Offers consulting in product/service design, marketing strategies, and technologies.

HOW TO APPLY:

Submit proposals using electronic form at the Web site.

Bold New World
7655 Sunset Blvd.
Los Angeles, CA 90046-2725
(323) 845-9111
Fax: (323) 845-9123
E-mail: info@bnw.com

Boulder Technology Incubator
Focus: Colorado technology start ups
Web Address: www.bouldertechincubator.org/

Looks for new companies with a unique technology niche that can sustain competitive threats through patents. Also values high growth potential without high risk and ventures that have attracted necessary start-up capital.

HOW TO APPLY:

Send proposals to:

Boulder Technology Incubator
Marine Street Science Building
3215 Marine Street
Boulder, CO 80303
(303) 492-8585
Fax: (303) 735-4499

or

Boulder Technology Incubator
1821 Lefthand Circle, Suite B
Longmont, CO 80501
(303) 678-8000
Fax: (303) 678-8505

The Business Incubation Group Inc.
Focus: Internet start-ups
Web Address: www.bizincu.com/

Provides business and operations consulting for start ups. Helps entrepreneurs develop a product/service concept, launch the company, and nurture its growth. Expects start ups to be past the incubation stage within two years. However, the Group maintains ties to member companies after incubation and continues to participate on a company's board throughout its development. Offers legal, financial, research and development, marketing, and communications expertise. Introduces young companies to angel investors. Leases office space and business equipment at discounted rates. Looks to partner with up to five new ventures in the coming year.

HOW TO APPLY:
Complete electronic form at the Web site.

The Business Incubation Group Executive Offices
99 Hudson St.
Suite 12R

New York, NY 10013
(212) 966-2500
Fax: (212) 219-8075
E-mail: info@bizincu.com

Cambridge Incubator
Focus: Business-to-business e-commerce companies
Web Address: www.cambridgeincubator.com/

Founded in 1999, provides seed funding, physical space, and introductions to business and investment sources. Requires start ups to be located at the incubator site, which is near the Massachusetts Institute of Technology. Can house up to 20 companies.

Targets emerging Internet companies. Funding typically ranges from $250,000 to $1 million.

HOW TO APPLY:
Demonstrate proprietary market position, managerial experience, high competitive barriers to entry, and potential for market dominance. Send proposals using electronic form at the Web site.

Cambridge Incubator
1 Broadway
14th Floor
Cambridge, MA 02142
(617) 758-4100
Fax: (617) 758-4101
E-mail: info@cambridgeincubator.com

Campsix

Focus: Business-to-business Internet start ups

Web Address: www.campsix.com/

Offers seed funding, physical space, and business consulting for Silicon Valley companies. Maintains a network with 40 area partners for marketing, business development, engineering, and other resources.

HOW TO APPLY:

Send business plan using the electronic form at the Web site.

Capstone Ventures

Focus: Business-to-business e-commerce and healthcare

Web Address: www.capstonevc.com/

Initiates or leads investments in start ups headquartered in the U.S. Takes a board seat. Targets start ups that use existing technologies in new markets. Investments range from $1 to $2 million in the initial round, up to $5 million total.

HOW TO APPLY:

Use electronic form at the Web site or send proposals to

Capstone Ventures
3000 Sand Hill Road
Building 1, Suite 290

Menlo Park, CA 94025
(650) 854-2523
Fax: (650) 854-9010
E-mail: gfischer@capstonevc.com, bsantry@capstonevc.com, or capen@capstonevc.com

ColumbusNewport LLC

Focus: Growth-stage and start-up e-commerce entrepreneurs

Web Address: www.columbusnewport.com/

Provides merchant banking and business services for start ups. Resources include seed funding, business loans, help with possible mergers or acquisitions, accounting and financial support services, human resource consulting and executive recruitment, and ties to legal expertise. In-house staff can help business people commercialize a new product or service and develop marketing plans for domestic and foreign campaigns.

HOW TO APPLY:

Send a business plan or executive summary. Address the size and characteristics of the target market, the business strategy, the company's product or service, the competition, and financial projections. E-mail the proposals to: ecplans@columbusnewport.com

ColumbusNewport LLC
2111 Wilson Blvd.
Suite 1200

Arlington, VA 22201
(703) 351-6620
Fax: (703) 351-6634

or

ColumbusNewport LLC
19200 Von Karman Ave.
Suite 500
Irvine, CA 92612
(949) 851-1700
Fax: (949) 851-1790

Cube8.com
Focus: Internet start ups
Web Address: www.cube8.com/

Invests in and incubates start up Internet companies. Offers investment capital and business mentoring. The latter includes business strategy development, marketing, advertising, product/service development, and financial growth. Especially interested in companies that sell Internet develop and support services, business-to-business and business-to-consumer e-commerce applications, and Web content providers. Will guide expansion efforts of U.S. companies into Europe.

HOW TO APPLY:
Send proposals to

Cube8.com
375 Coleridge Ave.
Palo Alto CA, 94301
E-mail: keesup@cube8.com

DigitalVentures
Focus: Business-to-business Internet applications

Web Address: www.digitalventures.com/

An outgrowth of a venture capital fund, Digital Ventures funds seed-stage businesses and guides them with the expertise of its executive staff. Core services range from developing business strategies to helping forge business partnerships. Helps in executive recruiting and finding follow on funding. Also offers legal, promotional, and financial resources.

HOW TO APPLY:
Send proposals via e-mail (preferred) to submit@digitalventures.com. Candidates can also send information about their businesses using the electronic form on the Web site or by regular mail to:

DigitalVentures
Attention: Investment Consideration
50 California St.
8th Floor
San Francisco, CA 94111
(415) 354-6200

DotCom Incubator
Focus: Internet companies
Web Address: www.conxion.com/promo/incubator/Incubator.asp

A joint venture among technology and banking companies Conxion, IBM, Silicon Valley Bank, Garage.com, Mercury Interactive, and Servicesoft Technologies. Offers Web site hosting and data center services free of charge during incubation period. Helps cultivate funding and develop products or services to the proof of concept stage.

HOW TO APPLY:

Complete electronic form at the Web site.

.COM! Ventures

Focus: Atlanta-area developers of Internet applications
Web Address: www.dotcomventuresatl. com/aboutus.htm

Charges a mix of fees and an equity stake in return for consulting on strategic business development, funding, and commercialization. Incubator resources provide offices, high-speed communications, and support staff. Will help start ups write business plans, select technologies, and recruit executives. Start ups aren't required to be housed physically within the incubator.

HOW TO APPLY:

Send ideas or full business plans to webmaster@dotcomventuresatl.com

or to

.COM! Ventures

1103 Riverbend Club Drive
Atlanta, GA 30339-2811
(770) 612-9190

Doublespace

Focus: U.S. and European Internet companies

Web Address: www.doublespace.com/

Founded in 1979, incubates domestic and European companies. Provides seed funding and services for creating business prototypes, marketing and branding programs, as well as contacts with international markets. Offers its branded Internet Hotbed services, a package of strategic and technology resources for quickly growing Internet companies.

HOW TO APPLY:

Complete a series of electronic forms at the Web site. Reports interest in a proposal within a week

Doublespace

601 West 26th Street
14th Floor
New York, NY 10001
(212) 366-1919
Fax: (212) 366-4645

duoDesign

Focus: Electronic businesses based in the Midwest
Web Address: http://www.duodesign.com/ index.cfm

Provides as much as $450,000 in capital and business services over six months. Takes a minority stake in the start up company. Services include introductions to angles and venture-capital fund managers. Provides in-house expertise for marketing, communications, software development, technology selection, and business strategy development. Manages offices, conference rooms, office equipment, and support facilities for as many as 25 start ups.

HOW TO APPLY:

Send a business plan via the electronic form at the Web site.

duoDesign
1007 Church Street
Suite 510
Evanston, IL 60201
(847) 491-3000
Fax: (847) 491-3100
E-mail: info@duodesign.com

EC²
Focus: New media and communications
Web Address: www.ec2.edu/

Affiliated with the University of Southern California, the EC² Occupant program gives entrepreneurs offices, multimedia production facilities, technology services, and introductions to other new media companies. Production resources are open to members 24 hours a day, every day of the week.

Technical services include Web and DNS hosting, an intranet, non-linear video editing, 3D computer animation hardware and software, as well as audio recording and editing capabilities.

Start ups can remain in the incubator for three years or less and are subject to annual development reviews. The incuba-

tor generally takes a share of 5 percent or less in each new company.

HOW TO APPLY:

Candidates are chosen by the strength of the business concept, commercial potential, the quality of the business plan, managerial talent and experience, and potential synergy with USC. Send business plans to Jon Goodman, Executive Director, at *jgoodman@ec2.edu*

EC² Incubator Project
746 West Adams Blvd.
Los Angeles, CA 90089-7727
(213) 743-2344
Fax: (213) 746-1226
E-mail: info@ec2.edu

Ecolony
Focus: Business-to-business e-commerce applications and services, as well as Internet infrastructure technologies
Web Address: http://www.ecolony.com/

Offers financial, infrastructure, technology, business strategy, and partnership consulting and services. A joint venture of venture capital and technology services companies. Helps early-stage companies develop executive teams and hone business plans. Facilities include offices and equipment plus phone and Internet infrastructure. In-house expertise covers managerial, staffing, technology, financial, and promotional disciplines. Targets young businesses with strong managers.

HOW TO APPLY:

Submit an executive summary to ideas@eColony.com.

eCompanies
Focus: Web-based services
Web Address: www.ecompanies.com/

Founded in 1999 by Sky Dayton and Jake Winebaum, veterans of Internet ventures EarthLink and Disney.com, respectively. Manages a network of business- and consumer-based Internet associates. Operates a venture fund and an incubator that accelerates business, finance, executive recruiting, technology, and marketing development. The incubator provides executives who act in short-term management roles in start ups. May move a start up from concept stage to commercialization in six months or less. Incubator graduates are considered for first-rounding funding by the eCompanies venture capital division. Considers internally created ideas and those developed externally.

HOW TO APPLY:

Forward business plan using the Web site's electronic form.

efinanceworks
Focus: Web financial companies
Web Address: www.efinanceworks.com/

An incubator devoted to creating electronic financial services companies. Offers business consulting, funding, and infrastructure.

HOW TO APPLY:

Introduce your idea using the electronic form on the Web site.

Efinanceworks
601 West 26th St.
8th floor
New York, NY 10001
(646) 486-9000
Fax: (646) 486-9090
E-mail: info@efinanceworks.com

eHatchery
Focus: Internet start ups
Web Address: www.ehatchery.com/

An Atlanta-based incubator established in 1999. Invests capital, provides business consulting, and becomes involved with start up management. Helps companies address marketing, technology, human resources, and legal issues. Takes an equity stake in the start up, but not a controlling interest.

HOW TO APPLY:

Considers proposals sent online via the Web site's submission form. Note: Does not consider business plans submitted through regular mail, e-mail, or fax.

EHatchery
621 North Avenue, NE
Suite C100
Atlanta, GA 30308
(404) 487-1200
Fax: (404) 487-1201

eIncubator Inc.
Focus: Emerging technology businesses developing information technology, software, e-commerce, Web-based services, networking, hardware, telecommunications, and wireless applications
Web Address: www.eincubator.net/

A for-profit incubator that helps companies target business ideas and write a comprehensive business plan that addresses the target market. The incubator's staff also participates in building a managerial team and constructing a viable financial model. Takes an equity stake in start ups. Other resources include early-stage funding and networking with appropriate business and professional contacts.

The Web site publishes advice on incorporating businesses, writing plans, and choosing professional services.

HOW TO APPLY:

Looks for a clearly defined target market and plan to exploit that market. Candidates should have a well-developed summary or business plan that outlines the capabilities of the founders, revenue projections, and the uniqueness of the company's technology. Begin the application process by completing the Web-based admission form. Reports on interest within 10 business days.

eIncubator Inc.
6066 Leesburg Pike
Suite 500
Falls Church, VA 22041
(703) 845-8500
Fax: (703) 845-8454
E-mail: info@eincubator.net

GasPedal Ventures
Focus: East Coast start ups from New York to Washington D.C. Considers Internet proposals or non-technology venture with a unique marketing, content, or strategic business idea
Web Address: www.gaspedal.net

Opens Internet entrepreneurs up to its network of business and financial contacts. In-house staff assists in managerial decisions. Helps find funding sources, but doesn't make capital investments. Takes an equity stake in a start up.

Each incubator participant is assigned a staff member who cultivates sources for potential funding relationships, partnerships, and business alliances. Other staff members spend more than three months with the start up to help it with office, operational, and technical needs. Ongoing marketing, human resources, and financial support remains available during the incubation process.

HOW TO APPLY:

Forward a business plan or executive summary and managers' biographies to Andy Sernovitz, president, at andy@gaspedal.net. Encourages "cocktail-napkin" ideas.

GasPedal Ventures
461 Park Ave. S.
12th Floor
New York, NY 10016
(212) 447-5700
Fax: (212) 202-4105
E-mail: info@gaspedal.net

Ground Floor Ventures
Focus: Women-owned software and e-business ventures based in Hoboken, NJ
Web Address: www.groundfloorventures. com/

Targets software and Internet companies where a woman owns a significant stake in the business, those that were founded by a woman, or those that are commercializing an idea created by a woman. In addition to influential involvement by a woman, candidate companies need to offer a unique business niche in a market with $100 million or more in sales. The business should also have a sustainable competitive advantage from a proprietary technology or intellectual property.

Will invest seed funds. Strategic partners provides office space and technology, operations, and business mentoring. Depending on the start up's condition, the incubator pays for the support services outright or subsidizes the costs.

HOW TO APPLY:

E-mail an executive summary in Microsoft Word format (note: the organization doesn't read any other word processing format) to netimken@groundfloorventures. com.

Ground Floor Ventures
720 Monroe Street
Suite E-209
Hoboken, NJ 07030
(201) 420-4446
Fax: (201) 420-9176
E-mail: info@groundfloorventures.com

Hampton Roads Technology Incubator
Focus: Hampton (VA) area technology companies, including those developing remote sensing instruments, distance learning software, wind tunnel instrumentation, non-destructive evaluation techniques, satellite design and analysis tools, and Web/virtual reality related applications
Web Address: www.hr-incubator.org/

Targets companies bringing to market technologies create at NASA's Langley Research Center, local universities, and other research labs in the Hampton, VA, area. Considers both new companies and spin-offs of established firms. In addition to the resources of the Langley Center, incubator companies have access to technical and business expertise from Hampton University, The College of William & Mary, Old Dominion University, Virginia's Center for Innovative Technology, and other nearby institutions.

The incubator also offers small capital investments to its members. Incubation periods typically are three years. Fees range from $5,000 for start ups to $10,000 to established companies developing a new product.

How to Apply:

Complete the electronic screening form at http://www.hr-incubator.org/form.html.

Hampton Roads Technology Incubator
24 Research Drive
Hampton, VA 23666
Phone: (757) 865-2141
Fax: (757) 865-0298
martinka@hrtc.org

HatchBox

Focus: Internet and e-business ventures
Web Address: www.hatchbox.com/

Helps start ups develop their business strategy and revenue projections. Creates competitive analyses and outlines capital needs. Assists in making presentations to investors. In-house Internet expertise covers on-line branding and content. The incubator also conducts beta testing of new Web sites and make changes to content and usability based on test results.

How to Apply:

Submit plan electronically at the Web site.

HatchBox
395 Springside Drive
Fairlawn, Ohio 44333
(330) 665-1716
Fax: (330) 665-1585

Hi-Tech Partners Group

Focus: Technology companies, including those commercializing Internet, e-commerce, Web hardware and software, telecommunications, and software applications
Web Address: www.hitechpartners.com/who/index.asp

A Georgia-based incubator managed by a group of former technology CEOs, the Group provides guidance to start-ups by taking board seats and participating in management decisions. Makes introductions to outside venture capital and angel investors, as well as potential business partners. Each of the CEOs also is an accredited investor and consider seed funding for participating startups.

How to Apply:

Typically accepts only those start-ups that have been referred by a known investor or business associate. Also screens candidates for business experience and ability to attract initial funding. To be considered, complete the questionnaire at: http://www.hitechpartners.com/questionnaire/forms.asp

HotBank

Focus: Technology start ups funded by the venture capital arm of SoftBank.
Web Address: www.sbvc.com/

Supports early-stage businesses with recruiting, legal, accounting, human resource, and information technology services. Offers links to other entrepreneurs, industry exectutives and world-wide companies under the SoftBank corporate umbrella. Provides mentors with experience in founding and growing technology companies.

How to Apply:

Send proposals to

SOFTBANK Venture Capital

200 West Evelyn Ave.
Suite 200
Mountain View, CA 94043
(650) 962-2000

HP Garage

Focus: Start-ups focused on the Internet, application services provider companies, and electronic trading communities

Web Address: e-services.hp.com/start up/garage/

Contributes in building, operating, promoting, and funding new companies. Provides as much as $2 million in financing for business equipment, including computer hardware and software and data storage and processing resources from Hewlett-Packard. The financing program waives payments for half a year and doesn't require any down payments. The incubator also helps develop business ideas, built the IT infrastructure, and launch pilot products.

Looks for new ventures with a viable business plan and financial projections. Also requires companies to have a stake of at least $250,000 in seed funding already committed.

The Garage program also offers ten scholarships totaling worth more than $1.5 million for ventures creating an Internet-based product or service. The scholarships include computer equipment as well as integration and installation services. Apply for scholarships at www.hp.com/go/escholarship.

How to Apply:

To be considered for the incubator program, begin by completing the electronic form at: http://e-services.hp.com/start up/garage/contact.html

International Commerce Exchange Systems, Inc.

Focus: Internet companies and traditional businesses starting Web subsidiaries
Web Address: www.icesventures.com/

Established in 1995, the Internet incubator can accommodate two dozen-businesses. Provides venture funding and expertise in new media business development. Advises companies from the seed stage through an acquisition or IPO.

Provides managerial advice, links to funding sources, and executive recruitment activities. Can also assist start-ups in building Web sites and getting answers to legal and accounting questions. Operates two physical locations in the Silicon Alley section of New York City for new ventures needing office space and infrastructure. Can assist international endeavors through its overseas offices.

How to Apply:

E-mail proposals to Jacob Gold, Executive Vice President, at jacobg@icesinc.com.

ICES Inc.
18 West 18th Street
New York, NY 10011
(212) 981-3605

idealab!
Focus: Internet start-ups
Web Address: www.idealab.com/

Established in 1996, the incubator currently assists 50 new companies. Offers office space, communications networks, business consulting, IT development, pro-

motional services, and legal advice. Also can aid start-ups in brand building strategies.

How to Apply:

At press time the incubator was not accepting new applicants.

idealab!
130 West Union St.
Pasadena, CA 91103
(626) 585-6900
Fax: (626) 535-2701

iHatch.com LLC
Focus: Internet companies based in Central Florida
Web Address: www.ihatch.com/

Targets e-commerce, communications, software, information services, application services and electronic infrastructure businesses. Offers a virtual (no physical space) incubator and investment capital. Staff includes professionals experienced in Internet start ups, venture and angel funding, and IT. Helps in building teams, recruiting talent, branding and marketing strategies, and locating follow on financing.

Investments usually range from $250,000 to $1 million for seed rounds. Will consider select later stage and mezzanine financing opportunities.

Seeks start ups with experienced entrepreneurs and businesses with the potential to reach $100 million or more in value within five years. To submit a Business Plan by e-mail: bizplan@ihatch.com

HOW TO APPLY:

Send proposals to:

iHatch.com, LLC
SunTrust Center
Suite 1850
200 S. Orange Ave.
Orlando, FL 32801

I-Group HotBank New England
Focus: Web business-to-business, wireless communications, and Internet infrastructure companies
Web Address: www.i-group.com/

An incubator for Internet start ups in New England. SoftBank Corp., a technology and media company, is a partner. Provides business strategy advice, introductions to potential customers, access to initial customers, and management recruiting. Also offers capital investments and connections to venture capitalists and angel investors. Investments typically range from $500,000 to $2 million.

Through its SoftBank affiliation, I-Group allows start ups to network with other entrepreneurs, as well as Fortune 500 corporations and executives from a variety of industries.

HOW TO APPLY:

E-mail business plans to Chad Jackson, director of business development, at chad@i-group.com.

I-Group HotBank NE
355 Commonwealth Ave.
Boston, MA 02115
(617) 638-3000

i-Hatch Ventures
Focus: E-commerce, new media content, Web-enabling technology, network infrastructure, and Internet services
Web Address: http://www.i-hatch.com/

Founded in 1999, offers financial support and business mentoring to Internet start ups in the NorthEast. Also works with existing Internet businesses to expand into Europe or to create spinoff ventures. Consulting services include introducing start up managers to executives at established Internet companies.

HOW TO APPLY:

E-mail an executive summary and biographies of managers to plans@i-hatch.com.

i-Hatch Ventures LLC
599 Broadway
11th floor
New York, NY 10012
(212) 966-1094
Fax: (212) 208-2576

i-nterpriseZONE
Focus: E-commerce and telecommunications ventures, as well as start ups with a

plan to use Louisville, KY's, United Parcel Service Next Day Air Hub
Web Address: www.i-nterprisezone.com/

Aids start ups in finding venture capital funds to build information-technology (IT) infrastructure and in finding angel investors to fund company growth. Also provides consulting in financial, accounting, and recapitalization initiatives. Incubator resources include such "back office" computer services as Internet connections, financial software and network firewalls. Physical space consists of offices, conference rooms, cubicles, and an administrative center. The incubator also accepts "virtual" residents who aren't located in the Louisville area, but still have access to the mentoring services.

Incubator residents pay for services with equity or with royalty agreements.

How to Apply:

Send proposals to Stephen Zarick, CEO and founder, at: szarick@i-nterprisezone.com.

The i-nterpriseZONE
PO Box 6386
Louisville, KY 40206
(502) 899-3227

Incubator, LP
Focus: Internet start ups in the Berkeley, CA, area
Web Address: www.incubator-inc.com/

Targets entrepreneurs with ties to the University of California-Berkeley or those willing to locate in Berkeley. Initiates relationships with venture capitalists, university faculty, and business people experienced in managing technology start ups. Business associates include executives with Inktomi, RentNet, VR1, and Cybergold. Helps incubator members develop a focused business strategy and recruit managerial talent.

Member companies can receive approximately 200 sq. ft. of furnished office space without rent. Included in the space are telecommunications services, voice mail, networked PCs, and a Web host. Traditional business amenities consist of fax machines, a printer, file cabinets, and a conference room. Members also are eligible for legal services and tax advice for discounted costs from affiliated professional services firms. Incubation services typically last for one year.

Start ups pay for services with founders stock.

How to Apply:

Show ties to the Berkeley community, as well as a business strategy that addresses a large and fast growing market and an ongoing competitive advantage. Complete the electronic form at http://www.incubator-inc.com/app.html, or send executive summaries to:

Incubator, LP
Attn: Submissions
1912 Bonita Ave.

Berkeley, CA 94704
(510) 848-6048
E-mail: info@incubatorlp.com

IncuLab
Focus: Internet businesses
Web Address: www.inculab.com/

Helps companies create viable business strategies and financial models for Internet ventures. Works with new companies and established firms beginning online subsidiaries. Provides strategic planning, operations and financial management, accounting resources, marketing and legal advice, and IT resources. Also participates in executive recruiting. Manages a network of international partners that can help establish new companies overseas. Co-invests in member companies with outside financiers.

Looks for a viable business model with solid financial projections. Prefers companies that can capitalize on a niche market with high growth potential.

HOW TO APPLY:

Complete the form at http://www.inculab.com/index_submit2.html. Attach an executive summary or full business plans in Microsoft Word for Windows format. Also accepts hard copy summaries and plans mailed to:

IncuLab.com, Inc.
Attention: Potential Investment

40 Wall St.
59th Floor
New York, NY 10005

Information Technology University (ITU)
Focus: Graduate school students building technology companies
Web Address: www.itu.com/

Focuses on graduate-school entrepreneurs needing early-stage capital. Investments typically range from $100,000 to $500,000. Will help attract additional funding with introductions to venture capitalists. Advises in business plan development. Organizes activities with other students who are creating technology companies. Participating colleges in the peer program are Columbia University, Harvard College, the Massachusetts Institute of Technology, Stanford University, and the University of California, Berkeley.

HOW TO APPLY:

Send proposals to

Information Technology University (ITU)
13101 Washington Blvd.
Suite 234
Los Angeles, CA 90066
(310) 566-7380
Fax: (310) 566-7382
E-mail: info@itu.com

Innovation Factory
Focus: Internet start ups

Web Address: www.innovationfactory.com/

Provides hands-on managerial advice, facilities, and capital investments for early stage Internet businesses. Targets electronic commerce ventures and those that target Web sites to specific audiences. Helps entrepreneurs develop products, staff, and business partners.

Investments total up to $500,000. Office space is at a 4,500 sq. ft. facility in Narberth, PA, near Philadelphia.

The incubator helps cultivate additional capital from venture capital funds, angels, and banks. The incubator creates a unique incubation program for each member, with development milestones and regular financial reviews.

How to Apply:

Demonstrate successful business backgrounds in the founders. Also, the business idea must have the potential for high returns. Founders must have a personal financial stake in the company. Send a summary describing the business case, the revenue model, competitive analysis, capital investments to date, launch strategy, and managerial backgrounders to bplans@innovationfactory.com.

Innovation Factory
201 Sabine Ave.
Narberth, PA 19072
(610) 227-2100
Fax: (610) 617-9316

Intellimedia Commerce Inc.
Focus: Internet-based companies in transportation, banking, chemicals, and healthcare
Web Address: www.intellimedia.com/

Targets Internet start-ups and established firms that are building an online presence. Established in 1996. Expertise covers a variety of technical skills, including database programming and systems engineering. Also advises companies in operations management, capital formation, and communications. Works with Cordova Intellimedia Ventures LP, manager of a $50 million private investment fund, to provide start-up and seed-stage funding.

How to Apply:

Use the electronic introduction form at http://www.intellimedia.com/contact/index.html

Intellimedia Commerce, Inc.
One Securities Centre
Suite 1300
3490 Piedmont Road
Atlanta, GA 30305
(404) 262-0000
Fax: 404-261-2282

Intend Change
Focus: E-business ventures
Web Address: www.intendchange.com/ie4/index.html

Helps start-ups refine their business strategy. Participates in raising investment capital, hiring managerial talent, and commercial launches. Takes a board seat and an equity stake in the new venture. Incubator executives also advise member companies in marketing plans, technology, and partnerships. Maintains close ties with large venture capital funds, including Softbank, Crosspoint, GeoCapital, and Odeon Capital, as part of the financial resources available for member companies. Also maintains a strategic alliance with an executive recruiting firm that specializes in Internet businesses.

Looks for businesses that target large markets with unique and competitively advantageous ideas. Also analyzes the talent and market experience of founders.

How to Apply:

Forward ideas to ic@intendchange.com.

Intend Change
87 Encina Ave.
Palo Alto, CA 94301
(650) 289-6600

iMinds Ventures
Focus: Primarily western and Silicon Valley area companies in Internet and related Information Technology markets
Web Address: www.iminds.com/

Established in 1995. Currently manages a $70 million fund for Internet-related start ups. Courts companies developing business-to-business or consumer sectors with electronic-commerce applications. Also considers new-generation communications companies and software developers targeting client/server, corporate enterprise, and Internet applications. Backs seed level companies and new ventures by established firms.

Invests from $250,000 to $750,000 for seed-stage funding rounds, up to a total of $1.5 million over multiple rounds. Also funds early-stage companies with investments of $500,000 to $2 million, up to $5 million in subsequent rounds.

Incubator executives work as interim managers in young companies and help develop marketing strategies, public relations campaigns, marketing programs, and financial initiatives. Also helps build the sales staff and technology infrastructure.

How to Apply:

Complete the capital application form at http://www.value.net/cgi-bin/cgiwrap/iminds/capital.cgi.

iMinds Ventures
135 Main St.
Suite 1350
San Francisco, CA 94105
(415) 547-0000
Fax: (415) 547-0010

Internet Capital Group
Focus: Business-to-business e-commerce start-ups
Web Address: www.internetcapital.com/

Provides management expertise and technology know how. Actively participates in the develop of business models and operations of start-ups. Focuses on companies in markets that haven't fully exploited new technology. These include the plastics, paper, and metals industries and small businesses.

Start-ups receive help in building technology infrastructures for electronic commerce among suppliers and customers.

HOW TO APPLY:

Send proposals to:

Internet Capital Group (Headquarters)
435 Devon Park Drive
Wayne, PA 19087
(610) 989-0111
Fax: (610) 989-0112

Internet Capital Group
One Market St., Spear Tower
Third Floor
Suite 307
San Francisco, CA 94105
(415) 343-3700
Fax: (415) 343-3740

Internet Capital Group
One Boston Place
23rd Floor
Boston, MA 02108
(617) 531-4882
Fax: (617) 531-4886

Internet Capital Group
Pencader Corporate Center

100 Lake Drive
Newark, DE 19702

Internet Capital Group
1201 Third Ave.
Suite 5450
Seattle, WA 98101
(206) 494-1100
Fax: (206) 494-1101

Iron Street Labs
Focus: Internet start-ups
Web Address: http://www.ironstreetlabs. com/

Incubation services cover office and technology infrastructure, technological expertise, professional services, and business strategy development. Iron Street executives help manage start ups through work teams that specialize in key areas, such as operations and finance. Help hone business models, recruit managers, and direct investment capital. Takes an equity stake in start ups.

HOW TO APPLY:

Only considers business plans submitted through its Web site. Log on to http://www.ironstreetlabs.com/submit_a_plan. html. Responds in approximately one week.

Iron Street Labs, The New York Incubator
648 Broadway
Suite 300

New York, NY 10012
(212) 871-0864
Fax: (212) 871-0747
Email: info@istreetlabs.com

iStart Ventures

Focus: Seattle-based e-commerce and Internet start-ups or those willing to relocate in the city
Web Address: www.istartventures.com/

Targets new companies that use the Internet to capitalize on new markets. Offers seed financing, an 18,000 sq.-ft. facility for office space, and managerial expertise for an equity stake in the start up. Provdies introductions to venture capitalists and angel investors. Houses up to eight new ventures at a time. Physical resources consist of PCs, communications, data networks, and administrative management.

How to Apply:

Send ideas using the electronic submission form at http://www.istartventures.com/index_submit_ideas.html. Applicants may follow up by e-mailing an executive summary or business plan. Responds to proposals within five business days.

iStart Ventures

307 Third Ave. S.
Seattle, WA 98104
(206) 264-7600
Fax: (206) 264-8657

iVention Group

Focus: Internet, technology and telecommunications industries
Web Address: www.iventiongroup.com/ivsplash.html

Offers residencies in physical headquarters complete with data networks, conference rooms, copy machines, and receptionists. Provides support with business strategy, technology, executive recruiting, marketing, finance and organizational development. Associated companies provide expertise in communications networks, site hosting, Web development, marketing, accounting, and the law. Invests up to $5 million in seed-stage ventures. Targets companies in Colorado and the Rocky Mountains, but will consider opportunities based elsewhere.

Looks for strong entrepreneurial teams seeking to exploit a large, well-delineated market niche. Expects entrepreneurs to have a clear understanding of its competitive strengths and weaknesses.

How to Apply:

Fill in the electronic form at http://www.iventiongroup.com/ivcontact.html

Companies may also attach a business plan or executive summary in Microsoft Word, Adobe Acrobat, or ASCII format to an e-mail message sent to businessplans@iventiongroup.com.

KnowledgeCube

Focus: Internet start ups
Web Address: www.knowledgecube.com/home.html

Based in New York City, the incubator targets next-generation Internet initiatives. Offers funding, business-strategy expertise, technology advice, and access to international technology partners. The incubator's executives have backgrounds in technology, entrepreneurship, business strategy, and venture capital. Through close links with the Massachusetts Institute of Technology and other universities, has access to technology advisors for the individual needs of each project.

Looks for new companies that define themselves by the uniqueness of their technology innovations and the technical knowledge and experience of the management team.

Offers seed funding and follow on capital as the start-up matures. Also introduces entrepreneurs to outside venture capital and angel investors. Takes equity in start ups in return for services.

HOW TO APPLY:

Send proposals to:

KnowledgeCube Group Inc.

One Rockefeller Plaza
Suite 1700
New York, NY 10020
(212) 632-3500
Fax: (212) 632-3501

KnowledgeCube US LLC

238 Main St.
Suite 324
Cambridge, MA 02142
(617) 441-2044
Fax: (617) 441-2043

KnowledgeCube US LLC

58 Charles St., Third Floor
Cambridge, MA 02142
(617) 494-0880
Fax: (617) 494-0872

KnowledgeCube Seattle

3216 142nd Place NE
Bellevue, WA 98007
info@knowledgecube.com

Los Angeles County Business Technology Center

Focus: Los Angeles area technology companies
Web Address: www.labtc.org/

A non-profit incubator guided by private business managers, university faculty, and experts in finance and accounting. Promotes regional start ups, spinoffs, and early-stage high technology firms. Maintains a facility where new ventures can house themselves and have access to entrepreneurial and technical expertise. Note: the incubation space doesn't accommodate wet labs or industrial ventures. Companies outside the Los Angeles region may become affiliate members, which entitles them to mentoring services and conference room space.

Residents pay a monthly fee based on their space and services requirements. Rent covers utilities, computers and networks, administrative services, office equipment, use of conference rooms, and mentoring resources. Start ups also may participate in capital programs through the center.

HOW TO APPLY:

Forward an application (http://www. labtc.org/page9.htm) and e-mail business plan to the Director of the BTC at rsaenz@ labtc.org.

Los Angeles County Business Technology Center

2400 Lincoln Ave.
Altadena, CA 91001
(626) 296-6300
Fax: (626) 296-6301

LycosLabs
Focus: Massachusetts-based Internet start-ups
Web Address: www.lycoslabs.com/

Provides funding and business expertise for companies willing to locate in the Massachusetts incubator. Only considers start ups with an application prototype or existing Web site. Aides in business strategy development, marketing, and company development. Considers E-commerce, in-frastructure, technology, and viral applications.

HOW TO APPLY:

Complete the application at https://www. lycoslabs.com/lab/form.asp.

The Massachusetts Innovation Center
Focus: Massachusetts Internet ventures
Web Address: www.massinnovation.com/

Offers a combination of free and discounted services to members. Legal, accounting, and marketing services are provided by partners. The incubator helps start ups write a business plan, develop marketing campaigns, create financial systems, and implement technology. The incubator maintains a 300,000-sq.-ft campus with conference rooms and office facilities. Communications resources include a direct, OC48 fiber optic cable for high-speed Internet connections. Managers have expertise in e-commerce, finance, consulting, marketing and retail development.

Typically invests from $100,000 to $500,000. Looks for businesses with high-growth potential and a sustainable competitive advantage.

HOW TO APPLY:

Send proposals to:

Massachusetts Innovation Center
One Oak Hill Road
Fitchburg, MA 01420
(978) 424-2500

E-mail: info@massinnovation.com

MobileSpring
Focus: Wireless Internet applications and services
Web Address: www.mobilespring.com/

An incubator that focuses exclusively on wireless applications for the Internet. Provides office space and assistance in financial, marketing, administrative, and strategic business initiatives. In-house expertise covers technical issues relating to building wireless infrastructures, including network connectivity. Able to guide companies that use a gamut of underlying wireless systems and hardware, including cellular/PCS, mobile data, and paging services paired with PDAs, WAP phones, CDPD hardware, digital cellular/PCS phones, and text pagers. Takes a "significant" equity stake in each start up.

Looks for new ventures with innovative applications of wireless technology.

HOW TO APPLY:

Send an executive summary in either Microsoft Word, Rich Text, or Adobe Acrobat format to bplan@mobilespring.com.

MobileSpring, Inc.
120 West 44th St., 3rd Floor
New York, NY 10036
(212) 391-6668
Fax: (212) 391-9566

Net Value Holdings
Focus: New e-business and technology ventures
Web Address: www.nvholdings.com/

Established in 1998, looks for business strategies that identify a significant market potential and managerial talent and experience that can successfully promote the strategy. A virtual incubator that accepts entrepreneurs from a variety of geographical areas. Maintains headquarters in San Francisco, but also has offices throughout the Northeast. Provides financial and technical expertise, which an emphasis on Internet ventures.

Current incubator residents focus on Internet infrastructure projects, business-to-business ventures, and business-to-consumer companies. Offers capital investments and business connections.

HOW TO APPLY:

Submit a cover letter and comprehensive business plan, including financial projections, capital requirements, and biographies of the entrepreneurial team to plans@nvholdings.com.

Net Value Holdings
1085 Mission St.
San Francisco, CA 94103
(415) 335-4700
Fax: (415) 575-4756
HQ@nvholdings.com

Net Value Holdings
601 W 26th St.
Suite 11S
New York, NY 10001
(646) 486-6000
Fax: (646) 486-6600
Contact - John Brine
john@nvholdings.com

Net Value Holdings
1000 Winter St.
Suite 1100
Waltham, MA 02451
(781) 895-1661
Contact - Tom Aley
tom@nvholdings.com

Net Value Holdings
Two Penn Center Plaza
Suite 605
Philadelphia, PA 19102
Contact - Denise Kapusniak
denise@nvholdings.com

The Northwestern University/Evanston (IL) Research Park Technology Innovation Center (TIC)
Focus: Seed-stage technology companies
Web Address: www.theincubator.com/

Works with companies that have yet to commercial their product or service and have yet to build a staff. Activities at the Center typically include honing the business plan, hiring top executives, cultivating markets, building the core product, and working toward a seed or first-round investment round. The incubator's business ties include professional service organiza-tions that provide free consulting in legal, accounting, investment banking, human resource, and commercial real estate matters. The Center also offers the expertise of Northwestern University faculty, and in-house executives.

Helps start ups apply for federal research grants and state dollars.

Approximately 47,000 sq. ft. of office space is available for members. Rents can be as low as $21.50 per gross foot per year, or $1.80 per month. A high-speed fiber optic network connection connects the offices to the Internet.

HOW TO APPLY:

Download an application at http://www.theincubator.com/html_docs/application.html, and mail or deliver the form in person to:

Tim Lavengood
Technology Innovation Center
Suite 100
1840 Oak Ave.
Evanston, IL 60201
Fax: (847) 866-1808

Orbit Capital
Focus: Internet start ups
Web Address: www.orbitcapital.com/

Maintains world-wide connections for international businesses through its affiliation with the Orbitex Group of Companies, an international financial services firm. Provides financing, managerial expertise, and office space. Each resident start up has an individual advisor who works with companies on strategic issues. Also offers business and technical services to off-site start ups through a virtual incubation resource.

HOW TO APPLY:

Complete the electronic application form at the Web site.

Orbit Capital

410 Park Ave.
Suite 830
New York, NY 10022
(212) 616-7988
Fax: (212) 616-7990
E-mail: deals@orbitcapital.com

Oregon Innovation Center

Focus: Technology ventures
Web Address: www.oregoninnovation.org/

A not-for-profit incubator that offers physical space, support services (including high-speed Internet connections), and funding. Aids start-ups in designing and prototyping products. Offices include prototyping facilities and testing equipment. Guides product commercialization. Offers "brainstorming" space and technology transfer resources. Maintains liaisons with area business, education, and government leaders. Through affiliates or in-house staff, the incubertor provides consulting in accounting, financial development, legal, management, marketing, and other subjects.

Core incubator program is the i2m (Idea to Marketplace), which is geared to entrepreneurs who want to develop an idea from inception to a global launch.

HOW TO APPLY:

Send proposals to

The Oregon Innovation Center

253 SE Salmon Drive
P.O. Box 1510
Redmond, OR 97756
(541) 504-2929
Fax: (541) 504-2930
E-mail: info@oregoninnovation.org

Panasonic Internet Incubator

Focus: Early stage Internet, multimedia, networking and software ventures
Web Address: www.digitalconceptscenter.com/

Maintains offices in San Francisco and Cupertino, CA, for start ups needing physical space on a month-by-month lease and access to executives with the incubator's parent company, Matsushita Electric. Members are also eligible for funding from Panasonic Venture Capital. Technical resources in the incubator space include local networks, a high-speed T-1 connection to outside networks, Web hosting services, and discounted telecommunications programs.

Members may consult with the in-house incubator staff, attend business development seminars, and make use of the incubator's connections to venture capital sources.

Potential members may tour the incubator Wednesdays at 11 a.m. by registering at info@wtc-sf.org.

HOW TO APPLY:

Only considers seed-stage and start up ventures willing to locate at either the San Francisco or Cupertino facility. Looks for unique high-potential technology, a well-developed business plan, and managerial talent. Download an application form at the Web site. Complete and e-mail the form with an executive summary and/or business plan to ehouser@vc.panasonic.com.

Panasonic Internet Incubator
19925 Stevens Creek Blvd.
Suite 200
Cupertino, CA 95014
(408) 861-3900
Fax: (408) 861-3990

Panasonic Internet Incubator
1207 Indiana St.
Suite 9
San Francisco, CA 94107
(415) 401-8531
Fax: (415) 970-5095

Phase 1
Focus: Internet start ups

Web Address: www.phase1.org/

Provides infrastructure and business services on a discounted or cost-free basis. Takes an equity share of the start up. Maintains a network of investment bankers, venture capitalists, accounts, and attorneys who consult with member companies.

HOW TO APPLY:

Looks for an attractive business plan, managerial strength, a viable growth strategy, and the potential for success. Introduce your venture by completing the form at http://www.phase1.org/form.html. Note: At press time, the incubator wasn't accepting new applications, but anticipated openings by end of the year 2000.

Phase 1
312 Laurel Ave.
Laurel MD 20707
(301) 206-2224
Fax: (301) 598-0769
E-mail: info@phase1.org

Pipevine New Media
Focus: Online start ups
Web Address: www.pipevine.net/

Targets seed-stage companies. Services consist of strategic analysis, engineering, financing, planning, design, marketing, strategy, new media, and e-commerce consulting. Participates in the start up's creation of business and financial plans. Depending on the need, the incubator's executives can advise entrepreneurs in executing the business strategy or take control of executing the plan.

How to Apply:

E-mail business plans to submitplan@pipevine.net or fax them to (212) 245-8074. Pipevine also accepts plans sent to its offices.

Pipevine New Media
250 West 49th St.
Suite 601
New York, NY, 10019

Rare Medium
Focus: E-commerce companies
Web Address: www.raremediumgroup.com/

Founded in 1998, offers financial investment and business mentoring. Works with start ups or established companies building an online presence. Services range from management consulting to user-interface design, branding, and technology consulting. In-house expertise covers vertical sectors such as automotive, entertainment, consumer goods and services, financial services, high technology, and healthcare industries.

How to Apply:

Inquire to ventures@raremedium.com

Rare Medium Group
1145 Sanctuary Pkwy
Suite 400
Alpharetta, GA 30004

(770) 576-4100
Fax: (770) 576-4200

Rare Medium Group
2207 Commerce St.
Dallas, TX 75201
(214) 742-7273
Fax: (214) 742-7274

Rare Medium Group
370 Interlocken Blvd.
4th Floor
Broomfield, CO 80021
(303) 474-1755
Fax: (303) 474-1756

Rare Medium Group
21 East Long Lake Rd.
Suite 102
Bloomfield Hills, MI 48304
(248) 433-0900
Fax: (248) 540-0483

Rare Medium Group
164 Townsend St.
Suite 4
San Francisco, CA 94107
(415) 957-1975
Fax: (415) 957-1976

Raza Foundries
Focus: Broadband networking and communications ventures
Web Address: http://www.razafoundries.com/home.html

Specializes only in broadband start ups. Looks for ideas using leading-edge technology, experienced managers, and short time to market. Incubator managers work closely with engineering and management teams at member companies. Finds outside technical and strategic experts to consul member companies to augment the incubator's in-house expertise. First team-building step typically is to combine incubator managers with start up technical personnel to create the central engineering group. Provides facilities and technical equipment and introduces start ups to business partners. Also helps cultivate capital funding.

Most interested in high-end communications technologies, such as optical networking, network and packet processors, hybrid fiber coaxial products, and broadband wireless data and media networking.

How to Apply:

E-mail proposals to plans@razafoundries. com

Raza Foundries

2480 North First St.
Suite 280
San Jose, CA 95131
(408) 432-8510
Fax: (408) 432-8552
E-mail: contact@razafoundries.com

Reactivity Ventures

Focus: Internet start ups and Web spin offs from established companies
Web Address: www.reactivity.com/

Offers design and technical advice through a full-time development team. Provides mentoring for business strategy and prototyping resources.

How to Apply:

E-mail ideas to info@reactivity.com

Reactivity, Inc. (Headquarters)

1301 Shoreway Rd.
Suite 425
Belmont, CA 94002-4106
(650) 551-7800
Fax: (650) 551-7801

Reactivity, Inc.

1250 Capital of Texas
Cielo Center, Bldg. 1
Suite 300
Austin, TX 78746
(512) 732-1000
Fax: (512) 732-1001

Reactivity, Inc.

One Kendall Square, Bldg. 600
Suite 324
Cambridge, MA 02139
(617) 621-0048
Fax: (617) 249-0483

Red Hot Technology Accelerator

Focus: New technology ventures
Web Address: www.redhotlaw.com/

An affiliate of the Red Hot Law Group of Ashley, a legal specialist for technology companies. The accelerator offers business and legal advice in return for a stake in the start up. Can accommodate a maximum of eight new ventures. Executives maintain ties with area professional associations, including the Technology Association of Georgia, Southeastern Software Association, Business & Technology Alliance, the Computer Law Association, Women in Technology International, and the Computer Law Section of the Georgia Bar.

How to Apply:

E-mail introductions to eashley@redhotlaw.com. Prospective clients may also telephone Evelyn A. Ashley at (404) 575-1900 or visit the offices in person.

Red Hot Technology Accelerator
The Biltmore
817 West Peachtree
Suite 400
Atlanta, GA 30308-1138
(404) 575-1900
Fax: (404) 575-1901

Redleaf Group
Focus: Mission critical Web applications for large corporations
Web Address: www.redleaf.com/

Focuses on business-to-business and electronic commerce products and servces. Offers investment capital, management, and engineering resources in exchange for equity. Founded in 1996.

How to Apply:

Send inquires to info@redleaf.com.

Redleaf Group
14395 Saratoga Ave.
Suite 130
Saratoga, CA 95070
(408) 868-0800
Fax: (408) 868-0810

Redleaf
100 First Ave.
Suite 950
Pittsburgh, PA 15222
(412) 201-5600
Fax: (412) 201-5650

Redleaf
Fairfax, VA 22020
(703) 689-3500
Fax: (703) 689-3505

Redleaf
999 Third Ave.
Suite 2424
Seattle, WA 98104
(206) 447-1350
Fax: (206) 447-1351

Redleaf
Los Angeles, CA
(310) 395-8484
Fax: (310) 395-8665

Redstone7.com
Focus: Seed-stage ventures based in the New York City area

Web Address: www.redstone7.com

A spin off of Trident Partners, an international investment management company that manages $220 million in investments. The incubator targets seed-stage ideas or products and will consider proposals by founders without previous entrepreneurial experience. Actively works with members in management, marketing, business strategy, technology development. Recruits staff and helps write business plans. Cultivates outside investors and partners. Takes an equity in start ups.

Backs only early-stage companies that have identified a viable niche in a large market and enjoy a long-term competitive advantage. Start ups must be based in the New York City region.

HOW TO APPLY:

Complete the application form linked to http://www.redstone7.com/gateway.html. Then e-mail a business plan to business-plans@redstone7.com (Note: the company doesn't require a formal business plan). Reports within two weeks of receiving the business plan.

Redstone7.com
45 Grove St.
New Canaan, CT 06840
E-mail: info@redstone7.com

Rensselaer Incubator Program
Rensselaer Polytechnic Institute
Focus: Technology start ups
Web Address: www.rpi.edu/dept/incubator/homepage/

Founded in 1980 as the first university-based incubator. Offers academic, research, and community resources for businesses. Start ups usually remain in the program approximately two to three years. Offers a total of 100,000 sq. ft. in two buildings for start ups to share. Provides office space, a laboratory, and light-manufacturing facilities. The incubation space, which is available on a month-to-month lease, has high-speed Internet connections, a receptionist, office equipment, conference rooms, a building security service, and mail handling.

Up to 225 sq.ft. of office space costs $250 a month for a one-year lease (more space is available at extra cost). Lab space rents for $300 a month for a one-year lease (again, additional lab space is available at an additional charge). Consulting, planning, and networking from the Program's staff is free to members.

Members can participate in the university's education program for technology start ups.

HOW TO APPLY:

Send an executive summary to: incubator@rpi.edu

Rensselaer Incubator Program
1223 Peoples Ave.
Troy, NY 12180
Phone: (518) 276-6658
Fax: (518) 276-6380

Safeguard Scientifics Inc.

Focus: Software, communications, electronic services, and electronic commerce
Web Address: www.safeguard.com/

Through its partner program, offers links to related companies, potential customers, testing facilities, sales channels, and incubator programs. New members receive a three-month development plan for defining goals, setting milestones, and networking among Safeguard's partners.

Safeguard helps start ups develop the underlying technologies for their product or services, recruit executives, hone financial plans, and begin marketing efforts. Takes a "significant" stake in new ventures.

How to Apply:

Demonstrate a unique business strategy and the potential to garner significant revenues and high profits. Also emphasis the expertise of key managers. Complete an application form at www.safeguard.com/entreplanmainframe.html.

Safeguard Scientifics, Inc.
800 The Safeguard Building
435 Devon Park Drive
Wayne, PA 19087
(610) 293-0600 or (877) 506-7371
Fax: 610-293-0601

Santa Barbara Technology Incubator

Focus: Internet services and software, computer software and devices, and communications
Web Address: www.sbtechnology.com/

Established in 2000, typically invests from $250,000 to $1 million in member start ups. Investors associated with the incubator may invest additional funds in some cases. Start ups typically grow at the facility for three to nine months. Members pay for services as they're needed. Incubator managers and start up investors perform regular reviews on the start up's progress and suggest changes in strategy. The 12,000 sq. ft. incubation facility, in Santa Barbara, CA, provides PCs, networks, and telecommunications. The incubator staff handles the details of incorporation, obtaining business licenses, and creating stock options plans for employees.

How to Apply:

Register at http://www.sbtechnology.com/html/index.htm to receive a password to reach a secure area for submitting a business plan.

Santa Barbara Technology Incubator, LLC
320 Nopal St.
Santa Barbara, CA 93103
(805) 564-8005
Fax: (805) 564-7188
info@sbtechnology.com

Sequoia Capital

Focus: E-commerce and healthcare
Web Address: www.sequoiacap.com/

Offers commercial space and capital investments (ranging from $50,000 to $10 million). Seeks start ups located on the West Coast that have targeted high-growth markets with the potential to reach $1 billion. Also backs later-stage ventures in the Boston and Austin, TX, areas.

HOW TO APPLY:

Considers third-party introductions the best way to meet new entrepreneurs. Forward business plans to:

Sequoia Capital

3000 Sand Hill Road
Bldg. 4, Ste. 280
Menlo Park, CA 94025

Shelter Ventures

Focus: Communications convergence and broadband applications
Web Address: www.shelterventures.com/

Offers business mentoring, funding, and a network of partners for potential business relationships. Provides office space, help with creating Web sites, and participates in finding managerial talent.

HOW TO APPLY:

E-mail a business plan to businessplans@ shelterventures.com, or send a hard copy of the plan to:

Shelter Ventures

c/o Business Plan Submission
10880 Wilshire Blvd.
Suite 1400
Los Angeles, CA 90024

Start uprx.com

Focus: Emerging biotechnology, information technology, and Internet ventures
Web Address: www.start uprx.com/

Founded to help in locating funding and provide advice on business strategy. Note: At press time, Start uprx ws not directly investing in new companies.

Bill Schatz

Start uprx.com
66 Witherspoon St.
Suite 177
Princeton, NJ 08542
Fax: (240) 358 -7465
E-mail: bill@start uprx.com

Start ups.com

Focus: Start ups with seed funding, growing companies, and business expanding into new markets
Web Address: www.start ups.com/

Take responsibility for facilities, computing resources, and administrative functions for new companies. Will locate physical space and creating a 401(k) investment program for start up employees.

Works with a team of partners that provide professional services at discounted prices. Member companies work with the incubator to develop a project plan that includes a budget and milestones. Offers project management tools in a secure section of the Web site. The tools delineate capital needs, bids from vendors, and schedule changes.

Fees to start ups vary by situation, but the minimum charge for the incubator's services is $25,000, not including costs of third-party services. The incubator may take an equity stake as part of its service fee.

HOW TO APPLY:

Complete the electronic form at http:// www.start ups.com/get_started/. Responds to initial inquiries within three business days.

Start ups.com

2400 Broadway St.
Suite 200
Redwood City, CA 94063
(650) 474-5400
Fax: (650) 474-5401
E-mail: info@start ups.com

StartUpStreet.com

Focus: Internet, telephony, hardware, software, networking, life sciences, and semiconductor ventures
Web Address: www.start upstreet.com/

Offers free business information for entrepreneurs at its Web site. Ventures that formally join the incubator receive personalized business advice. Members also may search a database of national venture capital firms and angel investors for potential funding sources. Takes cash and equity in return for services.

HOW TO APPLY:

Looks for companies with a distinct competitive advantage in high-growth markets, and have the potential to reach $100 million in five years. Complete the registration form at the Web site. Note: new members are required to sign a service contract and pay a $275 application fee.

StartUpStreet.com

112 S. Duke St.
Suite 4
Durham, NC 27701

Stevens Technology Ventures Incubator

Focus: Technology start ups
Web Address: http://attila.stevens-tech.edu/ tvi/

Housed at Stevens Institute of Technology, Hoboken, NJ. Offers an Incubator Advisory Board to help start up managers with business planning and development of market strategies. Members also may work with Stevens' faculty and top students, as needed. The incubator has helped 50 companies who have attracted more than $10.5 million in outside financing. Incubator introduces members to venture capitalists and assists in applying for federal and state business grants. Physical space is equipped with business machines and conference rooms.

How to Apply:

Contact Gina Boesch, director, at

Stevens Technology Ventures Incubator
610 River St.
Hoboken, NJ 07030-5053
(201) 216-5366
Fax: (201) 420-9568
E-mail: gboesch@stevens-tech.edu

Swauger.com

Focus: Electronic-commerce, Web-hosting, and other emerging Internet businesses
Web Address: www.swauger.com/

Introduces members to financing sources, legal help, executive managers, and technical expertise. Looks for companies targeting business-to-business opportunities and have a product or service that is ready for commercialization. Takes an equity stake.

How to Apply:

Send an executive summary or full business plan to BizPlan@Swauger.com.

Swauger.com, LLP.
26523 Brant Way
Fair Oaks Ranch, CA 91351
info@Swauger.com

Techfarm

Focus: Information technology start ups
Web Address: www.techfarm.com

Established in 1993 by technology entrepreneur Gordon Campbell. Becomes ac-

tively involved with start up management and guides financial strategies. Helps write business plans, recruit talent, cultivate funding sources, develop research and design activities, and locate corporate partners.

Looks for start ups capable of leading their markets within five years. Evaluates companies based on the talent and experience of business and technical managers. Also targets ventures with an ongoing competitive advantage based on intellectual property. Especially interested in "companies that are addressing 'markets in transition' where a major shift is occurring in a market that enables the rapid adoption of the company's technology."

Backs start ups based throughout the country and will consider foreign ventures. Typically appoints one of its staff to act as chairman of member companies.

How to Apply:

Submit a business plan or informal proposal to one of the partners. E-mail addresses are listed at http://www.techfarm.com/pages/cont.htm. They include Gordon Campbell, gordon@techfarm.com; Kurt Keilhacker, kurt@techfarm.com; and Jim Whims, jim@techfarm.com.

Techfarm
200 W. Evelyn Ave.
Suite 100

Mountain View, CA 94041
(650) 934-0900
Fax: (650) 934-0910

Techfarm
One Bowdoin Square
10th Floor
Boston, MA 02114
(617) 742-7707
Fax: (617) 742-7709

Technology 2020
Focus: Information technology
Web Address: www.tech2020.org/

An Oak Ridge, TN, incubator with associations with a number of area business organizations that offer resources for entrepreneurs. Will critique and participate in writing business plans. Provides consulting on funding and management. Conducts seminars and one-on-one sessions for entrepreneurial education. Offers physical space.

Through state programs and the TennesSeed Venture Capital Connection, help connect start ups with angels and other investors. Also acts as a network operator for the Small Business Association's ACE-Net angel capital network. Manages the SBA's Microloan program and the TennesSeed Fund, for seed-stage companies.

Incubator membership last for a year, with extensions granted for companies that require additional time and which are meeting their development milestones.

Looks for companies with strong business plan, the potential for growth, the likelihood of creating jobs in the geographical area, and the desire to locate the company's headquarters in the region.

HOW TO APPLY:

Submit a business plan and the completed application at http://www.tech2020.org/entrepreneur/busdevapp.htm. Note the organization will assist businesses in writing a business plan, but it won't consider applications until the plan is completed.

Technology 2020
1020 Commerce Park Drive
Oak Ridge, TN 37830
(865) 220-2020
Fax: (865) 220-2030
E-mail: info@tech2020.org

Technology Advancement Program
Focus: Biotechnology, information technology, medical equipment, telecomtions, aerospace, electronics, and environmental sciences
Web Address: www.erc.umd.edu/TAP/

An initiative of the Engineering Research Center at the University of Maryland College Park campus. Backs ventures that will maintain significant business activities within the state. The incubator provides offices and labs, plus support resources such as receptionists and some secretarial functions. Members have access to business equipment, PCs, and the university's computer network (computer time must be scheduled and may include a fee). In addition, start ups receive technical and business advice from university faculty members and student participation in the business.

Typically accepts start ups for residencies of one to four years. Charges between $.72 and $1.17 per sq. ft. per month for space, depending on the type and size of space required.

How to Apply:

Looks for companies developing an advanced technology with a strong management team. Submit a completed application from http://www.erc.umd. /TAP/appform.html.

Technology Advancement Program
387 Technology Drive
University of Maryland
College Park, MD 20742
(301) 314-7803
Fax: (301) 314-9592
E-mail : tap@umail.umd.edu

Tower Hill Capital Group
Focus: Internet ventures
Web Address: www.thcg.com/

Helps develop start up business models. Works with new ventures to create a marketing strategy, including branding initiatives. Aids companies in technology and operational issues, including workflow and budgeting.

Considers direct investments through its Venture Development group. Also helps raise capital by cultivating outside investors and directing company valuation and negotiation efforts. Will identify prospective acquisition candidates.

Also runs an affiliate in Israel that targets next generation Internet and e-business projects.

How to Apply:

Send an executive summary to NewBusinessCommittee@thcg.com or e-mail a complete business plan to business@ thcg.com.

THCG, Inc
650 Madison Ave.
21st Floor
New York, NY 10022
(212) 223-8272
E-mail: Adi Raviv, Co-chief Executive Officer, araviv@thcg.com

U.S. Technologies
Focus: Business-to-business Internet companies
Web Address: www.usxx.com/

Offers financial, operational, managerial, consulting and administrative resources. Makes investments of $250,000 to $5 million. Washington, D.C., facilities include high-speed Internet connections, phones, receptionists, and administrative services.

HOW TO APPLY:

Forward ideas of full business plans.

U.S. Technologies Contact Information
2001 Pennsylvania Ave. NW
Suite 675
Washington, DC 20006
(202) 466-3100
Fax: (202) 466-4557

Union Atlantic's e-Incubator
Focus:
Web Address: www.ualc.com/ad/eincubator.htm

Helps start ups that have received initial funding cultivate venture capital. Charges an upfront fee of $40,000 and options to acquire 5 percent of the start up. Services include writing a full business report for presentation to potential investors, creation of a three-year financial model, and a competitive analysis. The company will also create a formal valuation of the start up and design a Web site.

HOW TO APPLY:

E-mail an executive summary to eincubator@ualc.com.

Venture Catalyst Group
Focus: Enterprise software, e-commerce, and networking start ups
Web Address: www.venturecg.com/

Guides management team, helps develop business strategy and the start up's technology product or service, assists in setting growth milestones, helps write the business plan, cultivates financing. Maintains a network of attorneys, accountants, bankers, recruiters, marketing, and technical consultants that can aid new ventures. Takes an equity stake in return for services.

HOW TO APPLY:

Call or send a one or two page proposal. Candidates may also complete an electronic form at the Web site to introduce their companies.

Venture Catalyst Group
Suite 301
459 Hamilton Ave.
Palo Alto, CA 94301
(650) 322-8576
Fax: (650) 322-8577
E-mail: dave@venturecg.com

Venture Catalyst Partners
Focus: The Internet, software, Internal-protocol communications
Web Address: www.venturecatalyst.com/

Provides Silicon Valley start ups with an interim CEO, participation on the Board of Directors, and advice on strategic issues. Considers national and international ventures. Creates marketing plans, business plans, revenue projections, customer research.

How to Apply:

Send proposals to

Victor Anderson
Venture Catalyst Partners
2 Sandstone
Portola Valley, CA 94028-8033
(650) 464-9925
Fax: (650) 292-2329
E-mail: info@venturecatalyst.com

Venture Frogs
Focus: E-commerce, information, and tel-ecommunications
Web Address: www.vfrogs.com/

Offers investments and consulting. Invests $100,000 to $3 million per venture. Looks for experienced managers and an idea that targets a large market and has the potential to become a leader in that market. Prefers San Francisco Bay area companies, but will consider other opportunities. Manages 15,000 sq. ft. in office space with PCs, Internet connections, phones, conference rooms, business machines, and reception areas. Member companies can connect with legal, financial, and engineering expertise associated with the incubator.

How to Apply:

Send proposals to incubator@vfrogs.com. Note: At press time the incubator was fully, it anticipated openings in late 2000.

Venture Frogs, LLC
1000 Van Ness

Suite 201
San Francisco, CA 94109
(415) 345-6260
Fax: (415) 440-9865
info@vfrogs.com

Venturehouse Group
Focus: Business-to-business, wireless, and broadband network start ups
Web Address: www.venturehousegroup.com/

Based in metro Washington, DC/northern Virginia. Offers financing, business experience, and office space. Maintains links to venture capitalists. Expertise covers business strategy, finance, recruiting, technology, legal, sales and marketing, PR, creative, accounting, real estate, and human resources. Corporate contacts are international. Takes an equity stake in start ups.

How to Apply:

Send proposals to

Venturehouse Group
1750 Tysons Blvd.
4th Floor
McLean, VA 22102
(703) 883-9600
Fax: (703) 883-3987
E-mail: info@venturehousegroup.com

VenturePlex
Focus: Seed-stage technology companies

Web Address: www.ventureplex.com/

Provides a high-technology incubator facility and seed-stage financing for southern California start ups. Manages 30,000 sq. ft. in office space with furnished offices and labs. Members receive high-speed Internet connections, a central receptionist, and phone service. Business expertise covers accounting, information technology, legal issues, human relations, and public relations. Hamilton Technology Ventures will operate in concert with the San Diego VenturePlex to provide the support structure, facilities and management needed to successfully nurture seed and early-stage ventures. Our partners and assembled support staff have the background and experience necessary to oversee all aspects of venture value formation.

At press time, the incubator was developing an online database to post information for investors looking to back start ups.

How to Apply:

Complete the electronic application form at the Web site. Reports interest within five business days.

San Diego Ventureplex
9645 Scranton Road
Suite 240
San Diego, CA, 92121
(858) 552-3690
E-mail: info@ventureplex.com

VentureWorx
Focus: Electronic business
Web Address: www.ventureworx.com/

A Charlotte, NC, incubator. Helps develop e-business ideas, provides business expertise, and guides start ups to public offerings or mergers. Introduces member companies to partner businesses, including ones that can market test business initiatives, create Web branding, and analyze key markets.

How to Apply:

Looks for managerial strength. Contact via electronic form at www.ventureworx.com/contactus.html

Wazee Angel Investment Network
Focus: Information, media and technology companies
Web Address: wazee.com/

An informal network of angels who target Internet-based start ups. Usuually take on consulting or board of director's roles. Provides investments, business mentoring, and introductions to other investors. Helps develop business partnerships.

How to Apply:

Send a one or two page executive summary. Also tell the organization if a business plan has been written and whether it includes financial projections. E-mail to

Alan Brigish, President, at Mail to mailto: albrigi@wazee.com.

Web Capital Ventures

Focus: Technology and Internet ventures
Web Address: www.webcapitalventures.com/

Takes a significant equity stake in return for investments and business consulting. Offers space within a 120,000 sq. ft, 10-acre campus in Ft. Lauderdale. The facility provides Web hosting and design, systems inintegration, information technology management marketing, and public relations help.

The company also manages incubator resources in Los Angeles and Tokyo, and plans to expand into Europe, China and Hong Kong.

How to Apply:

Backs start ups with a clear competitive advantage and the potential to become industry leaders. Looks for strong managers and compatibility of the company within the existing network of businesses. Send proposals to bizdev@mailboxx.com.

Silicon Ft-Lauderdale (Headquarters)

1400 West Cypress Creek
Fort Lauderdale, FL 33309
(954) 938-8840
Fax: (954) 938-8668
E-mail: invrels@mailboxx.com
or

4344 Promenade Way
Suite 102P
Marina Del Rey, CA 90292
(310) 823-8088
Fax: (310) 823-0888
E-mail: webcapitalventures@mailboxx.com

Or call a member of the Business Development Team.

Robert Taylor

(310) 823-8088

James Verbic

(954) 938-8840

Jason Smith

(954) 938-8840

Women's Technology Cluster

Focus: Women owned or managed technology ventures
Web Address: www.womenstechcluster.org/

Offers facilities, business advice, access to investments, and expertise in technology, marketing, recruiting, and finance. Offers month-to-month leases on office space, conference rooms, multimedia presentation equipment, and high-speed Internet access. Member companies receive funding consideration from the Panasonic Venture Fund.

How to Apply:

Applicants must be cultivating Internet, multimedia, networking, or software companies. The company must have at least one woman founder with a large equity stake. Start ups must locate at the San Francisco facility.

Complete the application at http://www.wtc-sf.org/application2.html.

Women's Technology Cluster
1207 Indiana St.
Suite 4
San Francisco, CA 94107
(415) 970-5090
Fax: (415) 970-5095
E-mail: applicant@wtc-sf.org

Youngstown Business Incubator
Focus: Ohio-based technology companies
Web Address: www.ybi.org/

Helps develops new companies in the Mahoning Valley of Ohio. Established in 1996. Provides free or low-cost office space, business equipment, and technology, as well as access to administrative, management, technical, and professional resources. Helps connect companies with government loans and out investors.

How to Apply:

Complete the application at http://www.ybi.org/submitapplication.htm#Incubator Pre-application. Also forward a business plan.

Youngstown Business Incubator
241 Federal Plaza West
Youngstown, OH 44503
(330) 746-5003

SBA AND BANK LOANS

Taking money from venture capitalists and angel investors requires a leap of faith on the part of entrepreneurs. In return for capital, both want a piece of your company, as well as an influential voice in board meetings. If you're not willing to make concessions like these, you don't have to launch your dreams on a shoestring. Fortunately, a number of lending sources—both public and private—have discovered the benefits of giving loans of a few thousand to over $1 million to entrepreneurs.

SBA SMORGASBOARD

When it comes to lenders with deep pockets, none are deeper than Uncle Sam's. Through the Small Business Administration, the federal government helps thousands of private companies develop and grow through loan guarantees that total more than $10 billion each year.

Entrepreneurs don't actually get a check from the government. Instead, the SBA guarantees loans approved and managed by commercial lenders. The benefit for entrepreneurs is that more capital becomes available for start up expenses, real estate, equipment, lines of credit, and other business needs than if banks didn't have the SBA's security blanket to protect them.

Definitions of who is eligible for SBA loan guarantees are liberal. You must be a for-profit venture. The company must do business in the U.S. or its possessions. The venture must have owner equity. There must already be some money, such as personal assets, behind the company. Finally, the company must be a small business under the SBA's definitions, which vary by industry. For example, retail and service operations must have maximum revenues of $3.5 million to $13.5 million (variations depend on the specific market). Wholesale operations must have 100 or fewer employees, while manufacturers are limited to between 500 and 1,500 employees.

Overall, the SBA designs these loans so it takes less collateral and smaller down payments to receive funding than if you sought conventional business loans. Another big plus: SBA loans are fully amortized for their entire life, typically seven to 25 years depending on the individual loan. This means you don't have to face periodic loan renewal evaluations, renewal fees, or balloon payments that the open market sometimes requires.

The SBA guarantees loans to a maximum of $750,000, although the actual loan amount approved by lenders may be higher. The SBA evaluates loan requests by judging the business's cash flow, the experience level of the management, collateral, and owner's equity, among other factors. It also requires that investors with a 20 percent or higher stake in the company personally guarantee SBA loans.

Entrepreneurs negotiate loan interest rates with the lending institution that originates the loan. However, the SBA enforces guidelines to tip the scales in favor of fledgling companies. Fixed rates top out at prime plus 2.25 percent for loans of seven years or more (rates may be lower at the discretion of the commercial lender). Variable-rates are set to the prime rate or a special SBA rate that consists of a weighted average of what the federal government pays for loans. The end result for entrepreneurs is financial breathing room from the interest demands of commercial loans.

When applying for an SBA loan, entrepreneurs will need to demonstrate sound personal and business credit records. Supporting documents will include a summary of the business, including the number of employees and annual sales, the reason for the loan, three years of financial statements for ongoing businesses as well as year-to-date results for the current period, personal financial statements for owners, officers, and anyone owning 20 percent or more equity in the business, and cash flow projections.

Receiving an SBA loan is not without unique costs. Lenders may pass on service fees the SBA charges for loan processing. The fees vary by loan amount, ranging from 2 percent of the guaranteed portion of the loan when that portion is $80,000 or less, to 3.875 percent of the guaranteed portion over $500,000. Loans also incur a 0.5 percent annual service fee on outstanding balances.

Under these umbrella terms, a wide range of loan categories exists. See the main Small Business Administration Web site, at www.sba.gov, for details on individual loans. Application forms are available at www.sba.gov/library/forms.html. Some applications may be completed online.

Here's a summary.

7(a) Loan

For companies needing any amount up to $1.5 million. There are no restrictions on what business expenses the money can be used for, and both start ups and established companies are eligible.

LowDoc Loan

Named for the low amount of documentation required for application, this loan is a kind of 7(a) Loan Lite. Along with less paperwork, borrowers complete a one-page application, and LowDoc loans promise faster approval decisions than a standard 7(a), often within 36 hours. However, the maximum loan amount is only $150,000.

504 Loan

Companies negotiate interest rates on acceptance for this long-term loan targeted for big-ticket items such as land, production equipment, and offices. 504 Loan funds cannot go to inventory, debt payments, or working capital.

CAPLines Loans

These credit lines provide short-term and cyclical working capital. Individual CAPLine products target seasonal business fluctuations, general contractor costs, and cyclical growth. Each product matures in five years or less.

SBA Express Loan

With a maximum loan schedule of five years, the Express Loan is a revolving line of credit up to a maximum is $150,000. The money may be used for any business expenses and are available to start ups and growing companies.

Small Business Investment Corp. (SBIC) funds

Loans from private venture-capital funds licensed by the SBA. Targets companies seeking $250,000 to $3 million in equity funding.

Special Small Business Investment Corp. (SSBIC) funds

Same as SBIC, only funds go to socially or economically disadvantaged entrepreneurs.

BANKS AND COMMERCIAL LENDERS

Banks aren't just for simple checking accounts and Christmas Clubs anymore. Jolted by relaxed federal banking regulations that have opened up competition for commercial banks, the industry is working overtime to offer new services as it searches for profits and growth. One of the biggest targets: entrepreneurs. The size of the market and the capital needs of emerging companies offer banks an opportunity to stay healthy in today's changing financial environment. To do this, they're streamlining the application process for credit lines and business loans—often requiring only a minimum of financial records to evaluate a loan request. Banks also are stirring the small business market with easy-approval credit cards with limits from $50,000 all the way up to $100,000. For companies that decide that accepting sizable debt is better than giving up a piece of the company through equity capital from an outside investor, term loans, credit lines, and credit cards now are paying for prototypes and business plans in young companies, or inventory and equipment in more mature businesses.

The result: The top 100 bank and thrift lenders held more than $219 billion of the loans on their balance sheets as of June 1999, up 11 percent from the year-earlier period, according to a rankings report from SNL Securities LC. According to data gathered by the SBA in June, 1999, the bank with the most outstanding loans to small businesses was Wells Fargo & Co. with almost $9.88 billion. Bank of America Corp. and Bank One Corp. followed closely in second and third with $9.86 billion and $7.4 billion, respectively.

Banks aren't the only ones that understand the power of entrepreneurial businesses. Credit card companies, like Advanta, American Express, MBNA, and Mountain West Financial, are now aggressively marketing business loans, credit lines, equipment leasing products to small companies in addition to their traditional products. According to Wells Fargo Bank, four of the top ten lenders to small-businesses in 1997 were credit card companies, not commercial banks.

Competition means that entrepreneurs have a wide range of debt-capital sources to choose from, ranging from local banks that are plugged in to your community, to branches of national banks that use volume to offer competitive rates. The Web can help entrepreneurs research what makes a good deal in terms of rates and fees, as well as streamlining the application process by sending requests online.

One of the best first stops when researching is the Small Business Administration's Office of Advocacy at www.sba.gov/ADVO/lending/bk_tb_98.html. Each fall, the site posts a list of what it calls the banks more friendly to small businesses. There you'll find a ranking of the best banks nationally, as well as related lists that show which are the best banks for small businesses in each state. Even if you decide to go with a local bank that doesn't top the SBA's list, seeing what the leading small-business banks offer in terms of products, rates, and accelerated approvals will help you comparison shop and arm you with negotiating ammunition.

When you're ready to apply for a credit line, loan, or business loan, you should have some standard financial data at your fingertips. First, understand that a lender will evaluate you based on a number of factors, including your business assets, your business and personal credit history, collateral, general economic conditions as they apply to your company, and your personal and professional financial condition. Credit reports and loan repayment documents will help bolster your request. You should also come prepared with financial statements for your business if it's already up and running. You'll need data on the company's debt-to-equity ratio. According to Chase Manhattan, banks generally consider a maximum 3:1, debt to worth. Similarly, the ratio of current assets (i.e., accounts receivables) to current liabilities shows how liquid your company is, and banks look for a comparison of 1.5:1, assets to liabilities, according to Chase. Records showing your cash flow will also be important to convince lenders you can repay your obligations.

Many banks, including most of the top ten lenders in the SBA small-business rankings, require detailed financial statements like those typically for higher loan amounts or $75,000 or more. For lesser amounts, companies with good credit reports may need only to complete a simple one-page application to get tens of thousands of dollars for standard business expenses. Competition has its advantages.

The following directory lists the top five banks in the SBA's latest rankings with summaries of credit and loan products for comparison with each other and other lenders that serve your geographical area.

TOP SMALL-BUSINESS LENDERS

American Express
Products: Credit lines, business loans, commercial credit cards
Web Address: http://home3.americanexpress.com/smallbusiness/

Credit line lets approved companies write checks up to $50,000. Annual fee is $95, but no charges for individual checks. Monthly payments may be a minimum or the full balance. Interest is the prime plus 3.9 percent. No documentation or collateral required.

Business loans provide $10,000 or more with fixed-rate monthly payments.

The Corporate Optima Platinum card has no annual fee and a credit line up to $50,000. Interest is 9.99 percent. (See Web site for a variety of other commercial credit card products.)

HOW TO APPLY:
Complete electronic applications available at the Web site.

Wells Fargo

Products: Credit lines, equipment loans, business loans, SBA loans, and commercial credit cards
Web Address: www.wellsfargo.com/biz/

Credit line offers a maximum of $100,000 in revolving credit. Interest rate ranges from prime plus 1.75 percent to plus 8.75 percent, depending on credit history.

Equipment loans offer available credit that converts to a term loan when purchase is made. Equipment may be new or used. Repayment schedule is up to five years for new equipment and up to four years on used equipment. Interest depends on loan type. One time application fee is $150.

Business loans have a maximum of $100,000, with repayment schedules up to five years. Requires collateral. Interest can be fixed or variable at rates determined at approval.

Commercial Master Card has limits up to $100,000 at fixed rates of 19.8 percent. Annual fee is $55 per card.

HOW TO APPLY:

Equipment loan: When you are ready to buy, call an Equipment Finance Specialist 1-800-416-0056. Once you have decided to purchase equipment, you can forward your invoice or purchase order via fax to 1-800-340-7468. Once received, in most instances funding for your purchase(s) will take place within 24 hours.

Bank of America

Products: Commercial credit cards, credit lines, business loans
Web Address: www.bankofamerica.com/index.cfm

Credit Lines $2,500 to $100,000, with no financial statements or tax returns required for some requests. No collateral.

HOW TO APPLY:

Call (888) 400-6000.

Bank One

Products: Commercial credit cards, business loans, credit lines
Web Address: www.bancone.com/business/
Note: Bank products vary by state, the following represents a business in Ohio.

Cards offer limits up to $35,000 with interest rates of prime plus 2.9 percent and no annual fee.

Fixed term loans range from $5,000 to $35,000, with fixed or variable interest rates based on individual credit profile. One time fee of $75. Also considers loans over $35,000. Range from $10,000 to $35,000.Variable interest rates based on individual credit profile.

HOW TO APPLY:

Use electronic application forms at the Web site.

Chase Manhattan Bank

Products: Business loans, revolving credit, credit lines, equipment leasing, commercial credit cards
Web Address: www.chase.com/

Business installment loans start at $3,000 typically for one to five years. Interest based on the Chase Prime Rate. Requires annual review and annual fees. Business credit lines range from $5,000 to $25,000. Annual review and renewal fee. Leasing plans include a purchase option with terms of one to five years.

HOW TO APPLY:

For credit products, contact nearest branch for applications and rates (see Web site for branch locations). For leasing, send e-mail to leasing specialist@leaseoperations.com.

Fleet Bank

Products: Credit lines, term loans, commercial credit cards
Web Address: www.fleet.com/busbpplceb.html

Term loans and credit lines from $10,000 to $100,000. Simple applications don't require past financial documents in many cases, and the bank guarantees same-day decisions on loan applications. Term loans have repayment schedules of one to seven years. Will consider credit requests over $100,000.

HOW TO APPLY:

Use the online application form at the Web site. The site also has a link for checking the status of applications.

KeyBank

Products: Credit lines, term loans, commercial credit cards
Web Address: www.keybank.com/templates/t-ps3.jhtml?nodeID= I-1.23

Offers variable-rate credit lines that can be renewed each year without filing additional forms. Increases in credit amounts can be made with a phone call. Also offers credit lines and term loans using personal collateral, such as home equity.

HOW TO APPLY:

Use electronic applications at the Web site or call 1-888-539-4249.

U.S. Bankcorp

Products: Credit line, term loans, commercial credit cards, equipment loans, and SBA loans
Web Address: www.usbank.com/usbsol.html

Credit lines range from $10,000 to $75,000 and don't require collateral. Lines from $75,000 to $500,000 also available, require collateral. Loans range from $5,000 to $500,000. Secured and have a fixed interest rate. Equipment loans range from $10,000 to $500,000 with a fixed interest rate. The Staples Visa Business Card has a credit limit up to $50,000.

How to Apply:

Submit applications to nearest location. For listing of offices, go to www.usbank.com/cgi/cfm/contact/contact_us.cfm.

GO PUBLIC WITHOUT THE HASSLES OF AN IPO

Entrepreneurs are no strangers to the gambling instinct. Successful business owners are willing to bet their savings, their mortgages, and years of their life on a new idea. If you're ready to roll the dice for stakes higher than what the typical entrepreneur can handle, there's one more, white-knuckle way to raise as much as $5 million for your company.

The Internet and some relaxed Securities and Exchange Commission rules about stock sales have given rise to Direct Public Offerings (DPO), a small-scale equivalent to an Initial Public Offering (IPO). The benefits of a DPO are that entrepreneurs can bypass the complexities and costs of traditional SEC securities regulations and use the Internet to sell stock in their companies. Also, companies that aren't big enough or sexy enough to attract an investment bank to underwrite an IPO can still go public, if on a smaller scale than those listed on the NASDAQ and similar stock exchanges.

The SEC defines a number of DPO categories, depending on how much money you may want to raise. The first, known as a Regulation A offering, limits public offerings to no more than $5 million in a 12-month period. Prior to the stock sale, you must get SEC approval for a prospectus-like offering statement that you file with the agency. Potential investors must have access to this statement, which describes your company, any special business challenges it faces, financial history, managers' biographies, the business model, and other characteristics.

In return for all this upfront work, the SEC exempts you from the tedious and ongoing reports IPOs must file. Also, the financial data you are required to provide is less extensive than for an IPO, and it needn't be audited. Even the offering statement is simplified: Companies can choose to arrange the information in a Q&A format that's easier to write than a more formal prospectus. Finally, to save on accounting and legal fees, you're allowed to test market your company's stock sale—through ads, postings on the Internet, or similar promotional efforts—to see if there are enough interested investors to meet your capital requirements before you formally file the offering statement with the SEC.

A second direct-stock option is a Regulation D filing, which is similar to the Regulation A counterpart, except that the maximum amount of capital you can raise is lower: Rule 504 under Regulation D lets you sell up to $1 million in securities in a year.

In both cases, entrepreneurs can use the Small Corporate Offering Registration (SCOR) Form, called Form U-7, when filing with the SEC. The document was developed by the North American Securities Administrators Association (NASAA) and the American Bar Association—and later adopted by the SEC—to help entrepreneurs simplify registering their stock offerings in multiple states, which have a tangle of individual securities requirements. Now that all but a handful of states have adopted the SCOR form, entrepreneurs don't have to complete dozens of forms to open their offering up to investors across the country. However, entrepreneurs still must abide by unique state securities laws, such as mandating a minimum amount of capital to be raised before the offering company can dip into the pot.

A third DPO choice is Rule 505, which lets you bypass more stringent SEC laws when selling up to $5 million in your company in a year. Under 505, you sell to accredited investors—essentially people who meet the SEC's definitive of being savvy capitalists—and a maximum of 35 others who don't have to meet any financial litmus test. Also, investors must hold on to the securities for a year before trying to sell them.

Entrepreneurs can also use a Form SB-1 offering to sell $10 million in stock in a year. To qualify, you must submit audited financials and your company can neither have more than $25 million in sales nor $25 million in publicly held stock.

Finally, an SB-2 filing covers sales of $25 million in stocks for a year. Like SB-1, this category applies only to companies with no more than $25 million in sales or publicly held stock. You also must provide audited financial records, the previous year's balance sheet, and income statements from the last two fiscal years.

No matter which DPO offering you consider, none is a sure bet. DPOs require tens of thousands of dollars for upfront accountant, lawyer, and advertising consultant costs. After that, you still must compete with all the other stock offerings—DPO, IPO, and over the counter—that vie for investor money. In the end, gambling that you can negotiate a favorable loan rate from a bank or find an angel investor you can work with comfortably may prove more profitable than putting your fledgling business on the open market.

For details about DPOs, spend time at the following sites.

North American Securities Administrators Association

www.nasaa.org

A venerable international investor advocacy organization. Offers the Issuers Manual, a guide to completing the SCOR Form.

SEC Office of Small Business

www.sec.gov

Provides overviews and links to information about the various DPO alternatives.

WEB RESOURCES FOR ENTREPRENEURS

There's no shortage of information on the Web about starting, funding, and managing start ups and growing companies. Managers can research specific topics by using search engines at Alta Vista (www.altavista.com), Northern Light (www.northernlight. com), Yahoo! (www.yahoo.com), and others. The following addresses are for sites that offer especially helpful background information for entrepreneurs in search of capital.

GOVERNMENT

Small Business Administration www.sbaonline.sba.gov: In addition to background information about SBA loans, this site contains a wealth of usual information about funding businesses and seeking capital.

Securities and Exchange Commission www.sec.gov/smbus1.htm: An excellent site for funding in general and direct stock offerings in particular.

BUSINESS PLANS

Bplans.com (www.bplans.com): A site created by Palo Alto Software, a publisher of commercial business-plan creation applications, offers good advice on the elements of effective business plans, as well as samples of plans.

Small Business Administration (www.sba.gov/starting/indexbusplans.html): This section of the SBA's larger site provides an excellent business plan template and advice for creating financial reports.

Massachusetts Institute of Technology Enterprise Forum (/www.mit.edu/afs/athena/org/e/entforum/www/Business Plans/bplans.html): The business plan resource guide here offers a comprehensive list of Web sources that offer sample business plans, templates, and advice for writing effective plans.

SMALL BUSINESS WEB SITES

Entrepreneurial Edge (http://edge.lowe.org): An online community where entrepreneurs can discuss problems and seek advice from peers.

Entreworld (www.entreworld.org): A product of the Kauffman Center for Entrepreneurial Leadership, Entreworld offers advice and case studies on creating businesses, writing business plans, and tracking down investors.

The Forum for Women Entrepreneurs (www.few.org): A professional association for women entrepreneurs in technology and life sciences companies. Members benefit from networking opportunities with investors.

Idea Café (www.ideacafe.com): A business portals with a small-business channel that advises entrepreneurs on financing issues, as well as general business-management subjects.

Moneyhunter (www.moneyhunter.com): Free advice for honing business ideas, creating a business plan, and searching for investors.

National Venture Capital Association (www.nvca.com/): A professional association created for venture fund managers, but entrepreneurs can use the membership directory to scout out funding candidates.

Nvest.com (www.nvst.com): Extensive information about funding and growing private businesses.

Rutgers University (www.libraries.rutgers.edu/rul/rr_gateway/research_guides/busi/smallbus.shtml): A comprehensive online guide for entrepreneurs, this site includes sections devoted to business financing as well as links to related Web sites and an index to printed resources in the university's library.

Service Corps of Retired Executives (www.score.com): A non-profit group of former managers that offers new entrepreneurs advice and mentoring.

Springboard 2000 (www.springboard2000.org/): Dedicated to women entrepreneurs, offers business advice and opportunities for networking with investors.

Venture Associates (www.venturea.com/): Provides information on the full range of financing alternatives available to entrepreneurs.

Venture Capital Resource Library (www.vfinance.com/): A venture capital professional association, its resource library can help entrepreneurs stay on top of VC trends and new fund capitalizations. Business managers can also use the site to present their business plans to investors for a fee.

INCUBATORS

National Business Incubator Association (www.nbia.org): Offers links to member incubators by state or country. Also explains the role of incubators in helping start ups and organizes conferences.

Otaniemi Technology Park (www.otech.fi/ScienceParks.html): The Web site for this Finnish technology center lists URLs for incubators throughout Europe.

REGIONAL SMALL BUSINESS ASSOCIATIONS

A number of venture capital clubs that offer opportunities for entrepreneurs and investors to network exist throughout the country. Unfortunately, many do not have Web sites, which makes getting meeting schedules and membership information a little more difficult. The following organizations maintain directories with club addresses and phone numbers.

Association of Venture Capital Clubs
P.O. Box 3358
Salt Lake City, UT 84111

The International Venture Capital Institute
P.O. Box 1333
Stamford, CT 06904
(203) 323-3143

K. Williams Resources (http://kwilliams.bizhosting.com/vclubs.
html): Lists venture clubs by state.

MAGAZINES

The following magazines regularly cover financing for entrepreneurs with original content on their Web sites, as well as in their traditional printed publications.

Inc. Online www.inc.com

Fortune Small Business www.fsb.com

Red Herring Online www.herring.com

Entrepreneur www.entrepreneur.com

HOW TO DETERMINE THE RIGHT KIND OF FINANCING FOR YOU

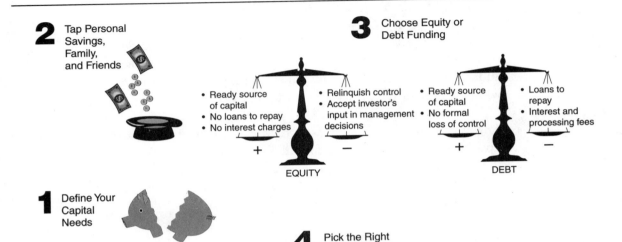

2 Tap Personal Savings, Family, and Friends

3 Choose Equity or Debt Funding

- Ready source of capital
- No loans to repay
- No interest charges

- Relinquish control
- Accept investor's input in management decisions

+ −

EQUITY

- Ready source of capital
- No formal loss of control

- Loans to repay
- Interest and processing fees

+ −

DEBT

1 Define Your Capital Needs

4 Pick the Right Candidates

EQUITY		
Amount	Development Stage	Source
Less than $1 million	Seed and Early	Seed Funds, Angels, Incubators
More than $1 million	Second Stage and Later	Venture Capital Funds

DEBT		
Amount	Development Stage	Source
$100,000 or less	Seed and Early	Bank Loans, Credit Lines, Commercial Credit Cards, SBA Loans
$100,000 to $1.5 million	Early and Later	Bank Loans, SBA Loans
$1 million to $5 million	Later	Direct Stock Offering

GLOSSARY

Don't know a red herring from a blue sky offering? Here's a glossary of terms common to small-business financing.

Accredited Investors—A formal definition created in the Securities Act of 1933 to identify investors who are wealthy enough and savvy enough to make investment decisions on their own, without some of the protections outlined in the act.

Angels—Wealthy individuals who fund early financing to start ups, sometimes even before a formal business plan is developed, in return for interest in the company and sometimes managerial influence. Typically, these investments range from a few thousand dollars to as much as $1 million.

Asset-Based Loans—Loans provided to companies that use the value of inventory or other resources as collateral.

Barriers to Entry—The difficulty competitors will face when responding to a company's new product, service, or marketing strategy.

Boat Anchor—Something that stands in the way of a company's success.

Bootstrapping—Creative or unusual strategies for funding a young company.

Bridge Loans—Interim financing that comes between formal funding rounds

Burn Rate—The rate at which a company spends money prior to generating profits.

Capital Under Management—The amount of capital an investor or group, such as a venture capital fund, has to offer entrepreneurs.

Common Stock—Company shares distributed in return for investments in a company. If the company dissolves, holders of common stock receive payment after preferred stock holders and creditors.

Debt Financing—Capital derived from interest-accruing loans (see Equity Financing).

Development Stage—Any of a series of growth stages companies go through as they evolve from start ups to mature ventures.

Direct Stock Offering/Direct Public Offering—Company shares sold directly to investors instead of through a stock exchange or underwriter.

Due Diligence—The process investors and entrepreneurs go through to validate the terms and representations made during funding negotiations.

Early Stage—The initial development stage of a company often focused on honing a business idea and developing a business model.

Elevator Pitch—A concise description of a business idea told in the time it takes to ride an elevator with a potential investor.

Equity Funding—Capital invested in return for a shares in a company and sometimes including managerial influence (see Debt Financing).

Expansion Stage—A development stage where a company begins to see growing revenues and initial profits.

Exit Strategy—The plan a company develops to recoup investments. Examples include an initial public offering or sale of the company to a larger corporation.

First Stage—An early, pre-profit development stage.

Incubator—A commercial or not-for-profit organization that offers business advice, physical space, business-services support, and funding to young companies.

Institutional Investor—Organizations, such as banks and retirement funds, that consider entrepreneurial investments.

Initial Public Offering (IPO)—The first sale of a company's stock over public exchanges.

Later Stage—A development stage of companies with an established market position; often just prior to an IPO.

Lead Investor—A venture capital fund with industry expertise or geographical proximity that allows for closer supervision of a company than is possible for co-investors.

Mezzanine Financing—Capital for an established and successful company, often just prior to an IPO.

Portfolio Company—One of a group of companies that a venture-capital fund is backing.

Preferred Stock—Special shares of a company that receive payment before holders of common stocks.

Rate of Return (ROR)—A measurement of an investment's success that takes into account the amount of capital invested and the length of the investment.

Red Herring—A prosaic name for a company's initial prospectus.

Recapitalization—The act of revamping a private company's capital structure.

Small Business Investment Corporation (SBIC)—An arm of the Small Business Administration that licenses private venture funds so they receive special financial considerations for targeting entrepreneurial investments of $3 million or less.

Securities and Exchange Commission (SEC)—The federal regulatory agency that oversees securities transactions.

Seed Stage—A initial development stage when business concepts and product or service prototypes are being developed.

Venture Capital—Private companies that pool capital from organizations and individuals to provide investment funds to growing businesses.

"Will the Dogs Eat the Dog Food?"—Essentially, is there a market for the new product or service?

INDEX